PRAISE FOR

HOW TO BE UNMOTHERED

"Camille U. Adams has written a truly astounding memoir that brings to light a portrait of cruelty that few others are willing to admit, and from which fewer still are able to break free. Little could have prepared me for how much I needed this book in my life right here and right now. I implore everyone read *How to Be Unmothered* for its uncompromising truths delivered with unmistakable beauty."

MARCELO HERNANDEZ CASTILLO,
AUTHOR OF *CHILDREN OF THE LAND*

"With a poet's lyricism and an eye for detail, Camille U. Adams is an incredible talent. *How to Be Unmothered* is a work of art, an excavation of memory, a blend of fierce determination, vulnerability, and a journey toward liberation. It is painful, beautiful, haunting."

JAQUIRA DÍAZ,
AUTHOR OF *ORDINARY GIRLS*

"Camille U. Adams' debut memoir focuses on the author's passage from girlhood to womanhood and from Trinidad to Brooklyn, a harrowing journey made even more difficult by various abandonments from the very adults responsible for taking care of her. Adams breaks taboos by refusing to keep family secrets that protect the powerful. She is not afraid to write about the aftermath of her 'unmothering.' But this is not a record of one's traumas. This book is a resistance—the reward of being brave enough to know the painful truth of one's own life. Each sentence is alive with poetry and bursts with the joy of survival; the voice of this writer is unique, indelible, and strong. In *How to Be Unmothered*, Adams shows us a path toward a better life can be made through stories. Instead of hiding, possibilities for intimacy, connection, and even love, come from being known. Read this book and then put it into the hands of someone you love who has ever felt abandoned as a child, by which I mean, any of us."

HOW TO BE UNMOTHERED

CAMILLE U. ADAMS

HOW TO BE UNMOTHERED

A Trinidadian Memoir

RESTLESS BOOKS
NEW YORK · AMHERST

Copyright © 2025 Camille U. Adams

Map of Trinidad (2019) courtesy of Olli Turho.

All rights reserved.

No part of this book may be reproduced or transmitted without
the prior written permission of the publisher.

Restless Books and the R colophon are registered trademarks of Restless Books, Inc.

First Restless Books paperback edition August 2025

Paperback ISBN: 9781632063953

Library of Congress Control Number: 2024953124

This book is supported in part by an award from the National Endowment for the Arts.

Quotation from "Down By the River" reprinted from Morgan
Heritage, *More Teachings . . .* (VP Records, 2001).

Quotations from "Leaving on a Jet Plane" reprinted from
John Denver, *Rhymes & Reasons* (RCA Records, 1969).

Cover design and family tree by Sarah Schulte
Text design and typesetting by Tetragon, London
Cover photographs by Solomon Battle, Kiara Bloom, Falombini, and LUNAMARINA.

Printed in the United States

1 3 5 7 9 10 8 6 4 2

RESTLESS BOOKS
NEW YORK · AMHERST
www.restlessbooks.org

to my Soul—
who never stops fighting
who always keeps writing
—I believe in your song

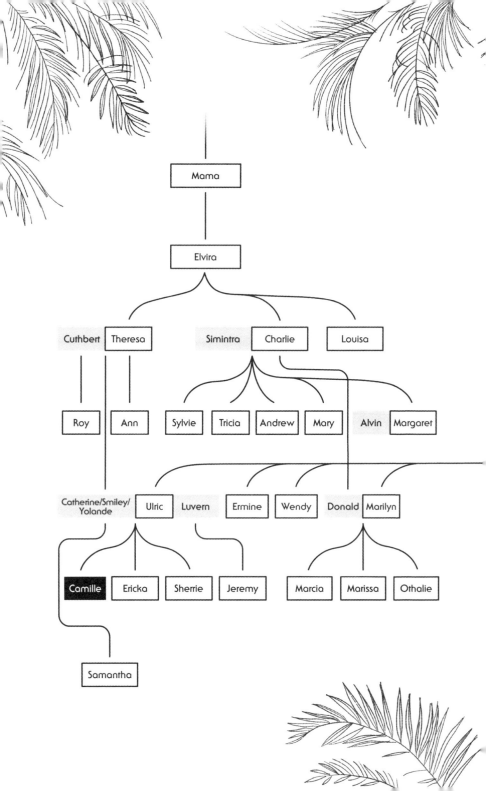

FAMILY TREE

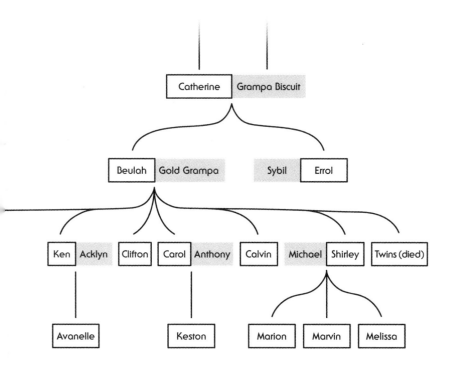

CONTENTS

1	Chenette Tree	3
2	Cotton Tree	43
3	Breadfruit Tree	87
4	Sugar Cane	91
5	Julie Mango Tree	99
6	Pawpaw Tree	125
7	Coconut Tree	141
8	Soursop Tree	155
9	Zaboca Tree	159
10	Bamboo Trees	193
11	Silk Cotton Tree	203
12	Sea Almond Tree	241
13	Pomerac Tree	249
14	Bois Canot Tree	253

Acknowledgements   267

She knew.
And now I know, too.

HOW TO BE UNMOTHERED

1

CHENETTE TREE

I am eight years old.

It's 1988. And it not even eight o'clock in the morning as we walking down Baptist Hill on Covigne Road. Walking to where my father car parked on the flat in Granny yard. Mummy and Daddy, and my younger sisters, Ericka and Sherrie. And trailing last behind in their duckling line: me. Starting out on this trip before the day even wake up properly.

Shuffling down the hill's steep on legs still asleep to go sit for a whole 107-kilometre drive from Trinidad head. From Trinidad's crown laying down on her arm stretched out in slumbering rest. All the way south where Trinidad's long, drowsing feet extend. Hours to traverse the two jutting peninsulas of our island coast's west. All for a wedding at which I don't self even want to be a guest. But we going, oui. At Mummy's behest.

Rear car window crank in my hand, its stiff 360-rolling finally inviting air to fan into the Ford's archived musk. The car's stored pungency combining with the new release just joining in from my father's bare feet on the gas pedal and brakes. Bare, as his size thirteens unable to take to the long road while sweatily clothed. So he say.

Mingling aromas from my mother's packed snacks—peanuts and sandwiches lined in sharp cheese paste mixed with tart mustard, to be washed down with citrus juice—still prove insufficient to douse the scent of my father's car. Its smell that would not relent, never far. This hot space housing and trapping each trace of his construction work jerseys and carpenter toolbox, locking in cement dust and the rust of wet mortar nails, and his underarm reek that never bails. No matter how much Breeze and Clorox my mother applies.

And is in this funk they want me sit for the whole three-hour drive?

This depart-at-dawn three-to-four-hour ride I had to miss *Who's The Boss* for last night. Sent to bed early. Not getting to watch Tony. For their down in the bush journey. For their departure from Covigne. This street where we live that I hate truly. Covigne Road. This place of loudness, gangsters, guns, wajang crassness, and fear. Where my parents choose to live. Of all the nice neighbourhoods, here.

But down Point Fortin even worse.

Point, with the thick swallow of crude oil on every inhale. Petroleum filling the air. And the few, the one or two business buildings, just spread-out, humble dwellings that say only country mouse does live here. And the bush everywhere. That have ears.

Point bush strange, and higher than the manageable bush near my father house, where we does pick rabbit meat weeds for our bunnies and get plum and guava and sugar cane. And we know the growth seasons of the sunning, shedding snakes. And clanking ting don't just walk out the grave willy-nilly so because it have streetlights lining Covigne Road that will make them expose.

Not so down south where Uncle Charlie live, in the hawking-up mouths of rivers kissing the Caribbean Sea. Down where alligators and caiman does hatch and breed. And manicou does squeak and feed on rubbish and food scraps. Where Uncle Charlie not even on the east side of our island that sea turtles does mount majestically and climb. To bring into the world new little leatherbacks calling Trinidad home aeons on aeons. Till the end of time. No.

We going quito quito. Behind god back. Because Mummy uncle child marrying, and de wedding go be a big lime. And, Uricka, family is family and daz a fact. My mother tells me. I, Camille, who do not agree.

In the driver's seat, my father turns the radio knob to the left, to the right. Trying to get the coordinates precise for Radio 100FM or 95.1FM to unstatically play. Him venturing away from the newsy AM choice. Here good, my mother says when she hears Bobby McFerrin's voice. And I lean my head back against the seat as "Don't Worry Be Happy," my mother's ears-blocking-lalala-staying-positive anthem, serenades her girl children three.

With this fake-Jamaican don't-worry command issuing over the airwaves, my father's wide hand lowers the handbrake to accelerate into the outstretched rays of the rising sun. In front of us, the grey car Tanty Marilyn just done save for and buy—that only her husband, Uncle Donald, does drive—is picking up the pace.

My father opted for second place in this duet of vehicles taking the complicated path from our neighbourhood of Diego Martin down to

Point Fortin. Uncle Donald should lead the way. It is his father house we visiting. It is his mosquito-biting area down south where we'll be staying. Though I begged to not go.

Though I begged to not be part of this caravan duo transporting first and second cousins on both sides. This duet of siblings and don't-even-like-each-other spouses. These sibling-and-cousins parents rousing our eyelids agape at the break of day to embark on a long weekend stay. In family bedrooms I cannot escape.

Their planned long country days ahead wherein their three girl children apiece—six in total that we could see—will wear white lace stockings and bobby socks. And sit in a church and ignore the clock. Till Donald sister walk down the aisle. Walking to the cassette recording of the "Wedding March" while her neighbours shoo-shoo about the dress revealing style. Us children waiting for the priest to say you may kiss the bride to finally get up and run outside. And play catch and hide under the tent where we'll sip Peardrax and pretend is champagne making us drunk through the reception's night.

But for now, the sliver of light on the horizon dapples the full, rusting barrels on the side of Covigne Road. Our starting point from which we'll go. Barrels of garbage still uncollected by the rubbish truck this Friday morning, and I must duck my nose deep into the neck of my flowery dress to suppress another assault on my nostrils. My poor olfactory nerves my father car done giving their fill. My unpointy nose, seeking relief now, breathing the baby powder from my chest as my father drives past Baptist Hill. And this ill-fated trip begins. This doomed four-hour haul down to Point Fortin.

Turning right from Covigne onto the main road, at eight years old, car sickness has suddenly taken hold. And I am a puppy with her head outside the window. None of my *Strange Awesome Facts* books for me. I must watch the passing scenery. Must engage with the wind's forcible entry. Up my nose. My brain standing sentry to airstreams imprinting encyclopaedic information. My pupils and adenoids portals to a mental mapping of Trinidad's locations.

Salt on my tongue and cartons of Orchard orange juice do not stave off nausea for long. And I reject the stretch of Mummy's right hand, two shades darker and only one size bigger than my eight-year-old one. Her hand offering a settle-yuh-belly capful of rum.

So it is my eyes that keep down my stomach's contents of breakfast boiled egg I tired tell Mummy I do not like. Of which she makes me eat every gagging bite. Eyes that remain trained on the flickering film reel of developing images that is the alternating terrain. Stretching from the urbane west peninsula. To the jutting barefoot of Trinidad, washed in the Gulf of Paria.

Leaving Covigne Road, where my father and all his siblings and cousins and aunts and uncles and parents and grandparents and nen nen build their homes. Leaving Diego Martin with it Spanish street names and driving along Western Main Road, we arrive in St. James.

This city baptised in a Catholic name. This town unfurling grey dawn. In ombre form. Across shadowy streets up to the lightening sky heralding morn. Grey galvanise roofs of one-storey, two-storey bars and stores. Grey galvanise glittering with spores of dew that cannot wash St. James anew. Grey dew that cannot clean the lives that stall under St. James' nectar, holding stumbling, vagranted men in thrall.

Rum shop after pub after bar, my father steers his car through the centre lane of bifurcated dark recesses on each side of the street. These taverns nightly facilitate the game of leapfrog from sticky stool to next-door pulsing stall. St. James, Trinidad's city that never sleeps at all. And I catch sight of the infamous bar that keeps spouses up at night. The bar at the heart of it all. The bar that is the larynx issuing the siren call—across cities, across boroughs, even across foreign, tugging waywards home.

This early morning hour, Smokey & Bunty's should be closed. But I lean out my head and watch it good so I can contribute my piece of bacchanal I see when the girls in my class talking during recess next week. Especially when Desireé want to play like I is such a baby and don't know ting. Always bragging. Cuz her mother young young and does dress sexy and does take her all over the place. And Desireé foot too hot and she go turn out the same way. So the teachers say. But today, I fill my quiver with arrows to show what I know outside the classroom to those girls lucky enough to go on adventures to Fort George and Blue Basin Waterfall. Lucky with parents who have money for their children cuz their father doh party and spend out all.

Is the red awning—spliced with brown and lettered with the white that also colours the vertical stripes of the du Maurier sign—that first calls my eyes. Is the same design on the pack of cigarettes my father smokes at night.

This same cigarette motif that repeats in the big umbrellas open over the patio seats on the pavement in front Smokey & Bunty. Their sheltering skirts are brake lights halting the gaze. These red parasols offering shade. Standing out in the white face of the bar's kitty-corner walls. Walls that also prop up a white ice machine with red lettering announcing the opportunity to all for getting drinks on the rocks through the night when the burgundy, criss-cross, steel gate not close up tight.

The actual sign, Smokey & Bunty's, is placed up high. I almost miss its inconspicuous size. Like a lidded eye under a Brooke Shields brow. As the sun now waking up, in its yawning glow, the bar doesn't look how I thought it would from newscasters' ominous tones. Reports of nightly stabbings and bussheads from bottles thrown. And this badjohn bar sitting under an upstairs white-gallery home. Who go want to live here? Where morning might be fair, but come sunset it raining bullet and big stone?

I doh know.

Forearm resting along the brown cushioned car door, I stretch out my head to take in some more. And that's when the pong breathes. That's when the stench rises in ghostly, curly tendrils from the streets. Gains shape and takes a courtly bow. Doffing his tattered cap in front of me.

This reek comes to the window to greet, to meet, me this guest to his stately seat. This reek, with fraying jester shoes on his feet, stands at my window open to his pavement.

Who would live in these used-to-be tenements? he asks. Where the scent of rum permeates. Who would dwell where the spirit of rum infiltrates? Everything? Where rum vapours annihilate the nothing. In the city of bars, in the dark, where sunshine in a bottle is needed. Even in a tropical isle of equatorial brightness. But sunniness is impeded.

Where the recipe for life's strife, the one still heeded, is: find joy's adjacent. That missive, that message those enslavers sent. This griot

Rum stench risen from the pavement, regales me. Me, whom he whisks back centuries, from 1988 to St. James' early plantations. Me, whom he bids, Come see . . .

And I hear the hoarse cries to uprise from the enslaved Africans of my ancestry slaked as booze snakes down their gullets in relaxing coils. Resistance foiled. Rum stemming the roiling pain as the sweet products of their toil get shipped beyond the constraints of their barrack-allotted soil. The enslaved's genius exploited when they put the detritus, the unwanted molasses of sugar cane refinement, to a boil. Exploited when they produced the very rum shipped as spoils.

Their invention made worms on the fishing rod, used as luring bait. In West Africa, rum paid to those betraying neighbouring tribal states. Firewater energising those who march more trafficked prisoners to European death ships in wait.

Rum bound in wooden caskets. Rum purchasing gaskets. Rum travelling the triangle "trade." Rum traversing the middle passage shackling millions as enslaved. Rum drenching the genetically inherited cells of those who first made the devil's brew.

Rum powering the waterwheel of the men and women in the fields when they reel from whips and hunger under the sun's heel. Sowing, hoeing, rowing, chopping, harvesting, grinding, binding the white gold for which Europeans stole them from their homes. Rum filling their dome. Rum softening the blow of staring out over graveyard waters to the continent that will not birth their daughters.

Rum spilling from cutlass-shackled African hands. Liquor leaching into the land. Alcohol the daily rations of those enslaved in iron chains. For centuries of sugar- and cocoa-harvesting gains.

Rum, transporting me back to see.

Rum spilt daily. Rum poured nightly. Rum addicted to over centuries. Rum scouring the eroded throats of African labourers. Those plantation workers making their permanent home in our isles. Those field hands with nowhere back to go after enslavement supposedly end. Here, resigned.

In a country, in a city, in a town where the very earth has been plantation-maligned.

This pungent Rum jester at my window to me explains who deigned stick my smarting nose into his terrain as my father drives through St. James. Rum sadistically grins. You overwhelmed, eh. Then he spins.

And my nausea satisfies his slanted shrewd eyes. Squinting eyes that prize the horror of that which he is making me apprised through the murderous montage he projects onto the darkened sky. Me who questioned a rum shop in disdain.

In my father's spectral window frame, Rum unshields his ghastly face. And reveals his homicidal role in centuries of ancestral shackled pain. And his trace. In the centuries of all the descendants he has claimed.

It is only when the car approaches the towering silk cotton trees, as we're driving past the police barracks' wide stretch of turf to leave St. James, that the stench of Rum fades. At last. My father's car heading for Port of Spain.

I have been quiet, while wicked Rum danced in my brain.

But my mother doesn't like me this way. My watchful, silent thoughts. Access to which she's always nervously sought. And her bulbous eyes swivel from the windshield, across Sherrie's wispy hair nestled to her chest, to the back seat. Where I sit concealed in dawn's shawl. Where I tuck against the door and defeat all her attempts to engage.

My mother knows two modes: unwashable, cloying honey. And rage.

Those eyes of hers, uncaged from the front, seek me out for something to criticise. To stimulate her dependent mind. Those eyes of hers want. They need. They seek to feed. I feel those eyes dismount ungracefully on me. An entitled plea. A say-something-observant-smart-daughter-of-mine guarantee. A distraction to quench the unsatiating greed of her commitment not to worry. Though she know we embarking on a trip on which my mind said no. I don't want to go.

A trip for which, will this mother be sorry?

But for now, my mother chirps. Her husband burbs. She waves a short-fingered, wedding-ringed hand. And giggles at her man with whom, this morning, she is forget-everything happy. The unopened door to my bedroom last night and her sappy sighs in my father's bed must be why. She is tender with Sherrie and smiling indulgently. And not impatiently answering Ericka's every six-year-old enquiry about what she spies.

Still, amidst her chuckles, this mother turns to observing me. Soliciting noise to puncture the unremitting gloom. Turns to me, in a boisterous car full of soca music, Daddy laughing, my sisters chattering, and wind blowing, that shouldn't have room for my silence's loud volume.

And before I turn my head to approaching Wrightson Road, which looms. To Port of Spain, our capital, that blooms against the pillow-cloud backdrop and the sun rising up. Before I recommit to keeping my head out of this car travelling south on this visit I cannot stop, I give my mother a sip from my cup. Something to pacify. So she will give me space again to be a child. A person who doesn't like to criticise and find fault in everything at all times.

I don my costume under her eyes' spotlight and make props of the men milling like moths under the streetlamps' bright. These mumbling, dribbling, ranting, chuckling at nothing said beyond the something in their heads men. Men with matted plaits, balding pates, and bent spines unrisen to the unflinching sky.

Men uneager to greet an unchanging day. Men with dry, flimsy stalks for legs, flanked by gabardine pants announcing their rank of vagrant in this caste-free place. Men in rough-hewn, brown fabric armed for the road. Men working nowhere, wearing Dickies against nights' brief cold. Men in crocus cloth that still must wear down at some point. Men in khaki bottoms with holes at the joints. And at the seat. Where their butts meet the street corners on which they sit. On pavements where they beg for a lil dollar to buy more spirits. Men adorned in only skin and bones. Men bare-chested, bare-backed, barefoot beyond the calluses making shoes of their soles. Men whose foul stench recoil promenaders who get too close. Men who left their flesh, their pride, their means to support lives, when they left their home. Men bound to the night sky. Men tied to day's scorching and rain's cry. Men fit to roam. Men leashed to a bar's opening and unmoored when it's closed.

These men I transpose into the play. Onto the stage of my mother turning to me, wanting, waiting, expecting, needing her salvation to say something to break the unsustainable flirty conversation between she and her chosen mate. I want to leave these men alone, but state, Wait, they does be drunk out here so early, too. Mummy picks up her cue.

And across the diagonal line of sight arcing from the front passenger to the back seat's right, Mummy's beady eyes delight. She gets to curl her slim lips in disgust. And steups loudly. She gets to thrust her sharp chin to the rolled-down window. She gets to look down her pointy bridge and cringe. She gets to peer and sneer at the spectacle that flares her tidy nostrils on her white-woman nose she wishes one of her put-a-clothespin-on children would grow. That proud receptacle that can smell the vagrants' unwashed bodies from here. Their odour reaching into her man's car in daybreak's unsmogged air. And my mother spits the words that declare, So dem is. With contempt.

And my retreat into muteness—now that I have paid the token, taken the ride, and surrendered a piece of my soul to the violent demand that I only observe the negative—wonders who the *dem* is that Mummy meant.

This disgusted dismissal is never spent, never in evidence for Theresa. A listening ear of compassion is always lent my mother's mother in Grenada. The light-skin mother of Carib or something descent. Mummy's mother who pays rent to the jumbie in her belly sending up daily entreaties for a bottle of 69% proof Clarke's Court Pure White Rum to reside under her liver roof. Her liver that never quiver at years of such abuse. That whispering for a bottle that never done.

My mother has all the sympathy, love, and understanding for this alcoholic mother of hers who pours wallets down her gullet. Reconstituting all the necessities she coulda buy. And my mother laughs when I ask her how could she accept this, ignore this. Send money. Enable it. And why. My mother throws back her head, fully amused, wanting me to join in too, in the family troupe. In agreeing that de rum does keep she alive.

But I do not lie.

We drive, on this trip of ill bode, to visit Theresa brother-something-so, past the National Flour Mills on Wrightson Road and their giant concrete silos. This beautiful blue steel and glass soul of Trinbago cuisine that milling our macaroni pie's wheat and our pelau's rice. And I look out the window at this elegant building coloured for the multiple shades of the sky. Artistically designed, aesthetically pleasing architecture. This sign of my country's booming industry, as we learn in social studies lecture. This pretty town-construction that always makes me smile. Though I will not know the price of Trinidad importing grain for a long while.

We drive past Licensing, where taxi drivers does buy they permit to make fares on the road. Past John D., where boys who can't hack it in academics and need to learn a trade does go.

My father's tan Ford car, following Uncle Donald's grey one—that he say he didn't want but he alone does drive, that he quarrel and complain and wouldn't watch his children all the while Tanty Marilyn taking lessons from Licensing so she wouldn't have to catch early-morning maxi taxis for squash-up rides out on Diego Martin Main Road to reach to the work that she alone does go—vrooms past the coral-pink Cruise Ship Complex. The port disgorging white tourists in whom we thankfully doh much invest.

And on this early-morning, down-south drive to where finger-big mosquito does eat you alive, we only now leaving proper town. Leaving behind the landmarks I have down. But is cool anyway, since, for we north people, anything past the lighthouse don't count.

Beetham Highway certainly don't. That stink stretch of La Basse that finally compel me to wind up the window. And, even in the car, hold my nose. Watching flocks of corbeaux circle and land. To feast on the perfume of death which to them sang. Watching hills of rubbish that little children sorting by hand. Black children. From nearby galvanise sheet hovels and particle board shanties and shacks. Children who crossed the no-traffic-light highway to scavenge, and must cross back. These children—descendants of the plantations selections. The plantations defections. The plantations rejections. The plantations resistance. Driven here. Germinating generations. On the outskirts of mind and government care.

My father driving past, my father driving fast. Nobody don't want to stop here.

Factories now drawing near. And that's where I sleep.

What the hell, I squeak. That startling, raspy, outta-nowhere voice creeps. From right beside me. Across my face, Rum's long, bony finger comes. Extending past a fraying jacket cuff, pointing out this is where he dwells. My eyes follow the arrow in a spell under the suddenly apparated finger directing my sight again out the glass windowpane to the right. Through which I see a wide, fat, aluminium vat. Sparkling, refracting the sun's light. Its gleaming height ascending several storeys. With companion tubings, pipes, ladders, and tangled machinery.

That right there is the Fernandes Vat 19 rum distillery. Rum speaks, like a tour guide's ancillary. Directly into my ear. He en hah tuh bodda. Nobody else in my father's car knows Rum is a passenger here. On their happy family trip. Nonetheless, directly into my appalled face he bends his chapped lips. And his fetid breath gusts as he shares.

My senses overwhelm with fear I'll never be purged of this sweet, burning cloy of Rum that comes from outside's oppressive air. Air drenched and overlaid with the brewing of alcohol night and day that forces itself into the nose of all those travelling this highway. This Rum aroma also leaking from inside. From out the pores of my companion on this interminable ride. Who apparently here to stay.

This Rum who I didn't see regain his wiry, muscled body. After he faded before the presence of the silk cotton trees. So, what permits this tenacity? This re-entry at seeming whim. And now inside the car interior's dim. What door is not closed against him?

This Rum who was submerged. Now lured into return. Into continuance. This Rum who has been conferred space to maintain his place. This rum materialised in my father's car. Occupying his own seat. This Rum playing host on this southbound journey. To visit my mother family.

Turning aside from perturbation that Rum hitchhike this drive, I tune into the car radio now playing Rikki Jai. Who so cute. And I fly up in my seat. Mummy, raise up the volume. Please. Hold the Lata Mangeshkar, gimme soca, aha aha. And I twist my wrists to screw the bulb and peck my neck in the freshened breeze. Dancing to the seductive soca chutney beat. The rest of the highways, roads, and streets pass in dream that Rikki Jai love song is actually to me.

Thus, I do not see. But I feel the gravel grater of Uncle Charlie yard grind under the slowing tyres of my father's car. Through the Ford's shocks, up to the back seat. Jolting me from oblivious sleep.

Feel the message-passing, whisper-warning of the tall bush leaves swaying in the tolling breeze. The bush stalks pointed heads above green round face bent toward each other. Distressed that my spine knows better. But has come to this place where the leaves witness in their dense midst events that efface being here is ever safe. The brown dirt at their feet keeps hold of every unhidden trace of violences in this place. Earth never forgets the DNA of a case.

I feel the back of my neck awake. Fully rouse consciousness from its drowse, from Rikki Jai's lapping serenade. Into silence. Alertness. Arrival. Unwanted sensations of vigilance that rival the dread at the inevitable rash that will spread with which I will itch in bed over the course of this weekend. From being made to bathe in a rusting galvanise-wall, outside shower stall. With a bucket of rainwater and Lifebuoy soap that don't rinse off. Because, as Mr. Holder teach us in science, rainwater too soft. And tap water hard. But Mummy say it not too bad. And I just fussy. Though I show her my skin red, streaked, inflamed, and bumpy. Every time we come by her Uncle Charlie.

But this is her family. My mother's. Smiley's. My mother's mother's brother-something-so. Smiley's uncle who took her into his own home. When she was nineteen. When Mummy was rebirthing herself as a Trini. When Mummy was leaving behind Grenada, her birth country. When Mummy was leaving behind her first abandoned baby. And the guarantee of a rash on her daughter's inner thighs and back is not bad enough to stay away up north, it seems.

This is her family. This Uncle Charlie. My mother mother something-so brother. And so it does not bother Smiley—this mother of mine who exits my father's car into radiant sunlight, displaying pearly whites—what I say I feel.

It does not bother Smiley that Uncle Charlie's youngest daughter with Simintra, his third or fourth wife, is a big fat bully. That Charlie and Simintra's tall youngest daughter, who only a year or two older than me, have an uncomfortable, ordering, show-me-yours way of playing tea. And that Charlie and Simintra son is a teen who don't need to be in the bedroom when we little girls getting dressed and ready. And the dyed-pink, one-ply toilet paper allotted squares never enough to stretch for putrid wooden-seat, outdoor latrine use.

And dodging Uncle Charlie nightly rum-lit fuse and his swinging cutlass that swear it going to chop up his wife ass cannot be forgotten the next day with a laugh. And the squads of mosquitoes and the dry standpipe. And the far away shop that require a hot-sun hike. And the high-up ladder to climb to the pink add-on upstairs just to get some ice is why I don't like taking a four-hour drive down Point Fortin to see this greying, paunch-belly, alcoholic Uncle Charlie. My mother's family.

But Mummy doesn't agree.

And so I feel nothing but disgust when she thrusts a pack of Bourbon chocolate biscuits in my face to lure me out her husband car and embrace her family. This Simintra she now hugging. Both Mummy and Charlie wife not coming up to five feet. Fat Simintra, biggest and broadest in the chest, with inverted triangle legs.

Pear-shaped Mummy, all-over-round and curvy and more hip-heavy. Mummy and Simintra. Two short pegs. Both with taller husbands of muscled arms, broad backs, and veiny hands. Two husbands' bodies honed into bludgeoning tools from working the land. The forerunners, Simintra and Charlie, who in their tangerine dirt yard stand. These people my mother demands me be happy to greet twice a year at least. More sometimes.

Because when Charlie son, Uncle Donald—my mother's first cousin—decides to take that long drive, my mother always becomes inclined to go down Point Fortin side. She never want to be left behind. My mother always becomes inclined to once again reside under the roof where these cousins first intersected their lives. Smiley and Donald forging a connection that would not die.

These two first cousins, Smiley and Donald, marrying two siblings, Ulric and Marilyn, who built their houses right next to each other. As is the way in my father's family of siblings who never leave the nest of their mother. The all-in-a-circle-of-petals way they reside, surrounding the mothering pistil, helping provide the two first cousins, Smiley and Donald, the means to abide next to, with, amongst each other for their marital years up Trinidad north-west side. The two first cousins, Smiley and Donald, having children nearly the same time. Donald's three girls a year older than each of my mother's. All neatly aligned.

It coming to pass that every time Donald impregnated Marilyn, his wife, this mother of mine and her husband also came to be with child. Now we are six girls, four spouses, two adult siblings, two first cousins returning to visit the house under whose roof they sprouted this design. Under Uncle Charlie roof where the two first cousins, Smiley and Donald, live initially physically intertwined.

Uncle Donald's grey car—well, his wife's—is parked to one side under a luxuriantly shading chenette tree. Tall, aloft, with branches drifting forth. Tall, aloof, with branches poised to observe the fury and noise Uncle Charlie's existence requires as self-evident proof. That yard spread around the chenette tree's roots, a sieve, a bowl, a basin of truth. Where rum, sweat, and tears glaze the urn of those who yearn to venture beyond its round perimeter. Striving, by all means, for a life out the blue board and concrete and add-on-a-piece house that have to be sweeter.

Into the cocoyea broom-swept ewer that is the dirt yard, Tanty Marilyn, Donald's wife—my father's sister—is beside their car's front door. Her gaze is trepidatious. Her gaze is not yet hard. And their three girls have already emerged to explore. These three girls who like their trips down south to their grandfather's house. These three girls whose view remains unmarred. Their enthusiasm never doused. Not after, nor before.

These three girls, my first and second cousins in this family that doesn't think anything weird of how our families interweave. This pattern I perceive. This intertwining like fungal roots. That bloom mushrooms. One day truths.

For now, us girls are all standing in the cars' and adults' shade. In the dirt yard. Awaiting the house's reception. Me, my two younger sisters, and my three cousins in sundresses and rubber slippers with already dusty toe thongs. My cousins, relatives on both sides of a square, Uncle Charlie's house keeps strong.

And I feel wrong. Being here. Where my mother doesn't hear. Where I don't share her eagerness to overlook all I see, smell, and funny-stale-water taste. All that chooks my brain. All that I cannot explain. All that impregnates the tumid air, with silent eyes watching me be steered into Charlie's add-on-a-piece, blue-board house, up the wooden plank steps.

Gapped steps over which Rum, out the car like a shot when it park, long since leapt. And disappeared. Melding, adept. Into the dark recesses shadowed and revealed through beads and lace curtains. Rum, fully materialised again here in Point Fortin. In Uncle Charlie house. Where Rum reception certain. In Charlie house. Where Rum's translucence disappears from view.

In Charlie house. Where Rum—animating everything, everyone, all that is to come—remains see-through.

Day is long down south. In the mouth of the afternoon, swallowed and regurgitated by the hours' unending throat, we hear the goat.

We children have been sent to go and play on our own. To get out the way. Out, they say. Out the space of the tent-pitching. And roti paratha on the tawa flipping. And gold streamers on the walls pinning. And collapsible tables' red cloth covering. And three-part, plastic champagne glass assembling. And all the busy fuss of the neighbours in and out setting up Simintra and Charlie big daughter wedding.

We have been sent. To roam. Us little ones. Go, with allyuh big cousins an dem. Charlie's bush clones. They who know the stretches of wilderness and weeds, flowers, herbs, and trees like the back of they hand and unscratchable knobby knees. They, these big cousins, Charlie clones, who know the buzz of different-colour bees collecting honey. They who know the chain-dragging clang of lagahoo walking upright like man. And know lagahoo monstrous sight. Having gained the ability after taking yampee from dog eye. Besides, they say, Dem does mostly come out at night. So we, the little cousins, don't need to take fright following these Charlie clones into the bush they know.

As long as we doh go alone.

These big cousins who show us which mango verre tree now good to touch and how much it ready to yield. Sweet, juicy mango spurting yellow. Dribbling down our happy chins and elbows. And these cousins know how to avoid the sharp fever grass we pass as our sticky hands look for something to wipe them on. And point instead to long, dewy ginger lily leaves fanning out from blushing, proud heads. We, little ones, mango-fed before the big cousins declare a game in these dense fields they able to read, of hide-and-seek.

And they run and they leave. Everyone scattering. Till I am awash, marooned at sea in emerald, waving bush taller than me. Bush thick with crispy tangs of crunched, munched grass. Sharp and sweet. Bush alive with nose-stinging brine of slithering scales. Companion snakes whose burrowed nests get wet in the last rain.

And through the shhhh-shhhing of green undulating in sun worship, in ecstatic, photosynthetic dance around me, I hear the agitated bleat. I peer through the sparser tops of leaves. The bush's middle an impenetrable mass of stalks and stems and reeds. Thus, I cannot see the feet nor the hooves. But I smell fur's frowsy, heavy air move. Toward me. Fur reeking like a closed classroom of boys after PE.

And locked in a sonic barrier of bleats and the funk of sweat, I am alone and cannot move my legs in any possible misdirection. To go farther to the left, to the right might be to stray too far from these wilds-knowing cousins.

Baaaaaaaaaaa. A prolonged blare and head-toss of short, jutting horns by which the goat declares those wide strong hands grasping round the eyes are unwanted there. And I don't know that man or the next or the other who have the coarse hemp rope round the goat's elongating neck. Its neck made to stretch as the goat backpedals from the direction in which the rope has kept flailing protest tied to the tree.

The tall shatine tree being made complicit simply by appearing stationary. The fruit-laden tree subverting the goat's back-wheeling attempts to be free. The rope pulling now. So tightly. Its strong weave making the goat's thick tan and black parting fur stand up spiky. As the fibres scrape and chafe the tender brown skin underneath directly.

No! My choked cry comes before my sentient hands rise without my command to block any further sound. Don't look around, the tall plants utter. Then provide cover to my quaking thighs. Lemongrass embracing my shin in blades of knives. The leaves' ripplings masking my screech and converting it into just the wind's sigh. Not my cries that belie the horror before my rounding eyes. My terror at those hands.

Those hands. Dry, rough, hard, and laughing. Big, veiny, strong, and passing a clear bottle of White Oak rum round. Hands lifting Vat 19 rum to chugging throats, Adam's apples swallowing down.

Those hands swinging up the cutlass dancing its silver pirouette. Schwing. Cutlass singing. Ringing its own musical accompaniment. Those lifted hands raising their underarms' charging battalion of fetid sweat.

While the goat is butting. Leaping rear legs struggling to eject those spread hands at its rump. The goat is screaming. Beating the scabby tree trunk to which the inch-wide rope has bound its undaunted hope.

And the sun up on high kisses the cutlass' sharp-edged blade in diamond light. Flashes that blind the eye beholding the fevered arc of iron's ballet flight. Iron fuelled. Iron frenzied by the drumming fight of the goat's heart racing blood through arteries dilating in width and height. Arterial walls stretching tight. Arteries that feed unsheathed iron's might in this its commandeered rite.

And my hands won't let go my gasping lips. My brain won't let my impulse to run dictate my legs take me out of this. Out of here. Into the dangerous sphere where the men's hands grasp. Where the hands straddle the goat's tail. Where the hands keep the fat, brown body from its flail. Where the hands do not suppress the goat's vibrating wail.

The goat's high-pitch pleads. The goat, in language we all speak, grieves. The goat, wide-eyed, terrified, begging to be let free. And the cutlass smiles. Dazzling bright. Iron happy at the sight of the rope-pulled throat of the goat who does not cease to strive to get away. No! No. No. My grasping fingers say. Holding the watery plants, I sway.

Moan. No. My tears lamenting having come this way. Of a bound sacrifice under display. Of the goat neck stretching, stretching high. Bawling bleating begging calls. To a deaf ear sky. Of my toes clenching, not in the spotlight. Where the sun's ray falls. Trapping us in its bright, hot thrall.

The hand drops. One, swift, singing chop. Ripping muscle, sinews. Crunching bone. The goat bawls. Alone. I gasp-gurgle. The tied tree groans. Those hands cheer sharp iron finding its precise zone. And leaf crowns bow under the spray of fresh-smelling, warm globules of blood. Arcing in a flood of red. A far-reaching libation radius from the fallen goat's head.

The goat is not dead.

On the padded receiving dirt, the goat's eyes that hurt stare up at the sky. At the bush-green sea. Stare up at me. Why did I have to be sacrificed? I cry. I don't know. But I will never forget your life. Why did I have to be killed? I'm sorry, I'm so sorry. You shouldn't have. They shouldn't have taken you. But I will stay. I will tell someday.

The goat's battling head bumps along the sodden clay pillowing its horns. The soil that was unable to foil a plot to end the goat's life to commemorate the joining of this husband and this wife. The soil that is the final bed of the goat's head. The head that ends its nerve-spasm dance. The head that remains in the last direction that its spurting, pulsing blood fed the plants.

The goat's head says its last goodbye on the grounds over which the cutlass was brought to soar and preside. The dirt where drinking, labouring men denied the goat's right to life I witness leach and depart. And enter my heart that drops my knees to the ground. And erupts my belly in reverse Crix and weak Milo tea sourly over my tongue. In retched oblation the earth has found unpleasing.

My cousins find me heaving. Tears, babbling, trembling as if I'm freezing. And the teasing of a little girl who cries for a dumb goat and too childish to watch a chopped throat sallies forth in robust guffaws. My cousins' bravado stomps in the walk through the blood-speckled stalks. The walk they navigate in long strides, shaky laughs, and darting eyes.

And I alone cry. All the way back to Uncle Charlie's house. Charlie house, where these big cousins who saying, Hush yuh mouth, iz just a schupid goat, doh worry dey go curry it good an yuh go see how sweet goat meat is reside. In the house with no room to hide.

My stockings and ankle socks are glowing white in the church's candlelight. Mummy's soft lap is next to mine. Shiny dark red and black covers her thick thighs. With an elastic line she sew down the middle of the dress on the inside. Creating the gathered, ruffled effect of a Chinese Shar Pei. This *Dynasty* dress that's in style. Though I asked her why, at her Singer sewing machine, keeping Mummy company. Why she was choosing dark colours for an occasion that supposed to be happy.

Mummy reaches across the bench and pinches my fingers wedged in the starch-stiff neckband of my light blue and white watercolour dress. She means to stop my fussing that's mussing up her Smiley big daughter look nice and fancy, yes, she do good fuh she self compliments. Yet, after a hardly-sleep night wherein burning cockset did nothing to fight off warmongering mosquitoes and my ears wouldn't close to howls on the wind and the din of Uncle Charlie boys throwing back rum and puncheon, I am fed up and scratching at these nylon legs apparently required to watch Margaret wed.

This Margaret. Second Dougla daughter. Of old Charlie and youngish Simintra. Offspring of Charlie greying, grizzled kinks and Simintra straight hair shining jet black with coconut oil after it final rinse. Black and Indian link. Producing Margaret bouffant curls, fibrous and wavy, afro puff and lengthy from their mix.

This Margaret of the big front buck teeth underneath the forcing themselves not to smile too wide dark lips. Charcoal lips contrasting against the milky Ovaltine skin of her smooth round face graced with long eyelashes, feathery sideburns, and the faint trace of a moustache that betrays the prolific hair of her half-Indian race.

This Margaret's phenotypes elevating her to a place, so she say, where an army man dripping sweat go still want to stand up in his Sunday best and vow to pledge his mature life to a flimsy wife. To this Margaret, his vibrating bride, who everybody down Point whispering wild wild wild.

This Margaret who they say tired trow way chile. And take man from San'do to Guayaguayare to Rio Claro. Putting on miles. Wearing and tearing on a body barely past twenty. And if her man, who was hide way in de army, know what good fuh he, he go take Margaret up north.

Away from the scorch of the love that still burns for the young fella she did supposedly want. The one who spurn Margaret when he learn just how desperate to leave Charlie house she is that she turn her slim hips and knock-knee legs, her sultry voice, high-pitch laugh, and big standing-up breasts into assets. So she say. So she excuse, and so she plead. This Margaret of my mother's family. Who say is need. That make her turn her slender body into a commodity. A means to exit Charlie blue board and add-on-a-piece monstrosity.

This Margaret wedding her army man before me. This Margaret, my mother's family.

See the couple gazing deep in each other's eyes. Standing at the altar, wreathed in smiles. This Margaret and she army man both dressed in white. Him in his glorified uniform, back straight, striving fuh young-boy height. She in fitted sateen down to her toes. She not baring a trace of immodesty, capitulating to Simintra who does cry she en raise no hoes.

Formal attire covering Margaret up with nothing to show. Except for the wide-netted lace over the neck and shoulders and arms and chest.

That put you face to face with the peaking breasts that have no place in a church her neighbours shshing to say of Margaret dress she had the seamstress make just so. Huh, so we know how she ketch him, the whispers curl like candle smoke round the rim of the vaulted ceiling supervising this couple standing then kneeling.

This couple pledging vows they add on. Suffused in streaming mid-afternoon sun. Incandescent in candle flame. Lit within by love. So they claim. Inside olive-green walls that have me appalled somebody actually choose this colour as I look around for the Roman figures clock to stave off slumber. Ticking time to the number of beats before I can get off this hard seat and out this stifling heat.

Repeat after me, till death do us part. The preacher reach de heart of this mamaguy ceremony through which clenching has been unrelenting from my activating belly cause the wind outside on pause. Like if my ears stuff with gauze. Like a noonday showdown. Streets empty. High-beam sun making a mirage of parked cars and buildings turned hazy. And I awaiting weapon draws. That, coming. And Mummy not listening. Cause she too busy face-forward-viewing and celebrating. And my tugging on her soft arm irritating. And her shrug off of my hand accuse me of fidgeting.

But the sparrow sit down right there on the windowsill. Still still still. And nothing in the road moving. How nothing in this village moving. Why beyond the church so quiet. Dropped into the riot of honking horns and bullfrogs and crickets and barking dogs gone. Silent. And the whole atmosphere holding it breath. In violent absence of stirring life. This not right. And from outside to inside, through the window, it crept. The hackles, the shackles pinning me to knowing. Something. Growing.

You may now kiss the bride. This couple slides on yellow gold bands. And takes two minutes long to tangle they tongues. Margaret whoops and raises her bouquet in triumph. We marrid now. The congregation exhales. Relaxes their poise. I listen to the bush's missing noise.

Well, after rice done pelt and Margaret party gyuls done cheer and yell. After, arm in arm, the holy matrimonied couple done laughingly, relievedly run through the white-balloon arch of the church doors into the swell of setting sunlight, the real wedding—de fete—take over the night.

De fete. The feast to which everybody near and far doh require they get no formal invite. Wedding keeping, the whole village passing through that night. Long as gold rum out the Vat 19 drum flowing. Long as the slam of domino tiles on gathered tables of ply still knocking. And the all-fours card game still going. Long as man-high, boom-box speakers vibrating, shaking, and shocking. Making yuh half deaf when yuh pass too close to they length against the wall. Long as vinyl records on the DJ tabletop spinning. And sweet Percy Sledge crooning, issuing the call to dark corners for a wine and slow grind away from the naked bulbs revealing who horning with who man they cyah name mine.

Long as felled silky coconut branches, interlaced and standing sentinel, turning they green face into the additional reception space erected by dry wood bamboo poles, hold and fold young couples, running children, and the gossiping old into togetherness. Long as Michael Bolton "That's What Love Is All About" keeping the women romantic. And Mighty Duke when-I-hold-yuh-tonight "Thunder" giving the men opportunity to chook, hard and frantic. While the mothers laugh and shout to children, doh look.

Long as stew fish continue to cook. And chicken fat still hitting de grill splat. And barbecue smoke still burning yuh eye. Long as dem people curry goat and dey bottle of pepper sauce doh run dry. Long as the babies and all dancing. Stamping they lil foot on the upraise wood stage. Sounding loud as horse hoof. And when they fall, none of them doh look to cry in de crowding rampage.

Long as soca blaring. Pelau and Chinese fry rice sharing. Parents of bamsee-shaking teens not caring. The *cksshhh* of garlic and onion throwing in the pot hearing. And silky shiny starchy good clothes still faring. Long as White Oak rum eh sparing lash in de glass, then nobody care who foot get mash. And the fete cyah done. Whole night it run. Till we return inside Charlie house for a five-hour nap or thereabouts. Walking in, laughing at all who tired and buhn. Just on the cusp of the rising sun.

Whole night everybody have fun. Meanwhile, that whole night Simintra, in she electric blue, ruffle and shiny, fake satin dress, stay worried. Fanning sheself in sweaty anxiety Charlie might come.

That Charlie might wake from the coma of Puncheon and White Oak rum.

Wait. Wasn't he . . . there? This Charlie. This mother-mother-brother. This retained uncle of Smiley's. My mother's cherished family. Wasn't Charlie there? In the ghost-green church to hear his second daughter with his third-ish wife declare her betrothal? Her belonging. Her transference from her father's care to her husband dear?

Wasn't he there? Charlie. To watch Margaret marry she man. The man who name Alvin, if yuh must know. Though yuh doh really hadda, if truth be told. But we will allow him this slight space. And believe, for the length of the night, the love for Alvin reflected in Margaret moon face.

Anyway.

Wasn't Charlie there? Under the sky of tented tarpaulin drape over the ballroom scene of dancing Margaret, who change een a tight popcorn dress two inches below she bamsee. Wining and flashing the guests she panty. There to see Margaret take her first dance with wazhename as husband and wife about to embark on the rest of their life?

You mean to say, Charlie didn't show he face as day make space for night and the whole of Point Fortin, it feel like, come out to celebrate his daughter's last rites as a single girl? Charlie couldn't self manage to unfurl himself from the claim, the grip, the untenuous slip of rum to eat some roti. And come and dance with his wife relatives in they best dandan and dhoti?

Not this loving Charlie. To whom my mother clings so obligingly. As her family. And make me sit down, hot and sweaty, for a four-hour drive down to the bush where mosquitoes does eat you alive. And rainwater, latrine seats, and gigantic flies does break yuh "first" daughter out in rash and hives.

Because you have to prioritise the mother brother of your family and not yuh child who say in the church something lurking and coming. But you try to make that daughter feel like she crazy. And ting she does see and feel not right. Though is this same eight-year-old daughter bed yuh does crawl in at night. To cry and say, Yuh know meh mind did tell me not to marrid yuh father.

But in daylight, when you in denial, is right behind this self same man yuh does humble and flirt and crawl. And tell yuh imagining-things daughter yuh never say them things at all. So she wouldn't trust what she knows she must. About this family. This Uncle Charlie.

Who, indeed, where is he? And why Simintra, whole night, so worried? And why she tell she big son, who eh yet leave teens years behind, to make haste and go and hide the cutlasses over the Petrotrin oil pipe. And the knives. And the ice pick. Hurry up and run, quick. And doh get licks. By this Charlie who could still use his iron fist. And when rum swell he head, he doh resist adding metal to make his dent. This is the uncle my mother bring us down for a weekend to spend. Responsible ent?

Anyway, we was studying where this Charlie could be, off on a rum bend.

So. Where oh where could he be? This uncle of my mother's. Who seemingly couldn't be bothered. To attend the festive ceremony. The she-damn-lucky sealing of matrimony. For his wild, screeching-laugh daughter. For whose wedlock the fatted goat has been slaughtered?

Is when we outside. After the catnap and everybody refresh for the drive. When breakfast done eat and bags done pack. When Mummy and Uncle Donald and Daddy and Tanty Marilyn promising Simintra and her children that they go soon come back. And school holidays not too far away and allyuh could come up for a stay. And my big toe signing the dirt, no way. That the bush begin to sway. That the bush begin to say. Winds of rage on the loose. But I don't know how fast or how bad or from where that rage coming through. And what I supposed to do.

All I holding on to is Charlie didn't reach the reception the evening before. He didn't come home to the board and concrete house that night. He didn't shake the unconcealed galvanise and wooden beams with his drunken snores. And now is the next day. And I thinking we making it out safe.

But is when Margaret dragging her bags for her honeymoon holiday out from the bedroom she share with her sisters. Share before they all start to find quick-moving misters. Fast men to get them out from under Charlie roof and the up-ladder kitchen for ice.

Is when the crowd all assemble outside to say goodbye.

Is when, in a circle in the orange dirt yard, we standing. Cars parked. Us six girls leaning on bonnets, sitting on trunks, leaving sticky prints of tiny hands. Big people talking over last-minute details. Nervous lips, eyes roaming while they lavishing praise. Simintra yuh eh play yuh give yuh big daughter a nice nice wedding day.

Is when I collecting my snacks I need to munch on in the back of Daddy car. Governor plums, five finger, and pomerac for the drive so far. Especially for when we passing through central plains. And that sticky, burn sugar smell waft over everything, and the cars and all it invade. From where it emanate out Caroni Ltd factories processing sugar cane. Turning juiced stalks into exports of white grains.

Is when I in my thin-strap, swishy little frilly dress I love. Imitating denim cloth. But soft. With happy pink and yellow ruffles. My oh gosh leh we go nah stares being muffled. By the thickening air. That the parents not saying, not explaining coming from where. Like we can't see. Like I can't feel. Like tension not leaking from their tight-shoulder bodies.

Is when the grown-ups talking in loud darting eyes. Simintra metallically laughing and beaming hectic smiles. While Margaret husband, arm around the waist of his wife, talking a mile a minute. With unmicrophoned authority. Like he commanding his military. And Margaret giggling at everything her husband saying, laugh ascending like bush monkeys. Increasing the birds' chattering cacophony.

Is when I, with dry Crix and weak Milo unsatisfied, wondering if when we reach back Mummy will have time to cook macaroni pie and half-bake-half-fry chicken. Or if she gonna take the easy way out and make a weekday white rice and stew beef even though I hate how chewy that meat is and how is in my back teeth it always sticking.

When the bush inhale stiffen.

And dirt-streaked white-jersey Charlie and his standing tall, answering its blood-call cutlass emerge.

Man-high stalks reclose around the birth. Reseal upon the veiled path that Charlie serge pants, back pocket loaded with a bottle of Vat 19 Rum, swathed. Before disgorging him into the receiving yard bowl that feel the coming Charlie. Stealing ease from the breeze, relaxed limbs from the trees.

That Charlie arrive standing in front of we.

And here I see Rum once more. See Rum's vaporous form. See Rum having gained a solid body into which he's been absorbed. Charlie's, before me. I see Rum's animus through Charlie's red orbs. I smell Rum's dancing spirit through Charlie's dry pores. I hear Rum's wicked cackle coming through Charlie's maws. I taste the ancient one on the air in tangy iron gripped in Charlie's paws. And I know now why Rum joined this journey. Here is his prescient cause. Here is the real reason Rum endures. He fuels. Rum is the excuse to channel the abased truth of those obeying his laws. Rum opens existent evil's doors.

Charlie arm lift up. Charlie cutlass drop. Shrieking chop.

Groom straight back folding in. Right arm tucked like a broken wing. Still on his feet. On bracketing legs. That dare not bed into dirt gorging on his gushing spurts. Running. Bowing sweating head. Baying cries to raise the dead. Hobbling to green arms. Dripping red. Bush thrashing. Twigs snapping. Revealing. Rising falling waves of leaves swallowing relaying decreasing speeding. Of a red trail. Never to be seen in Point Fortin again. Tell yuh you didn't need to remember Alvin name.

Freezing frame. But my legs run me to hide behind the car from sight.

Margaret stays. In the front yard. Right where her father dispense with the husband she love so bad. Margaret stay within the arm span. Of Charlie going mad. Cutlass switch to the left from the dominant right. Charlie close his thick, blunt fingers into a fist crammed tight.

My dress tremble. Charlie pull back his big, brawny arm. Roped with angry veins. Charlie ram his giant fist into Margaret temple. Charlie punch the full force of his strength into Margaret doe-eye face.

I tell you yuh going anywhere? You en leaving meh kiss-me-ass house. You knock-knee bitch. Somebody send you to take man. And you playin brave. Ah go kill allyou dead here today today today!

Margaret father drop her where she stand.

Margaret don't crumble. She falls straight down like a capital letter I. One cuff. Margaret nosedive like Wile E. Coyote in those cartoons my sisters watch. And I never like.

Margaret doesn't scream. An automated response if your lungs have air to breathe. A sound Margaret don't have oxygen to make. Faster than anaesthesia, consciousness behind Margaret rolling up white eyeballs vacate. Consciousness withdraw from her motionless state. From her sprawling body lying in the harassed dirt. And Charlie smirks.

Everyone—these people, my mother's family, her husband, his sister—lurks. In a circumference. From a perimeter of distance to observe. I watch them, the big people, from the out-of-view side of the car. Where my knees tap out Morse code on the Ford's rust sealed with tar. And in the centre, far from none of the hands reaching to do something, red springs.

Into Margaret floral honeymoon dress, rusted blood begins to seep. To bloom. Margaret dress like the white sheet the documentary says the new wife shows off to prove. To prove in blood her fidelity to her groom. Blood that Margaret father makes flow as he looms. Blood Charlie exacts from his daughter who he will not relinquish from under his roof. Charlie being the man who extracts the blood exhibiting on cloth being publicly viewed. As he really wanted to do. Charlie staking his claim that will not be removed. As blood on his daughter dress for the honeymoon blooms.

Whose? Margaret blood? The goat? The groom? Who blood it is display? On show. Unshamed. From which none of the balcony, mezzanine, house spectators turning away. This family of mine, they stay. They neck craned. This morning after Margaret good good wedding day.

Hungry cutlass swinging round. Yous my fuckin chile. Margaret body unmoving, untwitching, on the ground. Yuh not blasted goin nowhere. Simintra's wailing pleas the loudest sound. You name woman in dis place? Margaret blood her father tore, dripping down. Allyou chirren an you modda belong to me. The parents gently dissuading, the big people stationary like points in Charlie crown. Allyou mudda cunt is mine. Charlie's rage their flaring sun. Like revolving planets they orbiting around. And you go dead here today. No one challenging Charlie to end the cutlass song. In my fuckin house. My thighs weakening at crouching down.

Rum extracted from his back pocket to quench Charlie's laughing tongue. Slurp. Gulp. Belch. Backhand against mouth to wipe. Dis Vat 19 rum need some ice. Rubber garden boots pound dirt and gravel, stems, flowers, and travel around the house's left side. Toward the backyard oil pipe.

The tableau reactivates when Charlie's dirty-jersey shoulders lope out of sight. My parents, my cousins' parents, turn and look at each other and begin their game of not I, said the fly. As Margaret's slender frame, in the hard dirt, lies supine. Black hair plastered against brown face unflushed with life.

Tanty Marilyn say, I doh want this kinda energy and badness in my place. Not all this kinda ruckshun and behaviour in my house.

Uncle Donald—Charlie son, Tanty Marilyn spouse—spout, with clenching jowls, Nah nah sorry I not getting in de middle uh dis. Daz between dem. I cyah help out.

Daddy—mouth pull in a U-shaped frown upside down, his head dip to face the ground, and his fingers scratching the back of his neck while he interject, when they look toward him next—Well ahmm huh uhuhuhuh hahhhh, diz a big ting allyuh askin yes, hmmm, ahhhmmmm, huh. A big ting. Cyatrin?

And Mummy—Smiley, Cyatrin, Catherine—without hesitating, without wondering. Without pondering. Without drawing a pause at any uncircumspect cause, reply, Of course. We cyah leave her here. We'll take her. Right, Ulric? Yeah, as she shakes her head and sighs. And doesn't look around for any reeling child. Doesn't look to the car I'm peeping behind.

Margaret go come home and stay wid us.

Thus,

> no ambulance, no police, no emergency services are phoned. Quick, the men go over to Margaret body still prone and take hold under the armpits and around the ankle. The men wrangle Margaret body into the Ford's back seat. My mother rests Margaret's heavy, whites-of-her-eyes-showing head on me. On the lap of her big daughter whose wise soul mature enough to bear the weight. The strain of a woman head, dead or alive, whose awareness her father fist take. Eight car doors slam. Eight tyres squeal. Two cars about-turn, gun engines, spew gravel, erupt a plume of dust as they wheel at high speed. Before Charlie and his cutlass come back to feed.

Thus,

Ericka cries and asks questions. Sherrie sucks her tongue and drifts into sleep's rejection of the car's reality. And this mother tells me Doh make no fuss. As Margaret lolling head rolls and toss on her unsupporting neck that does not show signs of being undead yet. My father drives the sixty-five-plus miles. Stopping at no police station, no hospital. And makes good time back to Covigne Road. And our bags and our baggage, he and Mummy unload.

Thus,

> after this mother says yes to her family coming to stay, Margaret wakes. Margaret laughs when she realises she get away. Even farther than she anticipate from Charlie house. Margaret only asks one question about her newly wedded spouse. Margaret says she's afraid to bathe without someone to watch. Margaret asks my sisters and me to stand in front the open shower curtain while she soaps and rinses, touch and thrusts her rotund breasts to see how they bounce. Margaret flounces around the house in red negligee meant for her honeymoon. Margaret replies that Ah doh need no wuk because Ah go get some money soon.

Thus,

> after this mother retains unflinching loyalty to all the characters of her family. After this mother pledges unrelenting fidelity to all the people of this pedigree. After this mother doesn't stop to think, discern, or implement anything she may have learnt experientially in Charlie house whilst maturing supposedly. After this mother invites her wretched relations to stay with we, Margaret decides to pose. For a rag newspaper's

centrefold. For the *Sunday Punch* magazine. Legs spread wide open, inviting all to come een. And view. Margaret in her birthday suit.

Thus,

after this mother opens the door to her family, who done run through South, to come stay in our house and Margaret publishes her nudes, Margaret laughs and flirts and bats her long eyelashes and croons. Margaret moons over the Covigne Road men, the mechanics and dem, when they tape her naked centrefold to the wall. To the stretch of brick I and all the little girls being sent to the shop must pass. Must walk by while these men grab their crotches, their rum, their blunts, and shout, smallie yuh have a sweet ass.

Thus,

when this mother says yes and doesn't draw a boundary between her children and her perverted family, Margaret remains the same as she showed when she was home: nasty. Margaret limes all day and talks to these rum-guzzling, weed-smoking, gun-toting, blades-holding, supposed-to-be-car-fixing men I ignore. These stray men who stay on the road all day, all night. These men I pretend my eyes cannot see when I walk quaking to the store. Margaret goes into their galvanise mechanics garage with these men to touch, and kiss, and hike up her popcorn dress, and smoke and score. And when walking up the hill, Margaret wraps her arm round my shoulders to hold me still. While she tells these red-eyed, bare-back, salivating men that I am her little cousin and she training me up. And asks why I doh spend some time with them. This woman of my mother's family who solicits the attention of the men who terrorise me. And tells them If allyuh like that first setta picture and pose, it have plenty more uh those. Those open denim jacket pornographic pictures to me she shows.

She, Margaret, kept-family of my mother.

This mother of mine. Closing her eyes. This mother who smiles. This mother who denies. This mother who does get vex. Uricka, yuh too sensitive, yuh just lookin fuh ting to be upset. This mother eyes big and wet when her husband tell she, Cyatrin, Margaret not bringing in no money an she cyan just stay here doin nuttin permanently. This mother murmuring and offering pleas when Margaret cuss, and when Margaret put up a loud allyuh-have-no-heart fuss, and fling glasswares and figurines in a tornado to leave. Drunkenly.

This mother belonging to Rum Charlie and his blue house of hell. And all that within it dwells. This mother the same as the people to whom she melds.

This is the mother who yells—when another of Charlie's daughters send to tell of another betrothal to another beloved under heart's spell—for her daughters ~~four~~ three: Decide which nice dresses allyuh want to wear for this next trip down to see my family.

That, one day, will not include me.

2

COTTON TREE

I am nine. Paying for my crime.

It is because I want some me time. Because in that rectangular house on the hill—this house my construction-worker father blueprint and build with his own hands when he was twenty-five, that he bisect down the middle into three railroad-style rooms on each side, designed like a game of moral my girl cousins and I play from morning till evening time—I am reading.

Because I am fleeing the stench of tension being brewed in that cornflower living room. Where my six-foot-two father's bulging muscles poise, waiting for their food. The veined sinews of his broad back, arms and legs flexing at attention. Across the entire four-cushion couch and commandeering an armchair, too.

His large, sandpaper hands braced. Giving my alternating sewing and strolling mother a chance tuh make haste an organise something fuh meh tuh eat. While he watching Jet Li roundhouse opponents with exemplary hi-ya kung fu. Side-kicks and knife-hands my father practises after viewing how to do. And the Sunday martial arts shows will end at the strike of two.

It's because of my own time I am making my own use. The in-between leisure hours before the seven o' clock news. This period for entertainment before TTT broadcast another protested policy from Prime Minister Robinson who getting people feel more and more vex. That seven o' clock witching hour finding parents perched in front the TV with wringing hands to see which salary the landslide-elected man going and cut next. On top of the 15% Value Added Tax. More taking, more making big people feel like they wallet under attack.

It is because I decide on my own to take advantage of the interlude. During which Daddy in a better mood. Without worry. Free to leave his smouldering ashtray on the jagged centre table to cloud the air we breathe. While he watching his warring kung fu movie. It is because I cough, waving my hands in front my watering eyes frantically. Because I wrinkle up my nose, heave a sigh, stand up and leave the living room to get a reprieve. Because I don't stay in the tar-stink fog with muted Mummy who won't protest the release of his second-hand smoke. Mummy who don't say anything as I choke. Mummy who don't speak up to chide an environment children shouldn't have to abide.

Next on TV, *Bonanza*'s cowboys will grapple, then flat out drag "wild rebels" through the dust. And my father's baked breast, leg, and thigh, warm-from-the-oven macaroni pie, rice and pigeon peas, callaloo, coleslaw, green salad, and tall cup of orange juice, all to be brought to him on a tray by that looming showtime, are a must. My parents' power-struggle game, their anxiety-inducing stalemate that Saran-wraps the whole house, through which my humming mother secret-smiles, will end at the dooming strike of two o'clock.

Is because I duck into the second bedroom. I will not voluntarily watch oncoming karate chops. And my two younger sisters—who still widely shut their eyes, uphold those people's lies, and deny deny

deny—are outside under the cashew tree, plating red mud pies on long mango leaves.

I am in that second bedroom that I cannot term my bedroom. That my sisters and I cannot refer to as our bedroom. That we cannot name, claim, possess because my mother does get vex any time it's so called.

I am in the second bedroom that is, with my parents' own, perfectly aligned. In that abhorred style of rooms succeeding and leading from one to the other, with a connecting door smack dab in the middle of the floor, in the middle between theirs and mine. The door that my mother opens at all hours of the deep, dark night. To climb into my bed and rest her head on my pillow. The front of her body curling around mine like the branch of a weeping willow, in the children's bedroom that grants no security from my mother leaving my father's queen-sized bed. Right after her moans, giggles, gusty sighs, to climb into my twin instead.

Where she'd lay her head. And weep. And tell me of my father's unwanted hands grasping, how he does force. This bedroom where my mother would share how Yuh fadda doh take no fuh a answer after he come home stink uh he whores.

The bedroom where I have to say I love you more, Mummy, to get her to turn away from me onto her side and like that remain. To draw up into a four-foot-ten foetus as she said, Iz you does keep me from jess sticking my head in the oven again. Threatening her daughter with ending her life. The second bedroom where my teddy and I are hemmed up against the cold brick wall to keep my mother's protruding butt from resting on us all night.

The bedroom that I rearranged. Blocking the door from my parents' room to ours with a cedar chest of drawers, and passing the blame.

An artistic impulse that just take me is the cause for my sudden need for change.

The bedroom that I reorganised so the entry door would be the one off the kitchen. So I could listen. Hearing the jangle of bead strips announcing one of this mother's trips into my bed. And I could pretend to be asleep instead.

Now free, when I work to cleanse my somatised body of trauma memories, I am removing her hands from my waist. Her sour breath from my neck. My right shoulder rotates to shrug that mother off me. Throw the monkey from my back. To push off the big spoon pulling my spine to her pillowy breasts. Strangling my space. Launching her covert emotional incest attack.

This Sunday, in the second bedroom, dust motes dance in sunrays lancing the row of fancy blocks atop the wall. Pink Cabbage Patch curtains undulate in a whispering breeze visiting me through dirt-speckled louvres. The thick smell of soaked earth sinks me into its clumps, captive like it holds the entrenched house. Its outer bedroom walls stand just three feet from the steep, moss-carpeted rise of Baptist Hill that sends mudslides to reclaim its stake. Rendering our windows portals for toads, vines, spiders, and snakes. Those bedimmed windows also a gate through which, in daydreams and night visions, I escape. And, this day, *The Children's Illustrated Classics: Oliver Twist* is granting me a magic-carpet page to a new, dank, cobble-stoned place.

I am lain upon the top twin bed of the bunker mahogany-colour set my father bought from Standards furniture store instead of getting out hammer, nails, and saw. Not using construction tools from his work bag once more. Not making another squat, unpolished bed my mother called an eyesore. With its unsanded pine slabs for slats under the mattress that bore jagged splinters, which tore our bed-making hands.

That sturdy, early iteration my father crafted for the first of his inside and outside children is mine. My younger sisters share the thin bunk beds—four-year-old Sherrie on the bottom and seven-year-old Ericka on the top of a set that quivers as if made of ply.

This Sunday, I brave a daytime climb up the flimsy ladder instead of sitting with my mother—in the bedroom she shares with my father—at her Singer sewing machine. Or going in the kitchen to put some water on the stove to boil. So my father could see at least something doing. And my mother, approving, encouraged by the 24/7 company she needs, would get moving to make lunch for him to eat. Taking care of my mother is not my responsibility, not my feat. Just for this one day.

And that's why she makes me pay.

It is not my duty to protect my mother from my father's brutality she is baiting. Not only by waiting to cook, but in those snaring-his-attention-from-the-TV side-eye looks. In those swaying hips and twisting back the curtains in the living room, while blocking the television screen from his view, and the finding-ways-to-get-a-rise chooks. Poking that I can't understand. She does rinse out my ears daily with the vinegar of her hate for this man. Why she not getting his food ready? And her children's meals, too?

Everybody else in Trinidad done sitting down at their dining table to their week-awaited Sunday food. All my friends will be bragging tomorrow in school about the big piece of fry chicken they get instead of the regular small piece that was stewed. Why this fussing, hair-brushing, cyah-leave-the-man-to-his-TV-watching mood?

I not understanding the contrast between what my mother telling me every single day. The unending complaints she does make that Ah never shoulda marrid yuh fadda when Daddy at work. At his construction sites. And she does have me sit down next to her on the couch instead of going and play outside. Instead of going and play with my cousins down the hill or reading my books in the gallery in the calm sunlight. And diz what she now taking it upon herself to do. Teasing? She not fraid uh him? This whole thing puzzling. I can't wrap my head around the lack of logic. My mother purposely flirtatiously walking, laughing, and sporting, courting Ulric. She not making sense.

This was when I didn't know the purpose of distorting reality for your child. So your daughter will always be on your side.

But in bed with my book, here my gut is untense. This Sunday is when my itching back finally not interrupting to send electric shocks jolting my nerves into a fray while I lay on my belly, lazily swinging my feet in the stagnant air. And it will be five years before I can sneak a visit to a dermatologist who diagnoses this unseen, no-reason-for-being itch as overwhelming stress. I could have told him it was fear. Perpetually on guard for the next slap or angry word—indicating that their always-bubbling trouble erupting—my adrenaline levels never reset. Yet this Sunday, I am giving myself the peace those people, those parents won't let me get.

I cannot, I will not hear my mother's smirk-lipped humming above the turning of raspy, illustrated pages and the floor fan whirring. I cannot, will not hear my father's readying limbs stirring against the velour cushion covers my mother does sew every Christmas.

I make myself swallow back the acid taste of the regurgitating Crix and cheese breakfast. I make my ears relax their constant vigil and, now inside the book, draw level with Fagin's hooked nose. I circle the tall man, study his jutting chin, curved shoulders, thin arms, vulturous pose. My eyes trace his question-mark back and return to his face, where his lecherous leer stops me cold. Oliver, yuh doh see the slyness lighting up his eyes? How his fingers stretching past his raggedy shirt look like scythes? Oliver though, his height level with Fagin's knee, looking up at Fagin trustingly. Oliver Twist was orphaned. He was hungry.

It is because, this Sunday, I choose me.

Because I choose to read. Because I choose to flee her and my father steupsing, their under-breath cussing. Their issuing threats, their flirtatious fussing. Flee my father groping my mother's thick thighs and jiggling backside. As she walks past from their bedroom, through the living room, to the kitchen with her preening smile.

Because I gone in the second bedroom, daring to decide: I will not be audience to their mercurial theatre of sexual strokes and knock-out strikes.

But my mother does not like me quiet. She cannot abide me being remote, removed from the endless chatter she stokes, that she makes her child obliged to provide. She cannot tolerate a lack of perpetual company and deems my independence an enemy that requires her extinguishment. So, she contrives. So, she arrives in the second bedroom to vanquish self-reliance and distinguishment.

The bedroom door slams open, bouncing against the wall inside. Yuh eh hear meh calling yuh? The black door my father made a choonky bit too wide swings back behind her, shutting out steam smelling of rice, horse hooves drumming on TV, my sisters' distant giggling feeding their dollies out in front. As my mother comes to tell me what she want. No, I din hear yuh, Mummy, I mumble through mahogany bars.

Steupssss, dise cuz yuh pack up in here like yuh en have nuttin tuh do.

From the top bunk, she is a dome-headed dinosaur. High hair bump at the jut of her head. Short arms leading the charge to my empty bed against the opposite wall. Long, straight, white-woman nose, about which she boasts, spears the air. Her slim lips sneer. Everybody outside spenin time tuhgedda and you like yuh doh cyare if yuh sisters need you or if I want help doin sometin. She sits facing me. Her sharp chin grows hard corners when she speaks while sucking her teeth. The front one is not yet chipped from a morning my father will beat and beat and beat.

I reading the book we buy when we went in town lass week, Mummy, I cajolingly speak into the pulsing atmosphere. She turns the rotating fan to blow her straightened hair. Yeah, buh yuh nuh doin anyting. Big big Sunday an your foot cock up like everyting done do. Youse a lady in dis house? Look, come dong an go in de shop fuh meh now.

I peer the length of my body. I am dressed in a wash-out home jersey. Buh, Mummy, we make groceries yesterday. And today is Sunday. Spikes and them mussbe done lock up and gone home.

The day before, I got her up from watching her soaps to make sure we reach Kelly's Supermarket before they close. When she said she depressed and don't have energy to go, I reminded her Sam would be there. After I kept up the cheer through the narrow aisles and we ticked off all the food, toiletries, cleaning supplies to last for two weeks from the list I carried, we got in line. The one with Sam at the register, bagging on the side.

While I unloaded the red pack of Breeze, the tall bottle of Squeezy, the bags of dried peas, Sam smiled. He sweet-talk my mother, holding her small hands with the gold bands, and had her ducking her head like a child. Sam is tall, young, face in a perpetual grin. He know he handsome too bad with that smooth, black skin. And all Covigne Road girls tracking him. Though I was discomforted by my mother's flirting in front me, at least Sam's congeniality kept her from blurting unending digs to criticise Dah saga boy one who tink he better dan me, or Dah pisintail gyul who picky hair much thinner dan mine, or Yuh grandmodda watch meh funny las week so bess allyuh stay up home fuh de time being.

Just yesterday she was feeling up Sam biceps. She was laughing open-mouthed. She was sticking out her tot-tots that reach Sam waist thereabouts. She doh remember slipping him a few dollars on a palm caress when he bring all the heavy grocery bags up the road? The cupboard full. Why I hadda go?

Oh gosh, Uricka, doh be so. Ah din remember to put de peas tuh soak las night. She switches mode to coax.

Yuh cyah cook something else? Ent lentils doh take long tuh burst? This is not my first rodeo.

Yuh know how yuh fadda is. Ah could make a quick lentils buh we go never hear de end uh it. We. Making us a team. My mother drops her round shoulders in the sleeveless floral top. One she sewed in the seamstress class she was taking before she just suddenly stopped.

Sharp battle angles are gone. My mother looks forlorn. The long nose points down to the thin brown carpet. In the lines of her forehead's frown, I read the remembrance. The dejected script plays across her face and pitches me, without encumbrance, without time to seek balance, without the armour of resistance or allowed distance, into the memory she is conjuring. That episode to which she is obliquely referring. The buttercream walls above the stove and yellow plywood ceilings bear the evidence of that morning.

It was a weekday that time. The sun had just finish rise. There was no warm-up before Ulric wade in with his opening line. Cyatrin, whey de work shirt dat yuh was suppose tuh hang up here fuh me tuh wear dis morning? My father holds a scrunched-up, black-and-white-chequered ball he lets fall from his fist to the plastic vinyl of the kitchen floor. I know dis not de good good shirt you was suppose tuh press fuh me since lass night? His black sweat rings the collar. The shirt releases his pungent odour.

My throat gags in the way it does when he comes home from work and pulls me too close, too long under his arms for a hug. He had was to dig the shirt out the basket before coming to ask if Mummy didn't know iz this one he want. He drawls the bait on a sing-song jibe. My father tilts his head to the side. Laser focusses on my mother's backside. Compresses dark lips into his spit-gathering-at-the-corners smile. It does not reach his hard, reddening eyes. I slide into the cobwebbed corner to hide.

Outside the tension of the kitchen, birds trill sweet melodies. Uncle Errol cock crows from the branches of Rose Mango Tree, sweetly looking in on me, tucking my shivering frame in the safe shade she throws over the living room and gallery. Our resident stray cats down in the yard complain how they hungry. Within the confines of these sunshine walls to which I am pressed, I do not speak. My father's growl drowns my heartbeat.

Eh, eh Cyatrin. Like yuh nuh hearing me awah? Mummy stirs the contents of the pressure cooker on the back-right burner with a wooden spoon. She does not turn around. She does not look up from the steaming pot as my father comes farther into the kitchen beyond the beaded strips dividing it from the living room. Yes, Ulric. That's all my mother replies quietly. She keeps stirring the viscous peas.

And I freeze.

My father does not like to be ignored. She does not turn to face him. Her spine communicates she is bored. She does not see my father adopt a waiting stance. She does not see him loosen his thick, outstretched forearms. I see it in a glance, the bubbling volcano. On the opposite end of the kitchen, the half-doors bear witness also. They stand in wait. I am out of sight behind the fridge, hanging wet school socks on the hot iron grate to dry. My sisters in the bedroom at my rear, behind closed doors. Making themselves not able to hear. Lucky not to see. Not made into my mother's security, her ears, her eyes.

Ulric, you mean tuh tell me yuh cyah wear something else dis morning? She stops her stirring and spoons some of the brown liquid to her blowing mouth. Slurps, smacks. Shakes in more salt. Some annoyance seeped out in her last word. My belly makes a 360-machine-cycle turn.

At her tone, my father spurs his bare heels to slam the concrete. He steps closer. It is not yet seven o'clock. I checked the analogue face on our bedroom wall before I crawled out to brave getting ready for school. It was meant to only be ten minutes of interaction between these two. The blue VCR digits confirmed five minutes to go before my father walk out the door, trek down the hill, and get in his tan, third car that park in Granny yard. But then came the snarl.

He growls again and hits the counter. Hard. Lightning bolts bloom in the thin, white Formica. A jagged shard snaps off under my father's first attack. Wares in the dish rack on the metal draining board jump and crack. I swallow my gasp, turtle-pull my head back. His voice is rising, growing unbalanced, sharp.

Wah odda blasted shirt yuh wah meh wear, Cyatrin? I tell yuh de big borse an dem coming een dis mornin. How de ass I suppose tuh wear a jersey tuh de office fuh Cummerbatch meetin? The how-it-go-look gene has been activated.

Steupsss, wah yuh want me do fuh dat now, Ulric? My mother jeers. Does not placate him.

Bang. His hard, bare heels hammer on the concrete under his feet. His heavy tread is water to the cement in my belly. Cramps. Uneasiness hardens to dread. My ears lose sound to Silence's theft. Lungs cease intake of breath. My body spools a cocoon of vacuumed silence. Shocked suspension. Temporary hoisting from this existence. A child's short-lived resistance.

My ears pop when my father knocks the pressure cooker cover off the pot. The metallic clang to the draining board, its bang on the floor, its discordant tinny spin is like the bell rung for wrestling. His arm swings back from its rotator cuff to launch an open-palmed slap at the boiling pot of lentil peas. Brown explodes upwards as the pot careens off the burner. Emissions of steam hiss and blanket the kitchen in mist.

Flushing skin up his calves, biceps, neck, forehead, signal my father's blood rushing. The advance of his erupting rage. Let my mother gauge whether to be fresh now. Her shoulders hunch. Her neck contracts. She cows under his looming height, hemming her in at the hot stove. Ejected peas coat the walls and ceiling. The detonation draws me out from merely peeking. The food that was for him to eat when he come home this evening is the second target for attack. There will be no more on-your-marks-get-set objects for intimidation. I know that.

Splat. In a second my father's hand is a squeezing blood pressure cuff around my mother's soft arm. He heaves her shoulder to the brink of its socket. Tears cloud my vision. My feet emerge without my volition. My long fingers circle a third of his russet forearm. Stop it!

He scoffs at my hold in amused derision. Gulping sobs and rapid breath from my mother who only now seems to detect the threat. Her bulging eyes, swivelling from her peripheral to plead into mine, are wet.

Uricka, go an geh ready fuh school fuh meh please. Dis doh concern you. Yuh modda and I jess goin an talk in de backroom. He pushes the top and bottom double doors of the kitchen to go through. My mother is being borne against his body like a police officer apprehending a criminal. He drags her into custody. He relatches the double doors closed behind him after they step down into the washroom. He leaves me to watch a father haul a mother away. Her face suffused with impending doom.

There is a fault line in the washroom's concrete floor my father built. There is a fracture in the middle between the washing machine and the stone jooking sink on the opposite side. Hearing two pairs of feet drop into this crevice whereupon floor plates slide as my father takes my mother in the backroom to talk not in front my eyes. Hearing my father's furious whispers rise. Hearing dull thuds of impact carry on for minutes at a time. Hearing high-pitched, muffled cries, is buried inside. Of me.

I didn't understand those early, discreet talks in the backroom. But my terrorised body knew. Even as a child. Flesh-pocketed memories do not lie.

This she wields. It is this with which my mother dilates doe eyes, to effect the squeeze. As she asks me, in that second bedroom, to go down in the parlour, please. When I know there is no need to reach in the shop. Groceries done make and the shelves stacked to the top. But, Mummy, everybody going to be dress up fuh church. Iz Sundaaaay. I don't want to go out de road looking like dis.

I don't want to be recruited as an accomplice preventing her getting licks from her husband's vicious hands. Sitting on my bed, she asking me to done read cuz, Uricka, yuh big enough tuh understan. Getting Daddy something to eat, keeping the peace with a man she chose to marry and with whom she chooses to stay a family is not her responsibility. It is mine.

I am nine.

And it's months after Carnival time. Ash Wednesday put to bed. We shoo out Lent. Fish and fasting done. Church people could stop pretend they don't listen to soca now that they wave coconut leaves for the rising son. They don't have to bend up they nose and say Take that rubbish off the radio.

They get to show off they new clothes the seamstress have time finish before Palm Sunday. Red plaid aprons, two-foot-high silken yellow headties, lilac waist sashes, fitted white dresses with anglaise eyes. New patent shoes they take off on the concrete church steps to leave by the mat get put on display. Everybody make they name come Palm and Easter Sunday.

Now church service gone back to its regular sixish hours in which to dance, ketch power, kneel and pray. To shout aloud they praise as Spiritual Baptists couldn't legally do back in my great-grandfather, Grampa Biscuit, day. Now, ever since the ban lift, it's like they use every Sunday to proclaim the triumph of ancestral ways. These Covigne Road and Factory Road devotees—teachers, cleaners, accountants, secretaries, bus drivers, gardeners, mail carriers during the week—all assembling to lay they burdens at the foot of de cross and behold somebody standing there.

We hear them all the way up here. My grandmother's mournful warble leading the off-tune hymns. Tanty Marilyn scratchy throat sounding the duption riddim. Gold Grampa arthritic gold hands, still strong enough to massage jumbie outta neighbours' joints and work his fertile land, clapping like cymbals in a band. His unflagging energy issuing a command heard passive aggressively among the Dominic family to step up the pace.

Across the aisle's divide, the Dominics, Mount St. Rose's other family that only ever sits on the right-hand side, attempts to match, then beat the stride of this family of mine in their race to own centre stage. The claim to fame—a four-room church behind a tall red gate on a tucked-in corner of a badjohn road.

I hear the duelling choruses of Hallelujah, tank yuh lawd! goading more Praise you fadda, de Alpha an de Omega! and my mind shows these stooped little church people as jousters with Bible swords. Their shouts charge forward. The congregation's increasing volume mounts the air, jockeys up the hill, gallops into the bedroom, taking me out of there.

I laugh in my head. But I keep my face clear. My mother will sneer and ask What so funny, Camille. And then skin up her top lip and say psychology prove people with imagination actually crazy, she hear it on a documentary on TV.

And then she will bad talk those people who have community. These church people down the hill dressed in they boring whites. And she'll say all the reasons it schupid to pray and how she doh want to be in they old church anyway. Though three years later I will see her hide in the backroom. See her cover her head, light a candle, and chant psalm 27, tears sliding down her face, when she decide she alone need to escape.

It is because I am trying to have some calm. My own little joy. That I find it on the page. That it earns me my teachers' warm pride and affection for high advancement beyond my age that she comes. And she stays. My mother sits across from me scrutinising my face for the slightest fray. To tear.

Scans from my hair in one-one, big-belly plaits that she knows I don't like cause they make me look like a little child. Plaits she insists on putting while I always ask her on Sunday nights to canerow my hair in a some up-some down with a muff style that suits my face and makes my cheekbones look high. A request to look pretty and have some agency she denies.

She skims to my little gold hoop earrings, then the old comfortable jersey I am wearing. Across to my long fingers with grown-out nails holding my book aloft. I feel self-conscious as her eyes scan my big bambam that doesn't lie down when I do. The butt that hard-back men down de road call cocked. And then back to the top of my heels kicked up, with soft calves melding to my thick thighs.

I have her pear shape, her dark complexion, her full hair. But not her white people nose nor her protruding eyes. I have rounder lips, bigger feet, am growing taller than her and more lean. And my unbreasted chest is, at nine, already drawing the eyes of wutless men out the road counting off the time. Men inspiring my mother to put down my body and me criticise for the attention she now has to divide with her not-first child.

She, this mother, is still on the bare thread count sheets. Her googly eyes do not blink at me. They resemble the illustration in the last children's classic I just finish read. My mother's are both the size of the one hated vulture eye. That orb that drove the madman to commit his crime of burying the old neighbour and his loud, demanding, endlessly ticking heart. Their white circumference swallow up the pupils' dark.

My mother scans and skims my body and I brace for one of her well-meaning enquiries like Whole mornin yuh get up yuh mean yuh en go and clean up and even wash yuh pinkie. Nobody ever tell you daz de firse ting yuh supposed tuh do. Yuh doh wait quite till yuh bade in de afternoon. And yuh nuh gonna put on a vest self tuh hold yuh? Yuh doh want tuh get saggy too soon. And why yuh doh pull up yuh nose some more while yuh juss lying dong here? Yuh want it tuh stay so flat and wide? Allyuh geh dah nose from yuh fadda side. And yuh doh tink yuh hair back from yuh face does show off how wide yuh forrid is? And, Uricka, yuh doh tink is time yuh cut dem nails? If yuh want dem long yuh should take cyare uh dem like dis. While she stretches out her palm to demonstrate.

I brace, my muscles clenched against the rip current those questions always channel through the placid sea of a quiet room in which I have gone to read. Alone. But this time my mother is sweet.

Honey works better for flies. Ply them with acid and they're less inclined to be loving, to draw close, to stay in line.

My mother doesn't have to persuade me to go in the parlour. She doesn't have to coax me. I am her child. She is giving me a directive and I have to follow whatever invective I want to spew. Whatever grief I feel over what she's making me do. Whatever injustice rankles that I have to walk down Covigne Road and on a Sunday to boot. But she tries.

She smiles. Why yuh doh wear yuh nice lil Carnival outfit? Look how good yuh does look in dat. Remember how nice yuh feel when we went around the Savannah in it? It come out so good. She chuckles, we finish it just in time dat night eh?

The we is back. The plunge into memory's stream—its warm, lapping, nostalgic attack—prompts me to give the expected smile. It is close-mouthed. And I turn on my side to face my mother while I am silent, demurring in the face of the hug reaching out to me from her eyes.

We are connected across the rough-carpeted bedroom aisle by my cute carnival outfit that's a good way to remind us of all the time we spend together and the nice things she does for me and the ties that bind.

Yes, Mummy. Fifteen more seconds before I'll rise. Hold in the sigh. I could put on that. Let me just go and brush my teeth and hurry up and go before Spikes close. I could reach by Ounce and buy a *Sunday Express*, too?

No immediate consent. There must be a questioning before she relents. Wah you want de paper for?

She knows I like the Sunday magazine. That I read the in-depth features, the comics, the profiles of accomplished local celebrities, and most of all the stories. And that they can get the TV guide. But I still answer why. For the *Junior Express* section, Mummy.

She nods. Arrite.

It isn't a lie. My mother just isn't aware that I also get *The Express* or *The Sunday Guardian* to read her weekly Libra horoscope. If I could see what coming it might help me stay out of her way. Or buy extra chocolate and nuts Nuggle and Peanola bars to make her feel better on a particular day. Or it could let me know which evenings to leave the *Childcraft* reading and go down by Granny with my cousins to play.

And she, my mother, also wasn't aware that in a year, at ten years old, when I check out the gigantic *Children's Bible* tome from Diamond Vale Primary School library it's because the horoscopes wasn't helping me diagnose how it is my mother so.

How a mother could be so? Why when she's in the same room with me I feel swallowed up by a heavy coat pulling me down? And why she always want me sad when we sit around looking out the living room louvres?

And why iz always she telling me how she had to quit the sewing class? And again had was to leave the evening literature lessons. And wouldn't finish the instruction to get her high school certification wid dem people? While I am watching with crunching anxiety.

Watching every evening, to see down the hill into the street. To see my father grey van bend the corner by Sexy-Wendy shop who does sell pholourie. Waiting intently to see when he coming. So I could make sure my mother have all the snacks and one-more-day inspirational speech she needs. So I could go inside before he reach. Before my father breach the front doorway and the tension start to creak up the Popeye and Bruno high-striker tower to hit the bell for all hell to break loose.

Or why, when she's a little lighter, sewing at her Singer machine—not a serger, *steupsss*—and I just want to have a happy conversation with my Mummy, she's always telling me how Yuh fadda say he going and leave? Whereupon my belly does start to gripe me. Because how we going and eat when he's the only one with a salary?

And she does say he might still drop some money Buh he want tuh be wid one uh his new woman. And my mind grapples to understand how marriage could be so unsolid and left wide open to these possibilities where any day now a father could just pick up and leave.

She isn't conscious, this mother, that a daughter could have dis-en-right feelings and that there are thus answers I seek. That my dissection isn't built strictly on the information she feeds. My mother isn't privy to just how much I perceive.

Her you-so-wise-fuh-yuh-age appreciation is centred around the comfort I give her to deal with the man to whom she stays married. It is not recognition of an independent trait that I carry.

So, this Sunday when I am nine, before I move on to works of psychology that I find, I am asking to buy an *Express* newspaper, please. For research into this mother's personality. And as a treat to me to read for having to venture on a Sunday down Covigne.

She doesn't move, though. Now that the bargaining is closed. Her spine slackens and my mother leans back on her Squeezy-coarsened hands and locks her smushy elbows. She stays in the second bedroom as I lift up from repose, swing my legs to dangle over the side of the top bunk, still watching my mother's sloping forehead from on high.

I close the book on Fagin's strut, his swaggering stride. And I slide *Oliver Twist* under the pillow to retrieve and read in my own bed tonight. My own bed where I'll curl up. Knees in my chest. Tucked tight. Avoiding stretching my feet into the nest of slithering snakes at the bottom of the bed. Snakes gliding over each other's wet-looking scales as they settle in to spend another night with me. A pit of snakes only I ever see.

Why yuh doh wear yuh cute lil Carnival suit, she said. This mother who read my reluctance to go down de road and moved on to persuasion to goad me into wanting to deliver her from her husband's fists and feet by reaching in the parlour to buy a tin of pigeon peas that she suddenly say she need to make Sunday lunch for Daddy to eat even though is just yesterday we went in the grocery and we bring home bags and bags after I nag Mummy to not feel sad and let we go shop for the week at Kelly's.

She doesn't need to cajole. This mother. I am her not-first daughter, it is enough to be told. But my little Carnival suit conjures hours at Mummy's side while over it she laboured and sewed and delivered it with pride. Hours of me sitting at the edge of the bed in the louvre-filtered sunlight, listening to always-have-yuh-own-money life lessons while the presser foot sped to get the bias cut just right.

It conjures, this little brown Carnival shirt and short pants I am ironing, the hours I ~~couldn't~~ didn't stay back after school to dance and be fitted and costumed for Diamond Vale Kiddies Carnival band because six o'clock loomed and my mother needed her yuh-such-a-wise-old-soul daughter next to her at the Singer machine in the afternoon. Needed her not-first daughter to stay in the room to soothe the impending doom, the lurking dread. Of her husband's return from work whose boot crunch over the yard's gravel would jerk her fingers and knot up the thread.

It represents, this little coconut-tree print pants and shirt in which I am getting dressed, my mother's present to Ericka and me. A gift of outfits resembling the "Hawaiian" clothes of red-faced, touristing Yankees. An outfit resembling the tropical ensembles foreign visitors disembarking down Cruise Ship Complex in town does buy. To say they fitting in among the locals on their visits to our Caribbean isles. An outfit made of fabric purchased on a trip for Ericka and me in town down Queen Street in and out of Aboud Syrian family fabric stores where my mother implored, allyuh choose what allyuh like.

It reminds, this short Carnival pants into which I'm stepping—that, when I walk, does ride up my thick inner thighs—of me picking in Aboud fabric store a vibrant pink and red bolt of cloth I liked. And my mother saying it so coskel, dat en go look too right. And her choosing another and then finding its replica. The same print but in different colours. A bright lime green for Ericka, and for me a dull brown. Two different tones of the same polyester with coconut trees and the sun going down.

And I am nine and old enough to know what I like and remind Mummy My favourite colours are bright yellow and baby pink. And Mummy skin up her nose and aloud thinks: Ent yuh doh really like dis. Yuh doh find dem colours too childish. And purchases what she please. As my special present of a non-costume Carnival outfit for my sister and me.

Yuh nearly ready, Mummy now asks me from the kitchen. She eager for me to go down the road in the parlour for the peas and I can feel her make-haste patience shortening as I am buttoning up the shirt of this silky-sliding, mud-colour, coconut-tree, sunsetting, Yankee-tourist-and-they-camera-ever-outta-timing suit, sewn especially for me. A treat for Carnival earlier this year. And in the wake of her trill, I hear Daddy grunt in his throat in the living room. My back frissons in fear.

I hear the couch creak under his restless shifting position that is warning communication to Mummy he go want to eat soon.

Hear the clink of wares coming from Tanty Acklyn and Uncle Ken house above, in their upstair dining room. As they and all done sit down to Sunday lunch this afternoon. Hear my younger sisters in the yard moving on from mud pies and now making their toy leaves into cars that zoom. Vroom over and through the gnarly, exposed roots of the cashew tree. The roots that I slice for laglee. To stick my school projects in my copybooks when neither Mummy nor Daddy remember to buy Elmer's glue in the middle of the term. And I refuse to have incomplete homework when my teachers walk around to discern who here to learn, and I refuse to have to feel shame in class and make my eyes burn.

I squirm after I turn my head to the closed door. Then shout Ah coming. And my reply slithers through the inch of space between the wood and carpeted floor.

It is my chore. Getting food. Helping Mummy keep Daddy and his belly in a non-beating mood.

But you don't like these autumn colours, the wardrobe's full-length mirror pronounces. He announces this to my statue-still form, unable to put on my slippers and walk out the second bedroom door. I don't want to go. But this isn't what Mirror wants me to know. Landing like a pigeon on a bronze sculpture, Mirror's deliverances are my resentful mind's added visitor. Here to crown my reluctance, my anger.

I was reading good good in the bed. I hate walking down Covigne Road where these people choose to make our home. I hate all the nasty men and them sooting yuh and calling me Little-Ulric and watching my chest. And grabbing their groins and puckering their burnt lips into the sign for a kiss and squinting their watery eyes, blazing red. And I tell Mummy what they does say. And she does only answer They harmless, juss ignore dem, try and be brave. And then rub my back to show she understand.

But if Mummy understand I wouldn't be going down the road and having to pass man after man lining the pavement. If Mummy understand she would know that the scent of weed does get me scared. And she would care my neck does get itchy in fear. Suppose one of them would grab me or hurt me, and they always high.

But Mummy say I is de oldest child, I living here all my life. I safe, and is just some fellas who like to lime. And I tell her about cocaine and what the advertisements and encyclopaedias say it does do to your brain. And how these men have no impulse control.

And this Sunday Mummy still tell me to get up, put on my little Carnival outfit, and go out the road.

When my mind say No.

The rough carpet tickles my soles. My eyes watch my long fingers in the glass making fists. You know the real reason you don't feel good in this outfit, Mirror unrelentingly interjects. Do I really need him to pile on causes for me to be upset? He who knows I need to feel I looking my best at all times. And that my clothes need to match my vibes, or I does just shut down and don't feel right.

You want to know why? Mirror persists.

Insists. Though my eyes see nothing of him, and my scrambling mind fills the fading Grenada suitcase under Mummy bed. Wondering how much of my clothes it could hold, and if the buckles would keep, and where the money in my piggy bank could reach. Not far enough for me to tread. Trinidad too small. Everybody know badjohn Covigne Road.

No, I don't. Lemme just go.

I never want to know what Mirror waits until I am alone to show. To whisper, to unveil, to tell. Looming Mirror who does just watch me steadily and tickle the back of my head until unease spread throughout. When I come back up the hill from my grandmother's house. When I reach back from a lime spending time with all my cousins, aunts, uncles and them, and saying to my bed-readying self in the glass how that was nice. On these days, Mirror waits. Then Mirror displays a dirt path in his frame. A grass-lined lane I walk down, recalling, analysing, unignoring the tumult in my belly, and un-normalising my family's every claim. Admitting what they say feels wrong. In my body, under words' opaque throng.

So, what's another insight? It's either now or he'll reveal it tonight. Yes, Mirror, tell me the underneath reason this cute little Carnival suit don't feel right.

Those are your mother's colours, Mirror deeply intones. Crisp, melodic, echoing, and sage. Confident, unfailingly, in what he knows. Wise voice of a long past age, Mirror responds to my inquest. Remember when you asked her why she always gets sienna oranges and maroons and copper-brown cloth for each and every dress? And she smiled and pulled you to stand in front her dressing table and look into her reflection and said, while stroking your hair, that for us with dark complexions these colours look best. You remember? You thought it was jest. You didn't see dullness as what properly suited you at all. But she hugged you and her arms felt warm. And she told you these dangly earrings of hers would soon be yours. So, you left it alone. Now look, you're dressed like fall.

Satisfied he's summoned sight to the surface, Mirror ceases to talk.

This Mirror, always so loud. Quietly. Just to me. Piping up when other people aren't in the room. Just a glass in front Mummy or Daddy, too. My sisters never able to see. This Mirror telling me look into my own eyes when I saying iz not so bad, exhaling irritation, inhaling reasons to be happy, to justify. Like when Mummy choose me to stay up after eleven p.m. and watch *Cagney & Lacey* with her alone. Or my cousin Marlon want to go for a walk to catch guppy, and I don't like the dirty river nor the slippery stones. Or Ericka make Daddy rent *Annie* on VCR again for the twentieth loan, and they all say Just let her have this nuh, Uricka, daz yuh lil sister. The one whose Carnival outfit is sparkling green and brighter. Not the dull brown that is to me assigned. Because Ericka light complexion and hazel eyes make a better fit for shades that glow in sunshine.

And now it is time. Turning away from Mirror—who does never put water in his mouth when he want to bring about the confronting rise to my eyes of something my belly knew—I bend to search for a pair of out-the-road slippers among our shoes.

No clanking beads and foil-tipped canerows fall in my face as I bend down now on this occasion of my wearing the cute lil Carnival outfit today. Not like the first time I wore it when Ericka and I got dressed in our matching shirts and pants. And Mummy took us to watch the pretty mas bands and lime in The North Stand.

Not like that Carnival Saturday, with Mummy and Tanty Carol heaving picnic baskets of pelau, coleslaw, and green salad, cheese-paste sandwiches, peanuts, and Orchard orange juice in hand. Not like that time of us and cousins and aunts and family. And other children and making new friends and clambering over and running between wooden plank seats. And the savannah dust tightly embracing our feet and legs. Savannah dust galloping in little whirlwinds besides us as we sing along to "Free Up," running up and down pavilion steps.

And us laughing and smiling and shouting over the loud sun and soca bass. And us pulling handkerchiefs out to wipe crystal streams giving chase over our foreheads and necks and backs and top lips. And the sharp scent of fresh cooking curry when vendors selling roti chunkay they onion, saffron, and garlic. And, from under pitched tents, the hissing tendrils of corn soup on the breeze calling out to me to spend. Come and gi dem my little allowance and find room for the corn soup filling warmth in my belly. And us oohing and ahhing when feathers and crowns and flags and wings make us stand still to rate which one is we. And which one is the best and which one we wearing next year when we gonna be dressed for the stage and we go be deciding road march and making we name.

No, not this time.

This Sunday, wearing the cute lil outfit of that Carnival Day does not conjure the friends and family and music and screams and play, and my ignoring the collared shirt of my suit that isn't adorned with the sequins and beads and ribbons onstage, and my laughter upon gripping the North Stand bars in sweaty hands to dance in conga lines and "Bump & Wine" in the Queens Park Savannah sunshine.

This second time wearing my mother's cute little Carnival outfit, I am alone. Plastic bag in hand. I walk out the front door to go to the parlour to buy a tin of peas my mother suddenly remember she need when I pulled out *Oliver Twist* to read.

On my way to Spikes' parlour,

I pass—

> Through the narrow, half-cement, half-dirt track from my father's house to the hill. Through the track where there is a seventy-five-percent chance I will see a snake. Usually a brown non-poisonous length, awake and stretching itself in the sun. But where I could just as easily bounce up one of the coral variety. Like the pretty, banded, bold piece of curiosity that slithered right up to my big toe last week.
>
> I didn't even see it fus I was busy looking up at the yellow cashew on the tree just ahead of me. Peering through the leaves to detect if it ripe already since I left for school that morning. But something was horning in on my ability to move. I froze for no reason that I knew or could prove. It was the colourful coiled neck awaiting my next step, relaxing its readied poise,

that startled me into recognition and noise. I ran into the house to tell my mother, the one now sending me down in the parlour.

I pass—

The fraying hemp rope—that usually restricts Alice the goat from straying beyond the scope of the plum tree's shade—bounding someone new today. A man stand up dey. Margaret-the-neighbour man, only clothed in a short pants, his beautiful oil-black skin on display. This thick, scratchy rope instead tying Sheldon neck; Sheldon who Margaret-the-neighbour breaking up with and letting go. Sheldon who cannot cope. So he say. So he shouts, so he screams. Sheldon tied to the plum tree leaning out over the hill's grassy steep. The verdant hill over which creeps wildflowers and vines for boiling for tea, to relieve fever, bring in breast milk, and purge bellies that gorged on too many confectionery sweets.

The rope knotted maybe-kinda-not really tight around Sheldon neck. His tendons raising in the breathing room as Sheldon cries out to his ex. The heavy, beige rope spooling its length down into Sheldon's open hands. Him threatening Margaret-the-neighbour—owner of Alice the goat, eye-rolling receiver of this wailing throat—who in her half-finish gallery stands. Sheldon arms spread, dangling the dancing rope, weeping his warning oath to Margaret-the-neighbour how sorry she will be if she doh take him back as her man quick-fast and in a hurry.

I pass—

Tiger dribbling jowls. His sharp canines. All their points exposed by vibrating lips pulled tight to snarl as I come into sight. His ears laid flat against his striped skull. The fury in his eyes not dulled by recognition of the sharp scent of my triggered Teen Spirit sweat. Deep bass growls reverberating from his corded neck.

Uncut claws digging grooves into the cement pathway. Whipping tail shredding hibiscus, stinking suzy, morning glories bordering the house's front lane. This dog that races from the back of Ms. Dick's yard to push the rusting entryway to its expanding brink every time I try to slink past the washed-out pink gate, terrified this will be the day it gives under Tiger's muscled weight.

I pass—

White, soft fluff skirting piercing black seeds. Puff upon puff clouding the leaves and branches of Ms. Owner's gnarled cotton tree draping over the asphalt hill. Her filled clothesline sagging with dripping garments pulled from the stone sink in her front yard. I don't even think of picking one of these punishing buds whose cushiony fuzz makes me wish they wouldn't chook so hard. Instead, I bend to smell the sugary, red Ixora, pluck a delicate flare, and suck the sweet nectar before jewelled hummingbirds suction their share.

I pass—

A curved, brick perimeter wall at the foot of the hill. Painted green, it still doesn't blend with the St. John's and black sage bush, bad-luck pawpaw tree, and that other hollow trunk one with the fanned-out, scratchy dark leaves. The painted and repainted brick, smooth with layers of thick pigment the Baptist church spent its collection to buy in an effort to hide all the illiterate "fock" offending its flock's eyes, is a bulletin space for passers-by.

That brick wall too rude. Bordering a church, a hill, decent people family homes, but right outside Philip mechanic shop also, the brick prefer to remain crude. The brick wall opposite Philip repair garage choose to barrage passing women and children's gazes with skinout centrefolds from *Sunday Punch* pages.

The *Punch*, the people newspaper for they jokes and they rages. And even if is Tambu—in his African prints and wide pants and wise lyrics and Bélé dance—did win the road march, charming everybody of all ages. Is really Crazy soca that claim the backstreet stages. "Nani Wine," sing Crazy. Nani Wine, the title for this *Punch* centrefold skin up wide. Nothing that hide—parted legs showing a wet bikini. That is the picture in the *Sunday Punch* centre this week. The image that the brick wall forcing all the young girls to see.

This Sunday, the young girl sent down Covigne Road is me.

This is the road, twisting like a congoree in muck under an entrenched plant pot, dwelling in darkness, feasting on leaf decay and corkscrew worm waste, its black-brown carapace rising and falling like hills of sugar cane, with tributary peaks and lanes and treads that extend to the east and to the west like the congoree's million crawling legs.

This is the road where wild men and wild dogs roam. None of them with no home. Lining nonexistent pavements. With their depravement.

Tunnelling passers-by through their wall-of-bodies xyst. Funnelling pedestrians through their body-constructed long portico they landscape with guns and blunts at their hips. Panting. With unsheathed phalluses and froth at their lips. Roofing their arbour with barks, with growls. With salivating, with howls. Shepherding you into their tight packs on the prowl.

This is the road where rum does drink and dice does roll. Where dominoes does crash and cards does fold. The place where Girlsin and Boysin run away from they home to come. And open up shop. Because they is cousins, so Mummy say, and they was too young—even for Indians living in the country—to set up house and marrid. So they family say stop. But cousin-loving is nothing in Covigne's hilltop.

This is the road where Renee—we second or so cousin who does do a lil yard work and cleanup—get chop. And when he survive that cutlass and get up, couple months pass before somebody throw pitch oil and light a match on him in his one-room shack. And it was straight to POS General Hospital he had was to go back. This after Renee win a big hand in whe whe, so Tanty Shirley say. And dem men and dem wanted they mattress share before the whole uh it spend, dissolved in a White Oak bottle again.

This is the road of a concrete basketball court, fenced in wire diamonds, providing sport for its misled youth. The court where the fellas and them does gather to take a sweat any chance they get when it not in use by the tall, yellow madman who do too much school, so Daddy say, and was never again right in de brain. And daz why he does wear a grey mechanics onesie to do dem funny, twist-up position ting and meditate with de whole stalk uh plantain on he head for hours straight. The court where this wiry, muscled man is the first I ever see maintain stillness and pose. Disregarding green fig sap dripping through his halo afro. Never unbalancing from one heel tucked in his groin, and all his body weight atop one slim ankle joint. The hot court that does not scorch this man's seated, folded thighs. The court from which he dips his head and says Peace sister when I stare, passing by.

This is the road of an old river and remembering streams. Where gullies and tadpoles and dragonflies teem. A place of wildflowers, birdsong, and fecund fruit trees. A place of lush mountains, jungle gardens, and of open fields. Of waterfalls, of canyons, of chickens, and pet monkeys. A place of dollar cabs, fry chicken, fry fish, and pholourie. Of apple dunk, children carnival fete, bazaar stalls, and back-in-time red bulb parties. Hosted by tight-clothes Sexy-Wendy. A place where her man, Tex, old enough to be her grandmother's ex. Who so happy he get she, so Calvin say, that Tex give Sexy-Wendy a shop she proud to open up instead of having yearly babies like the girls she does sell sweet drink and chicken and chips to. Them and they out-the-road man and they duckling brood.

This is the road of bussing bamboo. And launching calypso. Of football games, standpipes, stray cats, shedding sheep, and bleating goats. Of crumbling half-construction, abandoned to the claim of bush when Covigne's realities manage to push out the few hopefuls who ignore the nightly news stories of gang murders, drugs, and armed robberies. These investing builders disbelieving all this possible from one little street. From one winding road whose name does make people do the sign of the cross throughout Trinidad and Tobago. One of them places you must never go, so my teacher says. Yet it is the place where my better-than-them family keeps residence. A place where my father's house is mere feet from my great-grandfather's red-stepped home. The road in which five generations of this family's roots take hold. Planted in its hills and valleys, where daz yuh cousin too, I am constantly told. This place I am living at nine years old.

This is the road of seven or so church and about five auto repair garage that does buss price when they charge, though they never fix nobody underbelly or soul. A place where one of those kinda mechanic shops can grow. That one, worse than Phillip's, that I does always ask Mummy and Daddy about. And they does just say Make sure to never go in dey and then hush they mouth. One of those businesses that never open and never closed. Two storeys of iron eclipsing the sun, casting out cold. Sitting at the blind bend in the street. Cover up in yellow and blue tarpaulin. The better to hide from infantry police with loud-booted feet. Concealed by army sheets tied to dense mango and chenette trees. Draped in disguise from circling helicopter eyes. The kinda mechanic shop with its body plated in windshields, trunk lids, and van doors that does never again release any cars or maxi taxis sucked into its gated maw. The type of garage that does chew up steel and spit out fidgety men. Like Marvin and dem who cuss out Ms. Yvette when she demand her bus back, and chase her and call her a mannish ole whore. One of those creepy mechanics place I have to pass by on my way to the store.

Blue rubber slippers slap my heel. My soft toes clench the thin thongs that keep the slippers from sliding off my feet. My ankles strain against the terrain of one-inch rubber with no incline, no arch, no lift. A white plastic bag rustles alongside my right thigh, squeezing out between my balled-up fists.

I don't want to do this.

Past Baptist Hill and Covigne Road axis point. I turn right at the joint. Skip my fingers along Mount St. Rose imposing iron gate guarding its singing holy flock from that outside carousing throng and from those intoxicated reprobates. I hop the puddles pooling the pockmarked asphalt astride the dripping standpipe. And hold my nose as I walk by the barrels on the other side, full of garbage bags we does all pelt in at night. This don't feel right.

Something just off today, my belly keep clenching to relay. Go back up the road. It want me to obey. But Mummy say . . .

I band my shoulders tight. The vertebrae ache from giving them no respite to let my back be supple flesh. My spine is a rod the lasering sun cannot melt. Not yet. Neck in a stay-strong-be-alert brace, my eyes dart left to right as ahead I face the stripped-car-parts cave backed by a river and trees, into which more than one girl has been dragged and never again seen. Unfound by police. I can feel concealed men's loud stares spear out from its depth. And cannot breathe.

How to ease around the shadowed curve of this mechanic shop's tents that I never see doing any repairs, now that I'm here? Where I am roped to the kerb, unable to extend my leash into the middle of the street, knowing dollar-car drivers don't slow in approaching blind corners. And most of their scrap-metal assemblages don't have horns either. And some again don't even boast a muffler.

I don my invisibility cloak. I put on a dropped head that don't know what goes on in that place where the lights come on at night. And roll my arm sockets to the front like Ms. Turpin instructs in PE when she teaching us how to stretch our body so we loose and nice. My upper arms now conceal my chest. But I still let my arms hang, not fold. Can't look vex. Next, it's a must to restrain any swing my thick thighs bring to my hips. And I don't let my eyes slip out past their blinders, like those resentfully worn by Black Beauty and Ginger. I am not interesting. Might be a little slow. I have nothing appealing. Leave me alone.

From this point, I will not exhale deeply again till I reach back home. I am now in the thick of Covigne Road.

Still walking, the next trial I am face-forward ignoring is Tanty Carol husband sister family sitting in they upstairs and downstairs gallery, rubbernecking. Collecting the news. A pack of hyenas beady-eyeing everything happening. Never moved to action, always amused.

I can't subtly become bow-legged here where they'll stare and point and snicker. And, though using my fingers to pull my riding-up short pants back down would be quicker, any conspicuous attention drawn to my crotch would be red meat, a red flag to the glazed eyes of the men that watch.

And this is where my father choose to live. And why yuh doh wear yuh cute little Carnival suit is the consolation my mother choose to give for making me go in the parlour to buy the pigeon peas for hungry Daddy to eat, so she don't get beat when his Western finish playing on TV.

Breathe.

Aye, smallie. Pssssssst. Eh, darkie, come leh meh ask yuh a question, nah. Aye, gyul, waz yuh name. Yuh fraid? Doh frighten. Ah jus want tuh talk tuh yuh. Come, nah. She nice an tick, eh. Look at she backside nah. Ah want tuh beat it out. Sexy smallie, look over here, nah gyul. Ah ha something tuh gi yuh.

They laugh. I keep trooping past. Eyes and arms at attention. Don't blink back the heat in your eyes too fast. Hold on to the sweating plastic bag. Don't hear them, Camille. No shallow inhalation. Don't swallow again. Don't gasp.

Yuh feel yuh too high and mighty awah. Aye, bitch, yuh eh hear meh calling yuh. Come here, gyul. Yuh lil cunt. Is a big man like me yuh need tuh give yuh wah yuh looking for, yuh know. Darkie, doh study dem fellas, eh, I have wah yuh want. Right here . . .

A brown blur rushes out the corner of my line of sight. I am a marching Buckingham Palace guard, unseeing, unhearing, unprovoked. Without fright. Out of frame of my fixed gaze, a brown haze bounds back close to me. The very edge of the stretch of my vision is trained, inconspicuously, on the men lining the left-hand side of the road. They mustn't see me look.

Any interest will goad these men to take up the invitation of a nine-year-old whose eyes happen to fall on them. And I am alone. And the one or two simpering young women liming with those fellas won't be any help. And the men will book it from their perch on overturned beer cases and garbage bins, and cricket wickets and elevated rusting car rims. To come touch.

I have to keep my eye on them and make sure they too drunk and high to do more than watch. And I can't let all these people out the road see how much those nasty words getting to me. I can't be soft. Because the filthy words will increase if they know, if I show, if they see they have any power over me.

Xylophone ribs brush my thigh. And the brown smudge at the right, out of my peripheral sight, is now beside my knee.

A snarl reverberates. A growl from deep in the throat. Loud. Long breaths pant. Bristles scrape my calf. Something wet, pointy, sharp begins to puncture the side and back of my knee. Aaaaahhhh! No! Noooooo! I leap forward to run. Soft arms wrap around me. Jutting breasts stop my progress.

Hahahaha. Wham tuh she. Wuh it is happen dey. De dog just playing wid yuh. Doh frighten. Look she scared, yes. It good fuh she. Big gyul like you fraid a dog. Watch, he gone up he road. He gone. De ting more scared a you. Allyuh too damn sometimeish. Humble yuhself. Lil bite it gi she. Yuh eh hear how she bawl. Ha ha.

Breathe, dahlin. Look you drop yuh money. Here, yuh have a pocket? Watch me good, yuh know who I am?

Yes, Ms. Sybil.

My grandmother brother wife tells me to breathe again. Cushions me in the cradle of her pillowy arms. Hugs me to her vast bosom. She waits until my heartbeat slows. Matches the rate at which hers goes. Peers into my face till my wild eyes focus and can make out distinct shapes properly. Till I can see.

Ms. Sybil trains her gaze on my face till my bright white vision musters recognition. Until I am capable of communication with her who lives in the house beneath my father's on the hill. Of course I know her. But my body is trembling still. My lungs wheeze, puffing air through rattling teeth. And my brain is going on hold every time that brown fur tries again to come close to just me.

I am trying to make Ms. Sybil let go so I can run. She doesn't. And the insane dog not done. Again, it barks. Again, it comes. I back back, spin, shift, and hold on to Ms. Sybil's dress. Brown fur stands on end. Charges at me. Its sharp yellow canines drip spit. Ms. Sybil pivots, shouts mash dog, and blocks it. The dog does not want to play. That dog not going away.

Not much taller than me, Ms. Sybil leans my head on her shoulder. Where yuh reaching? By Spikes?

Yes, just there, I tell her.

And she turns our feet to head back down the street from the frenzied rotations I'd spun in my attempt to run. Yuh mammy mustn't send yuh to make message so young. She should wait till you older. Too much tings happening out dis road, chile. It not like it use tuh be. Ms. Sybil keeps her arm round me. And I do not hear the men lining the road that talk. I do not focus on the men liming on the road who gawk.

And my hiccupping gasps ease. Ever so slightly. As Ms. Sybil loud, nasal voice soothes my ears with her dahlin and sugah and hugs and head-touches to her auburn-dyed hair. And her gold bracelets' and gold rings' chime relax my spine. And the sliver of gold in her smile charms me every time it sparks in the sunlight. Suffused in orange and gold warmth, hair, and skin, Ms. Sybil walks me within a safe distance of Spikes' shop, stops, and lets me go in.

I am barely taller than the three-foot counter, wooden and wide that I am standing behind, waiting in the non-line as bare-back men laugh with Spikes. Men throwing back small glasses of amber rum into chalky mouths. Men ordering beer chasers, loose cigarettes, and other items I know nothing about being transferred with closed fists. Till I back away from this to the left of the tall crowd to stand in front the glass-door fridge holding Cheddar cheese, pennacool, ice cream, and sweet drink. Spikes' nine-inch TV blares a football game and I cannot think.

The stink of spirits and unwashed armpits chokes me in Spikes' boxy shop. Shelves of dry goods stack up behind the portly man whose eyes never rise above my neck, above the sleepy half mast at which his gaze is kept by weed. Under his shop's dark ceiling, its walls' loud blue paint, nude magazine spreads, and faded peeling Christmas decorations close in on me. I am the lone girl in the parlour on a day decent people does be in they house or in church or on a family drive. It's not the time, nor the day guaranteeing the presence of wives making small grocery instead of going all the way down the main road to that older supermarket or to Kelly's.

And the leers and the jeers, and the Aye-sexy-smallie blares, and men's inching closer with smirking lips and outstretching fingers to me; and Spikes not studying I asking for a tin of pigeon peas behind him please, and the bad dog waiting up the street, and Mummy sending me down the road so she don't get beat, and my father stretch out on the couch tick-tock hangry, all bring down my pee. Past what my bladder can hold. Past what my trembling body can any longer control. Past what my pride and intelligence can fold within me.

Fear drips down past my mother's cute little Carnival suit pants, courses over my nearly pierced knee, onto the blue rubber slippers. Making a small pool at my feet.

Standing in the puddle of my pee, I want to flee. If Spikes can't hear me, he'll see this green. The five-dollar bill and the red singles land amidst my interjected demand. Just this and a tin of pigeon peas, please.

These ice lollies I've taken out the fridge go in the plastic bag. The peas finally reach my hand. And coin change I leave behind.

Urgency that should have been heeded before there was no more time finally grants me Mummy's needed peas. I step out the gloom back into the sun-drenched street. Please don't let them be able to see.

My Carnival suit of burnt orange and brown could keep down suspicion. Can't it? Will suppress wagging tongues and realisation. Won't it? Squeeze my thighs. Keep the wet portion inside. Bend my head and hide. Don't survey the hungry wolves on either side.

I am a child. If nothing else, wetting yuhself will remind. Don't pay attention to me. Nothing to see. Nor laugh at. Splat. The next drop lands on my hand holding the bag above my waist so it drapes over the sodden pants. Two more end their descent on my clenched fingers. And the sun lances my bent neck.

Let these people, these high people, these drunk people, these stoned, boned, unhomed people; these snorting, guffawing, rough people; these falling down, dirty in the drain, tough people; these cloned people, these smelly, rum-belly, crusty, dusty, corn-foot people; these have no house, knockabout, slack-mouth people; these no education, no direction, aimless, nameless people, these I will leave and if ever I return to visit Covigne will still be here people; these on the road, always up to no good, rising to nothingness people—let these ignorant people who fraid a book, who hold me in contempt for my ability to read, not catch a look. Let them not see.

A hand lands on me. Soft, staunch, smushy. A hand of age, unhard. A hand old enough to have learnt to talk where words can't. The hand speaks calm to my lower back. The hand articulates comfort to my waist. The hand whispers, Brace. And I do.

Ms. Sybil's hand guides me—and the left-behind money, and the tin of high sodium dressed in green, and the cute little Carnival suit in which Mummy wanted me to preen to go down the road to save her from he who she choose to marry and with whom, in marriage, she chooses to tarry—up this road where Mummy and Daddy choose to live.

Ms. Sybil's hand guides me past Ms. Okee selling gas tanks and flour across the concrete and woodlice bridge. Past Sexy-Wendy who not selling pholourie because is Sunday. Past the upstairs and downstairs gallery full of my aunt husband family ready to bray. Past that mechanic's garage where girls remain unfound to this day. Past the Baptist church where I hear loud Gold Grampa shoeless on the altar saying Yes beloved, starting to pray. Up the hill. To my father's house. Where Mummy still waiting on me. To deliver her something for my father to eat. So she don't get beat.

No, dahlin? Ahright, daz okay.

I have just shaken my head at the sight of the gallery gate and front door. I don't walk to walk through there, where Daddy will be stretch out on the whole couch to watch TV. Where Daddy will be taking een his Westerns and his kung fu movies. And will see me. And will bark, Wham Uricka! when my wet rubber slippers squeak over the carpet. And I won't resist keeping my head bent, and I won't explain Why big gyul like you embarrass the family name.

No more. No added shame.

Ms. Sybil walks with me, her hand still shoring up my waist and my back that shakes and my spine that wants to cave in on itself. Walks with me around my father's house to the side door instead. To the white half-doors atop the gravelly, unsmoothed concrete steps that will let us into the washing room. The little jail-cell-size rectangle off the kitchen that holds the washing machine, the jooking sink, the cupboard, the beer cases, the buckets, the singing mop, and the hairy broom.

Cyatreen, good day, good day, Ms. Sybil calls into the curtain hanging down to the bottom half-door. The top half of the door remains open from wake to nightfall. This is the door Ms. Sybil sends her little grands to ask for sugar, some ice, or salt.

Today, Ms. Sybil asks for nothing more than for Mummy to come. Cyatreen, look dis chile here. Somn happen out de road. Ah had was tuh kerry she home.

She wants Mummy to come tuh explain yuh how it nuh good tuh send de chile out dere by she self, nuh. Doh mind she was lucky Ah was dey.

She calls to Mummy to come to tell her everything that went on. To come from the kitchen where she supposed to be cooking the food that not done. The Sunday lunch Daddy belly tumbling waiting on, as his eyes eat their fill of white cowboys glorying in scalping their "wild Indian" kill.

But Mummy doesn't arrive from the kitchen's right side. That hand at my waist that matched my stride through tight-throat grief, while my eyes leaked and my wet slippers squeaked, has given my neck relief from its bow. I unlock the bottom door, stand on the threshold, and able to begin lifting my eyes a centimetre now.

Ms. Sybil didn't let them clown. Not when we passed Sexy-Wendy shop. Everybody liming ask if she going up the road. And Ms. Sybil tsked and said yes. Ah taking de chile home.

And Sexy-Wendy reply was to me. Gently. Okay, iz alright, yuh hear luv, doh study nuttin. Iz alright. And I didn't have to face my plight alone.

Now Ms. Sybil's tone—that caring, fretting, back-patting, there-there-alright note in her bright orange and gold voice—allows me to suppress the noise of blood rushing through my ears.

And I hear it when Ms. Sybil calls again.

Metallic forks clatter against glass plates. Muted clunks sound from wares striking wood over which cloth is draped. Ericka and Sherrie giggle between slurps and a story of their dollies they relate. Daddy chomps and smacks. A wooden chair scrapes over ceramic tiles.

Mummy appears through the kitchen door from the left-hand side. Her long pinkie fingernail picks a morsel of rice from between her incisors.

She smiles.

3

BREADFRUIT TREE

I am ten.

And is just after when Abu Bakr and the Jamaat al Muslimeen men stage they governmental coup. And Prime Minister Robinson and other ministers in The Red House get shoot.

It is 1990, and curfew now raise, and people now liming outside again with they rum money to spend. And inside my mother bedroom, I am just discovering my mother has another daughter, from way back then. Her daughter's picture hidden in her chest of drawers, beneath a writing pad and a pen.

And when my mother tells the story of ~~why~~ how she left her two-year-old baby in Grenada, she regales, she relates, she details, she pontificates. My mother illustrates newborn Samantha not swallowing her milk. My mother leaving being punishment for little Samantha being of that ilk of bad-mind child. Who dares make her mother suffer.

And I will perceive that this oft-repeated story is a narrative of a baby rejecting her mother. Who was only trying so very hard to do her utter best. Feeding her, nurturing her, nursing her from her own tender, swollen breasts.

So much so, Samantha puked. Samantha had diarrhoea. Samantha had regurgitation all in her newborn baby hair. All on the floor. All on Mummy good good dress.

And how it wasn't fair. That this first-time mother, trying to care, should have to deal. Should have to struggle with an ungrateful baby who reels. And gushes milk out her nose. Out her mouth, out her rear. Out her ears. Out of every orifice that could declare itself unimpressed.

And why my mother must stay there? In Grenada. Depressed. Why she must stay in this house with the yard full of breadfruit mess? This house under the breadfruit tree, eating oil down too too often that make from Breadfruit Tree best. In this house, with a baby who, when she was new, refused the golden, gurgling milk my mother's gargantuan breasts produced.

Why stay. For a baby who didn't value holding down what my mother's seventeen-year-old mounds poured forth. Into her daughter's mouth. Which scorched from the continuous, unrelenting stream of milk. The flow my mother did not relieve Samantha from receiving till she was filled to the hilt. And needed air.

And needed release from the heavy mammary glands remaining there. In Samantha's nose and mouth and face. Till white dribbled past Samantha's lips. Going to waste.

And still, my mother did not replace her daughter's prone form into one upright. And let her burb. And let her curl her tiny fists. And purr. Satisfied.

No. My mother kept squeezing that milk between Samantha's lips pressed wide. Looking into her child's flooding eyes. Listening to her choking daughter. Unable even to cry. Watching the pressure of liquid in this newborn rise. Beyond any measure that would reasonably suffice. For a newborn child.

While my mother's own mother harrumphed and spied upon the neighbours. And declined to teach the seventeen-year-old, first-time mother. Who couldn't bother to stop feeding her baby when it was clear Samantha had begun to be smothered.

But Mummy didn't know better.

Her eyes get wetter at this part of the tale. The part where she sniffs and inhales over her own mother's skin-up nose and eye roll and turning away that fail to help. That fail to tell Mummy how to nurse well. And what Mummy was doing wrong when she keep feeding and squeezing till milk spill to the ground.

And, at this juncture of being regaled, comes the time. When Mummy tears accumulate. The point has arrived.

I, the not-first daughter, must make a reply. I must hold in my mind the image of a helpless woman-child. Pitted against her own scornful mother, looking out the window, maccoing the neighbours. Pitted against the wilful, wasteful newborn daughter. Refusing being fed. Which distressed Mummy so much she took to her bed.

Lay down in weariness. And planned her escape to Trinidad in her head. While lying next to newborn, sick Samantha. Overfed. Little Samantha, the first daughter my mother left. The first daughter my mother fled.

And I, the not-first daughter, am glad that I succeed. That I always achieve. In how hard I always try to be good for Mummy. So I am never starring in her story. Of a baby who would not cherish Mummy properly.

I am not the kind of baby who could ever vomit up milk from Mummy. For spite. When Mummy didn't know better. And was just doing what she thought was right.

I am ten. And mature enough to hear these details of when Mummy left her first child. And can sympathise with Mummy plight. Can empathise when I ask, How could she do that. And Mummy tells me why.

Then three years later, at thirteen, I myself must try. To believe Mummy's tears. When she sings. And I hear: I'm leaving on a jet plane. Don't know when I'll be back again. And she tells me, Keep the faith. We'll be together again. Soon. Before she sends me off to school.

And boards a one-way flight.

Out Piarco gate. And I can only eat cornflakes and milk. For a whole year straight.

While this not-mother starts another new life.

4

SUGAR CANE

I am eleven years old.

Living on Baptist Hill, up Covigne Road. With my foreign-born mother and with my wife-hitting, wife-lip-splitting, wife-kicking father. And with my two younger sisters, Ericka and Sherrie. This is the nucleus of my extended family tree.

Above our house is Uncle Ken, my father's brother. Ken living with his wife, Tanty Acklyn, and their one daughter. His wife's sister living with them as well. Though I don't think Uncle Ken enjoy how she come to stay and having her there so much, so he say. But is a different story his forcibly close-pressing body to her does tell.

At the bottom of this hill lives my aunt, Tanty Marilyn, my father's sister, and her non-working, belt-jerking husband, and their three girls. This husband training pothound dogs on dragon blood to growl, and leap, and hurl.

Directly across the road from Tanty Marilyn lives another aunt, another of my father's sisters—this un-venturing-out family tightly, with insularity, populating each other's world.

My across-the-road aunt, Tanty Shirley, living with her alcoholic, wife-beating, funds-stealing, young-schoolboys-teaching husband, and their two sons, and their youngest girl. And a little farther up the road from Tanty Shirley is yet another of my father's sisters.

This aunt, Tanty Carol, living with her mister. Her new, fattening, weekday-living-room-sat-in husband who eye does slant and who lip does curl. This husband who don't say good morning and does let Tanty Carol do everything while over his belt a growing belly unfurl. This fireman husband, but auxiliary, and for-the-ladder-too-heavy husband, who so new. A recent addition who none of the cousins could bring ourselves to call Uncle yet, so just "Anthony" does do. Tanty Carol and Anthony and her one son and their just-a-little-further-up-the-road house being this sprouting-seed family's biggest move. This family that lives footsteps from each other's houses they build out of open shut doors and glue.

And next to Tanty Marilyn, at the bottom of the hill, in the same big yard, lives my grandmother. Granny—Beulah, the begetter. Beulah, the mother of my wife-hitting, wife-lip-splitting, wife-kicking father. Beulah, who keep her goodly daughters in church and ban them from being soca feters. Beulah, who let her sons run the streets as boys-will-be-boys go-getters. Beulah, bound to the kitchen, who make sure her daughters land good government jobs by keeping them focus on they letters. Beulah, who herself living within reach of her father's home; Beulah not straying far from her own, too. Generations digging in their Covigne Road roots. My grandmother living with my gold grandfather and, of her eleven surviving children, the youngest two.

These last two of Granny's children being so close to the cousins' ages it hard for us to call them Uncle or Tanty. So they's just Wendy and Calvin to we. Pious last-daughter, accountant Wendy. And Calvin who does tell the cousins about each different woman with whom he nightly sleeps. Calvin bringing moaning, groaning young girls back to Granny house. To his mother who don't say a peep. His mother who—when Calvin flips me and Calvin tickles me in my short, green silky nightie—her wide closed eyes don't see.

This is the family in whom I am steeped. Churchgoing family who don't see, who don't hear, who always aware; who don't share the secrets they keep.

I am eleven. And Gold Grampa does preach about the lonesome road to heaven at the Mount St. Rose Spiritual Baptist Church that sit down on the other side of the foot of the hill, giving Baptist Hill its name. Granny is a Mother in the church, and this is my paternal family's claim to Covigne Road fame. Though Granny being an esteemed Mother means that she is only helpmate to the Leader. But this chauvinistic edict still grants her powers to be judge and weeder. Deemer of who is fit for her family. That number being zero of those with enough of a virtuous mentality. This family's credo being stifling insularity.

My grandmother not wanting to mar the legacy of her father, Grampa Biscuit, who is a Reverend in the church. And her mother, who was also a Mother, once occupying the same hallowed bench where Beulah's Sunday sanctity does now perch. Our grandmother's mother having passed before we cousins lived. So Grampa Biscuit always telling our mothers to send us cousins to his house, to come and clean up for him.

Grampa Biscuit then sending us cousins down in the shop to buy Bermudez Vanilla cookies. His treat to reward, delight, and please.

He believes. For helping dust and do everything in that old, stuffy board house that a would-be wife must. Now the cousins don't like vanilla cookies any more, not their sugary scent, not their crispy crust.

It is the thrust and lash—impatient and rash—of Grampa Biscuit black, house-and-land umbrella. From which not his daughter, nor his grandchildren, nor his great-grands could shelter. That ensures we all obey. It is why my aunts and my grandmother attend their Baptist church for weekly meetings and spend hours there every Sunday.

But Uncle Ken, Beulah's son, does not go. Not to Mount St. Rose. Because he is converted—to Tanty Acklyn's Jehovah's Witness Hall. Conversion being the only means by which they could get married at all. Conversion meaning that in life, in death, and beyond the grave, Granny and my aunts will hate Tanty Acklyn with a venom that will appal.

Granny setting this generational course. Tanty Acklyn stole away her son; an unforgivable loss. Granny says so to me when I am helping her cook saltfish for the provision one Saturday. The sin for which—every cold, un-belonging day—they make outsider Tanty Acklyn pay.

I am eleven. My sisters and I also do not go to church every Sunday. Mummy does keep us home and away. Is from up the hill every week we does hear Gold Grampa preach. The church yearly Harvest is the only time we does reach. Called on to partake, called on by Granny telling our mother she must let us come and celebrate. Called on to help Granny display the bounty with which their god bless the family, in fruitfulness, from them going forth to procreate.

And look how they land well bless, too. The feasting table full up with Gold Grampa biggest garden tomatoes, and his best red peppers and sweet peppers, and dasheen and eddoes and tania, and mango doux-doux. And Gold Grampa long, ripe sugar cane from over the wall. The cane he does cut for us grands, laughing at juice slurping down our chins, the cane that his sweet hand does grow fattest and strongest of all. The cane the church does demand he bring to the feast to symbolise the long stretching arm of they lord. Their required Harvest supply pulling up the cousins' quota short.

That cane reduction is really the only bad part of Harvest for us, though. Well, that and the stifling dresses in baby pink or pastel blue or soft yellow. The scratchy, hot dresses so frothy and lacy and puffy and flouncy that Mummy does deck us out in, every year, to go. Obliged to wear what the rest of the cousins wear, what church people consider good going-out clothes. Though, from since I small till now, I hate these dresses and the white stockings Mummy does make us put on beneath. In Trinidad boiling heat. With the frilly, lacy ankle socks over the stockings and the shiny patent shoes that squeak. The very dresses and frilly socks I will wear decades later to study in, to lime in, to teach.

This dress code Mummy claims she doesn't like herself. As she makes my sisters and I bow-tie the matching polyester belts. Sashes that go around our waists and complete our fancy adornments' array. Required to wear this so Mummy don't feel shame in front the other mothers dressing their girl children in the same Sunday-best way.

Still, at least we does get to perform. At Harvest, we does recite Bible verses and we singing in the choir and acting out skits in front the church with the rest of the regularly attending cousins. And we get to belong. For the weeks of rehearsal before Harvest, my sisters and

I are part of the norm. Part of the grandchildren group when it is we conform.

My sisters and I also called out the reserve by Granny for Thanksgivings. To come attend church and add. Pulled out to grow the numbers, to swell the swarm for celebrations the church members have. Thanksgivings to offer up tidings of praise and acknowledge personal blessings, making church hearts glad. A Thanksgiving with a full table put on display. A Thanksgiving with an overflowing bounty that boast and say, come see how the lord does answer me nice nice when I pray.

A table weighed with bread, milk, honey, stew chicken, and sponge cake, with fruit, and snacks offered up to the altar to give deep thanks. My sisters and I not needed, not seated for the adult sermon section in the beginning. My sisters and I showing up for the rejoicing part of bells ringing, and bread breaking, and food sharing, and honey and oil pouring directly in our mouths. And for leaving with a food-stuffed paper bag that distribute to everybody who gather to glorify Emmanuel name and sing, and ketch power, and shout.

But my mother nowhere about. Not when tied Baptist heads bow to the north, to the east, to the west, to the south. My mother nowhere about. Not when bare feet stomp and throats drum and hands cymbal and rotund waists our young expectations flout. Raising that zinging, pinging spirit that defying English, defying age, defying manners, defying clout. With sweat dripping, cotton dresses wringing, candles streaming, holy water gleaming, flower petals creaming the concrete floors. With wooden doors closed to hold the ricocheting holy ghost within the writhing core. My mother not here, not to share in the feasts of the generous, grateful host. Not here for the fare of Peardrax and wine offered praising, drying, bleating throats. Throats celebrating, summoning for hours the Most High. My mother not here to behold these wondrous, shocking sights. My mother not here, not with my sisters and I. My mother staying home as Thanksgivings, as Harvests, as church ceremonies extend into the night.

Mummy say Baptist services too long. Mummy say For six or seven or eight or nine hours on a hard wood bench, with they feet on cold tile, chirren shouldn have tuh siddong. Mummy who say she is not a Baptist. Mummy marrying into a church family who do not like this. Mummy and Tanty Acklyn on the hated in-laws list. Hate over years, over decades, over generations, that will never not exist. And these are the grandmother and aunts, when Mummy flies away to her new life, she will leave her children with.

5

JULIE MANGO TREE

I am twelve years old. When Mummy cuss out Granny in Beulah's own crowded home. And I am still on Mummy's side. Until I learn my mother's real reason why.

On a cloudless day in 1992, we nice and blanketed under Trinidad shimmering heat. Granny quick and easy macaroni and scramble egg with butter and Matouk's ketchup done share and eat. Water-down orange juice from the mug done drink, and the brown sugar still sticking in my throat, fus the juice too sweet. Granny pack-up fridge and big afternoon Dutch pots resting now and closed to us for the day. Not till dinner they will share out again. Now, the cousins and my two younger sisters and I all munching on mango chow that we make.

Half-ripe, full, and green mango we pick from the yard's trees we climb. Mango slice we adorn with salt, pepper sauce, shadon beni, garlic, and a lil lime. One big bowl of yellow, of red, of orange, of green, of white. Chow smelling sweet and spicy and hot and brined.

Chow burning we nose and watering we eye. But we too grown for only a lil black pepper this time. So we keep reaching juicy fingers into the plastic bowl. All the while we sipping on air, *skuppssss*, to cool the grind. Our teeth set on edge and our tongues pickled by refusing to resign teasing and laughing and jostling and pride. Lest one of we get called by the other a little child.

And I am twelve. And my cousins and sisters and I are spread round, at, and under Granny pockmarked wood dining table. The one covered up by a plastic tablecloth cause Granny knows her three-a-year grands not able to resist spilling from chubby baby and toddler and adolescent hands. And Granny want to keep she things nice if she can. Even while she afterschool-caretakes her active children's children. As her eleven offspring work to meet their jobs' demands.

It is into this happy noise of giggling and mango-munching. Into this excited chatter about the coming weekend curry-q with paratha and chicken on which we'll be lunching. Into this squeaky, high-pitched blaring of cartoons on cable TV in Granny dining room. It is into this huffing and puffing of air from a cousin who try a scotch bonnet pepper too soon. That the scream rends the air.

And even though my time is finally mine. Even though I having a good good lime with my cousins and them. Even though I for once not tracking if Mummy getting overwhelmed. Even though, when dry so, from the circle of adults in the archway Mummy start keening. And my canerow hair parts begin feeling fire blazing my scalp. On this sunshine day, in the midst of all of that, I am only scared for Mummy. My alertness, my concern, my body pivot immediately. It is for her I fear. Mummy. For whom I am trained to care.

What could make Mummy scream like a trapped agouti? Here? Where we in the all-clear.

And I don't hear Daddy horn coming up Covigne Road. That horn signalling construction work done and he coming home. Signalling his food need to be hot and ready to go. Signalling his big, enamel plate better be there on the chair he build. The dining room chair he will pull up to the couch from where he will spread his long legs out and eat his fill.

That horn beeping twice, signalling time to ready Daddy rice, and peas, and some kinda meat and some kinda greens. And a whole mug of juice that might be Kool-Aid if the grocery money he give Mummy en make it till month-end. And we not getting Orchard citrus concentrate in a can again. Only limes and sour orange and passion fruit picked straight from the backyard branch and vines till then.

But it early enough after school. Still early enough in the afternoon when Daddy and all this family's men still on they worksites. Still doing labour that require they big biceps and physical might. And is only the women reach back from the office jobs that they does leave not too long after three. Leaving after promptly packing up their desks so they come up the road in time to give Granny a rest from watching all her grands. While my Gold Grampa sneak off down the road in his old gardening pants to the shop. Gold Grampa, going to bet on a Play Whe mark, though he promise he going to stop.

And is just Granny and all the tanties—her daughters, Daddy sisters—here talking to Mummy. Shoo-shooing in the kitchen where Granny over a big dinner Dutch pot with a wood spoon stirring. And they not even sitting in the good good living room with the AML floor fan whirring. Their conversation not requiring they move to that good living room Granny does keep for privacy and for her special company.

Those guests for whom alone Granny does pull off the noisy, sticky plastic covering the seats. Those newly revealed couch and armchairs Granny does offer her attendees after they feet squeak. After they feet creak on the plastic runner making an aisle in the lush carpet Granny determine going to remain the original amount of thick and pile. In the same condition as when Granny buy it from Courts in instalments she try to save. The layaway payments she accumulate from the little pension and garden produce Gold Grampa selling, and the money her eleven adult children give in a month-end wave.

Ent we down the hill, not in my father house? He not here, and we safe. And my belly untense without needing to try and stave off exploding magma that does course under Daddy skin. Waiting. To brim. Turning his copper complexion mahogany—that manifestation of rising molten rage. Flames over whatever insufficiency or inattention or lip Mummy evince that day. Whatever perceived disrespect Mummy display to provoke the eruptive blaze of spit. And Daddy boiling, clenched-teeth hiss. And Daddy veiny, calloused fists. Daddy's accurate fists that never miss.

Explosions I divert with jokes and encyclopaedia questions to ease their tension. And by being sure to stay at Mummy side. Keeping Mummy company. Though I want to hide. Keeping her out Daddy simmering way. Especially when he say he just want to cool his head after a long day and don't want to hear Mummy complain.

Though Mummy does keep pushing because Ah going to say what I have to say.

Even though my belly have no more room to barrel the strain.

To barrel their weight I am not under now, with *Little House on the Prairie* splayed in front of me on Granny plastic-draped table. Where I am able to laugh with my cousins who teasing me to explain how Almanzo and Laura manage to fall in love from getting lost in a winter storm while stuck in a sleigh.

Ent Daddy not here now? So how? That howl. That Mummy deep-belly bawl. Making my muscles brace. And goosebumps race. Here? In Granny place? Now? Like she did that day.

That day, a year ago, when I am standing in the corner. Squash in between the wall and space saver. That early-morning day the lace curtains still pull over the frosted louvres. So Ann and Ms. Sybil and Uncle Errol and them can't look up and see in the living room when they peep from their house below us on the hill. But they could hear still.

Daddy dressed for work in a plaid shirt Mummy pressed for him last night. He have his work bag with his favourite hammer and wrench, the wood shaver and beam level he using to not build the bench Mummy want for their bedroom. The bench Mummy want so Daddy could sit down there to take off his cement-dusted boots. Instead of putting his dirty jeans on the bed where she have to sleep. Daddy done pick up the keys from the kitchen table for his jeep that does park down the hill in Granny yard. All he have to do now is give everybody his obligatory spitty kiss that we does wipe off our cheek when he leave and say See allyuh later. Just that, nothing hard.

I in the corner. About to open the curtain and louvres. About to open this house to sunlight and fresh air, this house that does Hoover peace from my core. The TV on top the space-saver two feet from the front door. I watching the minutes change on the VCR till we don't have to be so tense any more.

Well, not again until night inevitably fall. And I hear the jeep coming-home horn. Its call I could identify anywhere in Trinidad, and have.

The horn blast at which I does tell Mummy he coming and tell my stomach to stop gurgling so bad. And does tell my sisters to finish cleaning up any mess they make. And does get my books and head for my bedroom, since I never like TV anyway. But does only watch it because Mummy ask me to keep her company when my younger sisters go down the hill to play. And I does stay because, as Mummy always say, I so wise and mature for my age.

I facing the kitchen, shallow-breathing, waiting. When Mummy walk through the strips. This beaded curtain separating the living room from the kitchen in place of a door. Nobody in Trinidad like to close off the concept of an open floor. The beads rattle and click when Mummy pass through. The height of opulent aesthetics in 1992.

The wood and plastic baubles making their own rhythm and blues. Beyond it, in the shared bedroom, Ericka store-bought bed squeaks. The refined wood weak. Like Ericka, prone to weep. While, having switched, Sherrie's bed is the pale and unyielding one which Daddy construct; the one that never utters a peep. The Standards-store, delicate hinge offering an audible cringe every time Ericka flip and toss. Sherrie bed—which cost Daddy only his labour and moulding in his favour from his know-how—saying nothing now. Their beds mimicking my sisters and their still mostly silent vows. My sisters who stay in their beds to cow.

Mummy passes back beyond their bedroom door, through the bead strips, onto the living room's thinly carpeted floor. Mummy wearing a yellow cotton nightie. She holding her morning cup of milky Lipton tea. And she stops diagonal to me. Right in front the gallon fish tank, sit down on the other space-saver that slightly leans and also shelves more books, the stereo, and glass figurines.

Yuh forgetting something? she question Daddy, who getting ready to leave.

Why? Why? We this close to being free. For the day. Why she feel the need to prolong this? Why she trying and make him stay?

Cyatrin, I doh have time fuh dis dis morning. Stop yuh shit, grits Daddy, ramming his ring of keys in the back pocket of his jeans.

Alright Daddy, just go now, my tightening belly pleads.

Stop my shit? Stop my shit! Stop your shit, Ulric. And what I suppose tuh do fuh de chirren?

Ent I give yuh grocery money de odda evening? Whey all dat gone arreday? Look, make some soup or sometin. I shouldn't have tuh tell you what tuh do. Yuh know tuh make some blasted food.

Daddy getting agitated. The slightest thing does make him totally overwhelmed and uncontainably irritated. Mummy say so all Beulah sons wid dey nasty temper ignorant. And I wonder if is true what I read in the encyclopaedia about Freudian childhood stages and underdevelopment.

Daddy shoulders tense up and his movements getting jerky. The whites of his dark hazel eyes starting to get murky. Like chum in the water. Daddy looking like a pressure cooker. One about to shoot its lid up to the roof. And erupt every piece a food onto the ceiling. All on the walls by the stove that still needing painting from his last exploding. He on the brink.

I watch Mummy watch him. Watch Mummy let it sink in that he near the point of no return. I watch Mummy eyes squint, her twisting lips calculate. Watch Mummy sneering face seek more bait to make the water churn.

Wah kinda man you is? Eh? she demands.

When that gauntlet lands, Mummy steps in Daddy's space. She looks up in Daddy face and curls her top lip. Past the bared canine. Mummy snips, Yuh radda take food out yuh chirren mout and give tuh yuh . . .

Slap!

My father palm—open, heavy, loud. He whip my mother head around. But she doesn't fall down. No, at first, Mummy stands her ground. And flings my glass of water from the space-saver up in Daddy face. This time, when he ring his hand across her cheek, Daddy makes sure to knock Mummy down to the floor straight. Her flinging-out arm takes with her that coskel glass vase.

The ugly vase Daddy buy, stuffed with plastic pink carnations, lies down at Mummy's side on the brown carpet Daddy chose, from which she doesn't rise. Mummy hits her head on the sharp, jutting edge of the centre table he picked that she always despised. And her voice warbles as Mummy throws up a hand to ward Daddy off from stepping closer. Nooo, Ulric! Noooooo! Oh god! Yuh's a monster?

Mummy clutching her ear. Daddy stoops down, leans over her body prone on the vomit-sienna carpet he still choose and buy when we say none of us like it. Daddy rears back and lets go a backhand that bust Mummy lip. And catch her upside her nose. That lays her head flat. Like she in repose. Like she just lie down there sleeping. Except for her snivelling, the crying, the weeping. That reaching my ears too scared to peek out past the corner where the fake-mahogany panel peeling back from the space-saver shelf. And I hiding lest . . . lest what? Daddy never hit me.

There are other ways to inflict pain on the body. Like witnessing. Like listening. Like hearing your mother wordlessly bawl. That haunting, mournful call.

Then comes the shrieks. Mummy's garrulous screams, Murderer! Yuh want tuh kill meh here! Yes, yuh want tuh kill meh in here today!

And the chant, Kill meh, yes, kill meh! Kill meh! Dey go do fuh yuh. Leh dey lock yuh ass up! Murderer!

Mummy sobs as she pummels her feet against Daddy's pants. Her nightie rides up her bare, round legs.

Daddy jeers, Look yuh! Watch yuh state. And then stands back up to his full height.

Daddy bites out from his mouth pursed tight, Hush yuh mout, Cyatrin! Hush yuh blasted mout! Stop all dat noise, crying like a suckin baby. Yuh want people tuh hear yuh? I killin you? Daz wah yuh want? Iz dat yuh go get!

And after he delivers this threat, Daddy lifts up his construction boot.

Help! Oh god, somebody help meh! He go kill meh in here today. Ah go dead today! Mummy yells. She squeals. She cries.

Mummy crab-walks on her spine. She crawls on her elbows. Backing away from my father, who's pendulating his steel toe. His gleaming eyes gone cold. His muscled chest puffs, blowing smoke. Those bloodshot eyes flash his imminent attack. Daddy snarls. His bared teeth broadcast his intention to kick Mummy in the ribs.

I jump on his back. I wade in.

With a moan, I grab him. Daddy. The one who used to play monster with me, and Ericka, and Sherrie. Daddy who used to pretend to be asleep when the floor was the sea. And we would reach out and poke his slumping hand. And Daddy would become a tickle-monster shark that could lift us up in strong arms. And didn't drop us when we squirmed to get away and swim back behind the headboard and sneak up on the shark again.

This Daddy I grab round the neck to restrain his bulging arm, his foot, his forward momentum from gaining stride. From kicking Mummy in the side. This Daddy shouts at Ericka and Sherrie to go back inside when they run out from the bedroom to cry, Stop, Daddy, please! And lie down next to Mummy.

This is the bring-a-snack-for-us-every-evening-when-he-coming-home-from-work Daddy who pulls me down from his neck and snaps at Mummy to get up and clean up yuhself. And go and look after de chirren and doh let dis mess be here when I reach home dis evening.

This is the Daddy who smirks when he picks up his bag. Steps over the broken glass. Looks sideways at Mummy. Glances at me. And leaves.

This father who is obviously, openly, incontestably malevolent in the sight of his terrified children. This man who my mother married and who is her match. Though I didn't know that then.

This is the day from a year ago locked in my belly. The one Mummy's howl in Granny's house now retrieves from etched memory.

When you're still a child. And your father beats your mother right in front your eyes. And you drop down to your knees. And you look to see if is anything worse than the black-blue bruise showing through her dark skin. And you help her sit up and you tell your hiccupping mother that you hate him.

And you ask her why we don't leave. And you grieve when she questions you how. And you try to figure a way out. And you hear your mother gasp in pain as she slings her arm across your shoulders. And you struggle to help her off the floor and to hold her.

And you tell your mother's shaking, retreating back Is okay. Go and lie down. As she was already heading for her bedroom door anyway. And you go and take care of your fear-struck, crying sisters who have to go to school. As do you. And, when in your uniform and back in the kitchen, that feeling you ignore. The presence of doom. The feeling bubbling in your belly when your mother on the counter leans. And sighs and sniffles that she can't do any more today again to get your lunch bags ready. And it's all up to you, you glean.

So you prepare the snacks, and the juice, and you make your younger sisters' cheese-paste sandwiches and yours, and you kiss your Mummy. And you tell her Don't worry, everything will be okay.

Before you run down the hill to meet the maxi taxi to go to school as Granny complains. Allyuh always late, she states. Irate. And always keeping back allyuh cousins who allyuh could give a care to. And Granny doesn't know or have any concern for what her son just do.

And you become the parent. That's who.

Till you learn that there is a name given to your mother and your father pushing your head down under their floodwater. Till you learn there is a term for them unfreezing their tableau, performing their looping domestic scene, and making you an unwilling actor.

There is jargon and vocabulary that effectively captures them reaching to embrace each other in their warring waltz. And ensnaring you as their dance partner. You learn there is language for these people who have made you their third, keeping their indulged dysfunction together.

But not then, not yet. That terminology isn't in the classic hardbound books you get from your grandmother's shelves in her good living room. That insight isn't in the *Little House on the Prairie* volume you was poring over when your mother decide to cuss out Beulah in her own dining room.

Almanzo was shaking Laura from sleep while tucking more furs around her in the snow sled. He was urging the horses on through the blinding blizzard to make it back home to the cabin, knowing if they stay outside much longer they all dead. Ma was knitting by the fireplace, worrying for her child. Paw was looking out the log cabin window, reassuring his wife. Almanzo is a capable man to court Laura and keep her safe in a storm. The patriarch declaring his opinion as pioneer law.

My cousin, Marlon, at Granny dining table next to me. Him asking Why yuh always reading about old, dead, white people anyway, Camille, when none of that doh make no sense. And if I en hear him asking if I getting pholourie in my curry-q box this weekend. Or geera pork, or if I brave enough for hot pepper on my curry chicken.

And I now answering. Telling him My body don't like pig and I does only eat pork for Christmas. And I not too sure if I could handle scorpion pepper sauce. When we hear a commotion coming from the grown-ups in their huddle. And we don't study it too much, although we never know them to make no big kinda fuss. But we brought up that big-people business is not thing into which we meddle. And we cousins go back to debating paratha or dhalpuri. When Mummy start to keen.

And my thoughts stutter. My muscles and time freeze. Sad and scared, my belly plunges to my knees. What making Mummy wail? So much agonising pain. Transmuting itself straight to the lump in my throat and my springing eyes. I can't bear to hear little Mummy cry. She not even a whole five feet in height.

With that same shortness, Mummy ducks under my aunts' arms akimbo. Dashes from Granny kitchen tiles' cold, through the archway, to the carpeted dining room, and in here continues to bawl her sorrow. My cousins' foreheads pucker and furrow. Ericka's worried eyes seek out mine. Shame tightens my skin out of which I cannot climb.

The Julie Mango Tree outside peeps through the old-fashioned windows to remind me of my cradle in her rough boughs. The arms of her branches where I lay and speak my diary, my dreams, my needs aloud. Resting on her rivuletting bark when nobody else is around. After Granny and all of them gone to church. And Mummy don't send us, and I am in search of quiet.

In Julie Mango Tree leafy limbs, amidst the riot of ants and bachac and lizards and concealed snakes resting in the stillness of the dwarf tree, I am saved. Granted reprieve from my coffee-breath mother not respecting my space. My come-and-keep-me-company mother needing to be braced in her thirteen-year marriage by making my brain the carriage of her regrets.

And in Julie Mango Tree's arms, when she done laugh at my too-short legs trying to climb to her crest as a way to impress my cousins, who does say I too girly and too nerdy all the time, I am mine. And she lets me be, hugging this girl who sings songs to her and praises the patience of her green mangoes turning ripe.

This selfness with her I find. Julie Mango Tree rustles her leaves and extends her watching eyes through Granny's window to breathe, to sigh on my bent neck. To me remind. To reinfuse. To re-inject the remembrance of the me-ness her sap imbues in my spine when I recline and watch, with her, our teal-painted sky.

Loving her, Julie Mango Tree, who Gold Grampa planted, and in whose boughs I recite the Anansi stories my golden Grampa does tell me with his loud laugh so bright. The stories that does always make me smile. Love beams through the window, transported on rays of yellow sunlight, girding me, as Julie Mango Tree and I watch my mother slide.

Down the wall to the floor. Like Mummy don't have strength to go on any more. What happening to her? Mummy never show this kind of emotion in front her in-laws. In front Daddy family who Mummy say never like she and always wutless to her.

Mummy always hold her head high. Always make sure her hair done to show Granny and them how thick it is and how it running down her back, like theirs never could no matter how hard they try. She always make sure she say, Good afternoon, Mammy, to Granny when she passing in after coming back from town, ever so polite. Always ask Granny if is anything she need before Mummy head up the hill for the night. Why Mummy go collapse on her butt in everybody sight?

Embarrassment wraps scorching tentacles round my face and shoulders, seeing Mummy drop to the ground. In front people she don't even too much want us around. My consternation sounds inaudibly, on waves of projected telepathy. Look around you, Mummy! Look at Ericka, Sherrie, and I. Always on the outside. You done don't let us stay here every afternoon like the other cousins get to do, eating Granny watery food, watching cable before Gold Grampa reach back to turn the station to the local news. The stinging tentacles tie into a noose when Mummy's out-loud reply is to let loose a bone-chilling cry. She does not rise.

The aunts make speaking glances over Mummy head with their wary, alarmed eyes. They never see Mummy let herself go in public before. It is what their clan dictate ensures. That nobody in the family is to carry on like this. Not where anyone can witness. Manners must be kept. We conduct ourselves with decorum and behave properly. Making a scene is not acting circumspectly. Take Tanty Shirley.

When Tanty Shirley—Granny daughter, Marlon mother—was inside her own house that lay out nice from Daddy blueprint design, she didn't abjure broughtupsy. No matter the price. Tanty Shirley keep quiet.

When, one Saturday, I was down by Tanty Shirley and suddenly, from my chair next to Marlon's in her gallery, I hear angry, hushed voices. And I hear tense, taut noises. But I couldn't quite glimpse past the glass sliding doors and thick curtains to see what began bothering him. Marlon. What have his face crumpling. His wild eyes pivoting. His sudden bloom of shame that was confusing but riveting. Till awareness in me start growing, obliterating unknowing. That I was bearing accidental aural witness to the drunk thumps of hitting. In that silenced house. Shirley didn't scream out.

In that house of how-it-go-look dignity that's etched into the coat of arms of this family. The code of respectability from which Tanty Shirley roused only some retained function of her drooping right arm and her left limping leg. Tanty Shirley didn't yell.

So at least Covigne Road and Tanty Shirley's priorly unaware niece didn't hear her beg. Beg that red, drunk-fish husband of hers, swimming in rum to his looming death. Because Tanty Shirley didn't tell.

In upholding governing decency, no one observe Tanty Shirley get kick in the ribs, thighs, and legs. Maybe her head. Not that Saturday morning when I went down to lime with her son in their garden-adorned gallery. Tanty Shirley maintained her family's propriety. And she didn't release a blood-curdling scream. As now does Mummy. Prompting her child—me—to attend to her. Fierce defender, sending in the cavalry. As Mummy small hands grip her belly to allow the howl to come out fully.

Doh fuckin touch meh! This to the impenetrable perimeter of aunts trying to restrain, retain, retrain Mummy in the centre.

I hover. And cannot enter. Mummy, though, find a way to exit the perimeter. She dash from the circle of arms confining her closer to the kitchen. Mummy reach the dining table, pick up wares, and start pitching. Granny grab Mummy wrists like she under arrest. Granny pull back her glass, though it not from her best set in the buffet. No more wares she letting go astray, no more get to go flying. Mummy start to toss her head from side to side, hysterical, frantic, crying.

Leave meh, leave meh, yuh ole bitch!

Mummy shove Granny hands off her arms, accelerating her flail. Mummy push back at Granny, who trying to subdue her against the cornflower wall and keep her contained. Against her wall that easy to stain. The wall against which we grandchildren can't stand, can't lean, can't play. Always told to stay in the toy room or go outside. But not today. The adults don't seem to realise we still all here. That their children could hear my mother spit at theirs, Haul yuh mudda cunt!

I do, though. I realise. And I know what coming. I know what brewing behind my father's family eyes. This family who unreceptive and unwarm to all in-laws and children born of women their prized sons marry, to the scorn of Granny, who form in her sons' minds that she is the one and the only, and that every other woman is a hussy of a certain variety.

I am cognisant. Mummy just make my sisters and I even more different.

The three little girls who emerge from a mother who come from Grenada. The ones who mother have a first daughter as a teenager before she meet my father. The ones who mother don't work and have Ulric minding her as a homemaker. The ones who don't go their church and does stay home on a Sunday instead they mother even self send the children to learn a little Bible story. The ones who mother does wear make-up when she ready. And long earring and fitted dress she does sew for she self.

The mother our aunts, uncles, grandparents never accept. The mother whose children they also reject. Now the mother who does use bad word, who does curse, who have no behaviour. It will all be so much worse when this fight is over. Living among this tight-knit chain of houses that Granny children all build mere steps from their mother's home to remain in her purview. This family hive comprised of hexagonal cells around a queen. This family of secrets, keeping quiet, not letting anybody een.

Mummy screams. She writhes, ducks, grunts as she can't break free. Granny tall, nearly six feet. Mummy does only reach five feet if she wearing heels. Granny can keep Mummy from moving, but she have heart problems and beginning to wheeze.

Buh Cyatrin, what is dis at all? I never know you so, Granny panting now.

Mammy siddong, siddong, Tanty Shirley whines as she guides her mother to a cushioned chair on which one of the cousins was sitting to dine. Lemme get some water. Hol on.

Tanty Shirley gives Mummy a cut eye when she passes her to go in the kitchen. That leaves Tanty Marilyn. Tanty Marilyn who still holding

Mummy's arms stretch out like Jesus on the cross. Like this family's saviour nail up in pictures on the wall against which Mummy's head turns and toss.

Fuck you, Marilyn! Mummy furiously spits. I see froth and droplets hit. Yuh know how long yuh have me in yuh craw?

I do not know this word, this phrase. And I can't infer based on its use like Ms. Goddard teach us to do. But this phrase lights a fuse. There is now spiteful glee. Now delight in Mummy's eyes that chills me. A maniacal fury in Mummy's orbs, bright and bulgy. A sibilant, tasty yessss. A purposeful channelling what seemed like uncontrollable distress. Mummy's despair sights a new target its radar traced. Mummy's rage aims specifically for Tanty Marilyn, in front her face.

A blooming snarl and smirk I am confused and saddened by, though I don't know why, are on Mummy's lips. They inspire shock and hesitation in Tanty Marilyn's grip. I feel something more, some presence, some history swimming under the surface. Something—of which I am not apprised—changing the current. Producing a rip tide.

No, Cyatrine, I doh have you in meh craw. Angry, appalled Tanty Marilyn boldly implores. Tanty Marilyn does not know yet what Mummy is projecting. Tanty Marilyn does not yet know the cause. Tanty Marilyn does not yet know the depths of this woman that is her in-law.

But for now Tanty Marilyn getting worked up, and the growing moles on her light brown face stand out in relief as her cheeks and chin shake. Denying vociferously. Outrage and a hint of shame, pushing back against this attack and trying to curtail the delicious bacchanal Mummy warming up to relish.

Hush and stop yuh schupidness, Tanty Marilyn shouts through lips gaping like the mouth of a fish. Tanty Marilyn wants out this scene turned hellish.

Yes, Ah know. Long time yuh have it out fuh meh. Doh fuckin tell meh tuh hush meh kiss-me-ass mout. Ah talking meh mind, Mummy bellows.

Quick as mercury moving up a thermometer at our equator, Mummy's tongue changes again to aggrieved. Her tone releasing pent-up sorrow.

Allyuh tink allyuh betta dan me. All uh allyuh does treat me like dirt in here. Allyuh not betta dan me. Allyuh not betta dan nobody in Covigne Road. Allyuh tink allyuh shit doh stink like everybody else. Leh meh go! Ah want tuh go.

Mummy recommences her tussling. Tanty Marilyn volleys back, while huffing, Jess cool it, Cyatrine, cool it!

And then when Mummy bends and growls and groans and shrieks and moans, and looks ready to throw their wrestling to the carpet, startled Tanty Marilyn exhales, Buh wah trouble is dis?

Then Tanty Marilyn begins to puff. And I wonder if she is going to have an asthma attack. Mummy looks ready to call her bluff. My crying sisters and protesting cousins are background noises, with voices that crack. Tanty Marilyn inflates her chest with a desperate breath. And pushes Mummy back. To hit the wall. Mummy butts Tanty Marilyn's forehead. And surges forward. Then Mummy bites Tanty Marilyn shoulder. And Tanty Marilyn backward falls.

Shoulder blades hitting the wall. My aunt looking like she going and topple over. Mummy always say Tanty Marilyn apple-shaped, with her two thin K-foot. And that she lucky her husband, Donald, even want her. Donald who is Mummy's first cousin. Donald who Mummy does smile and laugh wide with, happy at all his jokes she say so funny though the "jokes" always picking on somebody. Donald who Mummy doesn't find to be so grumpy. Like the rest of we. Mussbe as Mummy live with Donald for a year when she moved from Grenada and was staying with her uncle Charlie and his family. And she know Donald properly. Know and like him better than Tanty Marilyn, his wife, who Mummy say jealous she whole life that she not pear-shaped like Mummy. An apple and a pear, now going at each other with two opposing centres of gravity.

And Granny—downing ice water brought to her by Tanty Shirley, her good daughter, to her cushioned chair—interjects after every gulp and burb of air,

Eh eh Cyatrin, huh.

Then, Dis is not de way tuh go on at all, at all, at all, man.

And, Is take yuh take een, Cyatrine?

Till Granny swivelling eyes meet mine. Mine that done open wide. I just witnessed Mummy snarl and bite. I, her not-first child, hovering on the brink of a wrestling ring. On the outskirts of the scene. Watching Mummy. A mother I have never seen. Take een. Granny's eyes bid me, Step in, get through to she.

But why? Why is always me?

A grown woman screaming like a banshee in the middle of the afternoon. In Granny dining room. A grown woman uncaring her children are being brought into melee we cannot process. A mother unconcerned that she making us stressed. Making her children embarrassed and stand out from the rest. A mother apathetic to her cause and effects. That we would never want to show our face again after she make a mess of an easy lime.

After she spoil a nice get-together, where we was all planning what time we heading down the road on Saturday to collect our boxes of curry-q. A relaxing hang-out where we was all planning what games we would go through. How overnight would be Monopoly and Scrabble after we eat our curry Saturday late afternoon. And all-fours that the uncles would teach me to play. That card game I still haven't learnt to this day.

No. None of that have any sway.

Mummy not thinking about that.

So why I must have to wade in. Like I do. And pat Mummy on her sweaty back. And then hug her short frame into my arms and be a shelf that lets Mummy rest her mussed-up hair. My shoulders the shelf that bears the weight of Mummy's head and her sudden tears.

As Mummy settles her leaden breasts on my heart-thumping chest. And lets herself cry. Like her soul breaking and she just tired. And water gathers in my eyes. And my spine is heavy. But my sternum burns with shield-her fire. As Mummy's wet head doesn't rise from my shoulders. And my quaking arms enfold her.

Before Tanty Carol finally steps up. Tanty Carol, my favourite of the aunts, and my godmother, too. Tanty Carol who waves her small gold hands to shoo all my cousins, who had get up from the table to crowd around Mummy and Granny, out the dining room, out the playing room, and out to the yard.

Stay close tuh de house where we could hear allyuh. Doh go too far. Doh go past de pommecythere tree. And see allyuh doh over dat wall in de back.

Tanty Carol wants to keep cautious track of my cousins since nobody gonna be outside to protect, to watch them. And my boy cousins especially have the potential to cause problems. But even given this freedom, my cousins don't immediately leave. They stand solemn, staring, ready to make sure Granny okay. Their coaching they obey. To attend to the matriarch, their beloved grandmother. Granny who hasn't lost the starch in her spine as she rolls back her netted curtains from the open, old-fashioned, four-foot windowpanes. The windows through which Julie Mango Tree came. Granny opening her dining room to fresh air and ushering out the stale, the pain.

She awright, she alright, is okay, Tanty Carol has to say. Has to assuage my cousins' worries before they finally move to flee. Unhurriedly. Filing past, stealing quick glances at Mummy, whose bad words have, as their Sunday school does teach, made her unclean. My mother—still being held up by me, patrolled by Tanty Shirley—makes monkey face through her tears at my cousins as some shuffle and others hustle past her to leave. Maybe sticking out her tongue means the cussing and screaming done. My head is spinning and I need to lie down, I need a reprieve.

As my cousins exit the scene, Tanty Carol comes to me, from across the dining room. Stay and talk tuh yuh modda. Maybe you could get her tuh calm dong. She will listen to you. Mummy is sniffling, smelling sweaty, shuddering, mumbling in alternating volume.

At my frown, Tanty Carol asks, Yuh know what set her off? Yuh tink she . . . ? She not herself right now, right dahlin, but is okay. Tanty Carol is talking straight to me. My loudly weeping, wailing mother is absolved from speech. See if yuh could reach her and try to get her to see reason, okay luv.

And months later, when my mother leaves. Months later, when my mother packs up a suitcase and Trinidad flees. Months later, when my mother deserts my father and her children three. When I am only barely stomaching cornflakes and milk and can hardly get out of bed. Months later, when I need to be held. It is Tanty Carol who seeks me out with her doux-doux and her kisses and hugs—my endless, lonely tears to quell.

On this day, the day of the cussing, it is Tanty Carol's eyes I feel. Tanty Carol, the only aunt just as short as Mummy. She watches closely to keep me soothing Mummy, who begins her litany.

I sorry, I sorry, my mother weeps. I don't utter a peep. Mummy lifts her head, focussing her red, spilling eyes on me and repeats, I sorry, I so sorry. Sorry. Ah sorry. Forgive me? Say you forgive me?

Tell yuh mother is okay, Tanty Carol chimes in to say. I smell the food in Granny Dutch pot, delayed. I nod. Ericka and Sherrie, who come closer now, nod too. Immediately, Tanty Shirley motions to shoo. Motions to remove. As soon as she assesses the commotion passing and Mummy not gonna be relapsing into a full-blown flare. She starts procedures to get us out of here. The most churchy of the aunts, Tanty Shirley wants us gone so she could go pick, then burn some black sage, and smoke out, to clear the toxic air.

Mummy not letting go of my arm, of my waist. Won't stop resting her wet face on my shoulder. We trundle down the front stoop like this, me holding her. Tanty Carol hands Mummy's bag to Ericka through the back door of the playroom. My sister's eyes and nose are red and wet, too.

Allyuh go up de hill nuh, and let yuh mother get some rest, awright. Just take allyuh time and go up easy. By tonight, she should be feeling better, hear? Alright dahlin, see allyuh dis weekend, okay. Reach up safe. In her sweet singsong, Tanty Carol means to placate.

With that, and with the metal-latch clang of the closing yard gate, we are dismissed. Behind Granny and Tanty Shirley houses, in the gorge, canal waters hiss.

6

PAWPAW TREE

I am twelve years old. My aunts and my grandmother and my cousins on the other side of a gate now closed. And I am on the road.

Outside now, we walk pass Granny's, Tanty Shirley's, and Tanty Marilyn's houses. Pass the church at the foot of Baptist Hill. And up the hill's steep, past neighbours staring their fill. Thick, cliff boulders in my throat are standing still.

Wandering out there—

scratchy, gruff Bois Canot Tree stares. Dancing, red Hibiscus Bush peers. Stolid Black Sage looks. Tall, thin, hollow-trunk Pawpaw Tree chooks her fanned-out leaves down close. Her broad fronds listen to the quick dub-dub-dub-dub of my heart in throes of strain. My heart bearing the mantle that is Mummy, draped. Weeping, staggering, moaning Mummy, arm over my shoulder. Like a mapepire snake. Like an iron feather boa.

Spiky, pink Ixora Flowers taste my sweat. They lick at the beads running down from my neck. And sip on me. Ixora flips the normalcy of my picking buds from their star-studded crowns. My turning their strawlike style to my lips to drink down the sweet nectar they provide. My sharing with the bejewelled hummingbirds, festooned with long beaks to reach inside the flowers' ovaries replete with juice. Ixora Flowers put their heads together and deduce. Ixora Flowers whisper that this salt I produce is grief.

Tall, swaying Shango Bamboo Flags sync with the beat of our feet trudging piece by piece up the hot, asphalt hill. Fed, red Shango Flags astride green bamboo poles that shine. Slim Shango Flag poles wave in time. Happy from eating their fill of the offering that Ms. Ann, their devotee, pay on their holy day. Palm oil and cake. Gin. And something hot to stoke the flame of that orisha of thunder and might and wartime fire burning bright.

Cotton Tree buds sing in high-pitched notes that oppose the soft, white fluff of their blossoming pillows. Their sharp sopranos pierce my eyes. Their thorny pickers drop mucus down my snuffling nose. I cannot use their blooms to blow. My arms are occupied.

One arm around Mummy's waist, holding her upright. The other arm deployed in the fight to hold Mummy's small wrist and hand where it bands high round my shoulder blades. To keep my soft, squirmy mother in place. So secured, Mummy can tuck in her face from the Reverend sweeping the gravel dirt churchyard at the foot of the hill, and from all our neighbours along the sides of the steep's rise who outside with their heads tilt. Watching, listening, spectating their fill, to ketch de bacchanal, and then spill to whoever miss this parade of Cyatrin stumbling up the hill. These neighbours greet. And Mummy keeps her wail in place of speech.

These neighbours' eyes dart questions that assail my ears and brain and my prickling skin. Questions they begin to pose to me, Cyatrin big child. While their lips smile in concern and their voices warble with delicious savouring to learn what it is going on at all at all at all, bai.

But I keep the pace, keep my head straight, redistribute Mummy's weight, answer with a head nod in lieu of a wave. And become an adult this day. A twelve-year-old woman who greets with a lifted chin. Not a girl who waves and smiles and grins.

Razor Grass blades stretch from their barrier reefs on the hillside to slice, to strike, to stroke my quivering thighs. Their hairy little caresses sharp as knives. Razor Grass comforting the child who tells them sorry on weekends. The child who apologises when I pick from amongst their feet—careful not to tread on their toes—the so-called weeds we deem "rabbit meat." White-flowering greens to feed our little bunnies with all their fuzzy, twitching nose. Bunnies I think of cuddling as I am stumbling home with Mummy in seeming repose. With Mummy who can't her neck, nor arms, nor hips uphold. On her own.

Long Mango, juicy and full, glows ripe and yellow. Long Mango, luscious and bird-picked, promises tomorrow to drop in the track that is appendaged to the hill. The track that is the narrow pathway serving as a bridge to my father's house. Long Mango in heavy bouquets on tender stems promises me a few of them. We'll drop in the track's gravel for you to find. In the gravel that lines the track through which I must travel to return to the hill's rise and the neighbours' watching eyes in the coming days. We promise to fall and sweeten your tongue and fill out your round cheeks again. Look how yuh cheeks drooping now. Look how you walking under us and your head bow. Not so we does see you behave.

Plum Tree, leaning and unburdened today from a tied goat grazing or a hanging man crazing, releases her perfume of burgeoning flowers not yet in full bloom. She is giving me treats to look forward to—the coming season of my favourite fruit. Months to look ahead and embrace.

Months when I will stand face to face with bare cupboards that do not magically fill. But I can still walk out to the track and eat ripe, gold plums straight from the tree. And gather the half-ripe plums in a plastic bag to make chow or chutney. And soothe my rumbling belly and my empty chest rendered bereft. That Mummy will have cleft in two. When she does what my abandoning mother will always, to her children, do.

Cashew Tree turns her oval leaves, and squishy heart-shaped fruit, and hard C-shaped seeds into castanets. The rattling accompanies me—you are not alone—into the house's dark entry. Cashew Tree and the twining brown snakes in her branches standing sentry. The every-year-encroaching-closer Cashew Tree and her fresh-smelling snakes who proliferate wildly all watching me. Me bearing up Mummy on the left. My two younger sisters on the right. My mother's flaccid body borne, by three little girls, inside.

So one would think that Mummy—who seemed on the brink of collapse down the road and up the hill—would need to lie down once at home. And would go. That she would spill her tears over the fight in private. Collect herself. And leave her daughters, who survive it, time to catch our breath. Except, as soon as Ericka, Sherrie, and I step over the threshold of our father's house in gloom, into the living room, Mummy laughing, as good as new.

Yes, man. Mummy start to laugh, oui.

There would be no slipping into silence. Into privacy.

Come now. Peer through the fancy blocks in the walls' top. And watch. Three little girls in a semicircle. One perched on the edge of the couch. Not sitting back comfortable. Looking on at the tableau, troubled. That's me.

Pan to the next daughter sitting fold-up in an armchair. Let your gaze rest there. See her caramel fingers fidgeting in her lap. See a smile flicker in and out of focus to reveal the gap where her permanent canine is still playing shy. That's Ericka, who can't seem to keep her lips stretched. Benign. In a smile. Nor can she keep the crease from her ten-year-old forehead. That practised line. Ericka can't seem to keep a fun expression. She's overdone. And doesn't know now, in the third act, what is the Mummy-required emotion.

Scan now to the last daughter, leaning back against her own plush, comforting, cushioned armchair. Look at her skinny, seven-year-old self swallowed up there. Take in the muteness of Sherrie, observing this mother who minutes ago was crying. This mother who is now standing. This mother in the middle of the living room holding court for her daughters, with the centre table push to the side to allow her to fling her legs wide. This mother who for the stage's spotlight vies.

Zoom in now on this mother's smile. You see it? Adorning the lit-up face where the tears all done dry. You catch it? That special sparkle in this mother's eyes. As she letting loose a good belly giggle. Watch she in she element. Now, wriggle and press your ears to the carved holes in the blocks, and listen closely.

Oh gawd, ha. I en play Ah giddem, oui. Laughs Mummy.

She positively beams as she launches into her story.

Ah bring out de Louisa fuh dem. When Ah tell yuh, when Tanty Louisa get vex, de whole uh Chantimelle coulda hear she mout. All uh Grenada know my aunt. Hahaha. Yuh know what she used tuh do?

What? asks Ericka dully. Stultifyingly.

Huh, chile, Louisa used tuh ban she belly like so. Mummy mimes tying a scarf around her waist. And when yuh see dat, yuh know trouble coming.

Why? puts in Sherrie. Dazedly.

Mummy in her glee. She loves talking about her cantankerous maternal aunt. Repeatedly. Louisa, who everybody in their family village still fraid. Louisa, who made Mummy, her siblings, her mother, her neighbours, and anybody whose business Louisa make it a point to know, feel shame.

Why? Well, baby, when yuh see Louisa done tie she waist, de next ting is she used tuh puff up she face and brace she legs wide like so. Mummy adopts a shot-putter's stance.

She used tuh stand up like a man. And Louisa had some strong leg and dem. Yuh could see all de muscles in she thighs. Calves hard like stone. So yuh know she wasn't falling dong or sitting dong anytime soon.

Mummy laughs again, enjoying having a rapt audience to entertain. Enjoying unscrolling this history I've heard before. Me, familiar with her refrain.

Den when she done set up she self, Louisa used tuh trow she head back and bawl. When Ah tell yuh bawl? Bawl. She used tuh leggo one bawl like somebody killing she. Everybody would run out dey house and know someting upset Louisa.

And what she would do after? Ericka ventures. Ericka, who offers no censure to Mummy's behaviour. Ericka, who adjusts, excuses, accepts, condones. Ericka, who goes back to her Mummy's arms regardless of cruel fits she throws. Ericka, who continually seeks to quench the thirst to be the one her mother loves above all discarded daughters, and does put first. Then, now, always, Ericka disavowing nothing as her mother behaves worse and worse.

In her living room spotlight, Mummy smirks. Mummy throws back her shoulders to continue her tale. Mummy who before spit and curse, and now suddenly have words again.

Huh, den Louisa used tuh put all yuh business on de road. All who tief. All who have chile fuh somebody man. If yuh wearing a buss panty yuh doh want Louisa tuh know because she making sure she tell everybody de colour.

Ericka gasps. Fulfilling her part. Sherrie sucks her tongue and remains lapsed into dumb silence. I watch Mummy. Animated, enlivened, relaying her aunt's violence.

So she wutless, Mummy beams. Pride suffuses her face. Amusement sparkles in her eyes in which tears retain no trace. Tanty Louisa had everybody fraid tuh cross she. When Ah tell yuh she used to get on bad and put water in yuh eye. When she done so yuh cyah hold up yuh head fuh weeks. Shame? Shame? Huh, Louisa used tuh destroy yuh name in Chantimelle.

I feel a tug. An undercurrent ripple through me from Mummy's disquieting story.

Was she mad? I query.

No, just bad, she bad, is Mummy's answer to me.

Mummy scrapes off any encroaching rusted edges along her gilded memory. Brushes off my incorrigible question of insanity. Ignores any unease at the shame she endured from her own tanty. And resumes her unflinchingly jolly mood. Mummy brings her comparative narrative to a close. Mummy snorts a laugh and crows, Allyuh grandmother must be fraid me now, eh? Hahaha.

Ericka and Sherrie chorus the uncomfortable laugh Mummy's pause prompts. I don't laugh. I ask, Why you flip out like that? This is the insight that I want.

Why? is the question that will haunt.

Mummy's gaze switches to me and dons a mask to mime seriousness for the inquisition I launch. She begins, reply tremulous. And staunch. I doh know. I doh know, Uricka. Maybe I having a nervous breakdown.

Zoom out now. Adjust your field of view. Reorient to peer at this mother's forehead's frown. Train the spotlight upon the mother's dipping crown. Mummy kneels at my feet, takes my hand in her hold. Reiterates, I doh know. She does not produce laughter for me. I am not entertained by her Tanty Louisa story. Unlike Ericka and Sherrie. She picks another tactic to bring me into the fold.

Into my ear—separately—Mummy whispers her mantra to me. Keep the faith. The refrain Mummy always states. The phrase to my weary, seeking-love heart she always donates. The secret declaration with which she always placates, always consolidates my soul—that she besieges when she goes.

Into my ear—separately—Mummy's breaking voice whispers her phrase to seek to erase my scrutiny. Her phrase—Camille, keep the faith—that makes me not let go of her hands' grip on my own.

Until I am shown. And my heart mutinies.

Because what she is doing consciously, my mother knows.

I don't yet. I will later learn. The "craw" is the throat of a bird. To have something stick in your craw is to be so angered, so irritated, so deeply inflamed that you cannot swallow. You cannot breathe, the lodged item burns. When something—or someone—sticks in the craw of a bird, the winged being struggles to push out sounds or words. This I later discern, after the fight when Mummy's screams and wails and curses are heard.

Mummy saying Marilyn have Mummy in her craw. I saw perceptive Mummy detecting. Incensed, outraged, standing up for herself. I thought, Mummy is her willpower protecting. Strength rousing to strike back against injustices. I championed Mummy all her abuses protesting. So I am on her side. When Mummy wrenches this divide.

Months before Mummy boards a one-way flight.

I am on her side, before I am thrust into full light. And I learn that this mother is projecting. That this mother is electing to reverse and to accuse. That this mother is selecting and defaming the very wrongs she will be found to do.

Turns out, my mother is the bird. But she is something more, too. Something else that I alone will name. Though they all see what she do.

Step with me out of the frame, and train your long-focus view.

Years and years after the fight, the bite, the separating our family with a knife, this mother, this bird, will fly back over the border. This mother, too often having heard of Ericka drawing closer. Ericka, beloved daughter, in whom this mother has laid her eggs, maggots, worms, that will later gain legs. This daughter hopping over the divide to warmly again reconnect. So this mother says, Ah coming for a Carnival visit, back to Trinidad. To reunite with people she complain make her life so bad.

Then Tanty Marilyn and all the rest of them will tolerate this mother among them again. Following their Christian dictates to turn the other cheek and forgive former pain. So all the aunts will say Hi and they will closed-mouth smile. But really it will be their how-it-go-look mentality and their curiosity and their don't-talk-plain way of life that will make them abstain from turning my mother away, on this, her returned, purposeful Carnival stay.

And in that enfolding of theirs, in that re-welcoming they share, in that re-opening of the gate to the family compound, the true cause of this mother's fight on this cussing day will be found. The real reason for this mother's violence in Granny place, the reason for which we all had to wait, it will arrive. The reason, the treason that—years in the future—will survive. Just as strong as ever as the day this mother fights. This day she attack Marilyn for being, to this mother's first cousin, fixedly wived.

Come, put your eye to the bedroom's keyhole and see what they spied:

> Smiley's shed skin was done on the floor—epidermis ripped, hide stripped, peeled, red and raw, poised to feed, sipping on the draw—when they bust through the door. Her yellow teeth steep in his neck. His shrunken thighs immobilised under her thick legs. Her vulturous eyes swivelled and held. Locked on the appalled gaze of the intruders stalled at the threshold of the iron bed. Four posters railing the queen-size spread where ~~her~~ this Soucouyant's ripe barbadine breasts meld into the curve of his back. Where his wife's own now rested flat.
>
> His wife, Marilyn, who'd been brought to lay under Mount Hope Hospital barcode sheets that never warm, comfort, or conceal. Under thin white cotton that revealed just how much the oncologists steal. Just how deep they dig those trenches to halt marching cancer laying waste to the field of ducts which once nursed her daughters three.
>
> Those same daughters the gone-breasts decades ago fed and weaned now glared down at Smiley. As she peered over his shoulder slyly. Starlight illuminating vilely the obscene results

of a week's hunt. A week's countrywide search for a man leaving them, without qualms at his harm, in the lurch. A week's quest that lead to them finding their daddy undressed with she, Smiley, in this upstairs bedroom of a back-road home.

Iz salt they was supposed to throw.

In the mortar in the corner where her suitcase sprawl out, airline tags tonguing through the mouth of dresses and sandals and tight jeans to show her means of flying een and stunting on everybody in Covigne. Coarse salt. Not tears. Not Daddy how could you, and wid she of all people, too?

Soucouyant don't care.

But they did not believe me. Dem so doh wah hear. So they did not bar their crossroads with innumerable rice grain. They let ventricular connection remain after the first detonation Smiley aimed at their load-bearing frame wherein tumbling debris rained around her vanishment from Trinidad. Never—it was supposed to be—to be seen again by that family. But then when, decades hence, Smiley streaked across the sky, a red eye, atop the plane, a rotting ball of fire launching from JFK, the liar was re-welcomed into the bosom she claimed.

And, yet, Donald in their rented bed—drained of that on which Smiley fed—bruised, stooped, rising in the visage of the long-ago dead, head bowed before his revolted daughters he'd uncaringly fled, was not the bones Smiley came to collect. Not him. Not the trophy hollowed-out skull in which Smiley would build her nest.

That honour lay with her prey—the fatted sheep on whom Smiley feasts best. Mere bait he was on the mattress splayed from which Smiley ascended, red beneath her nails, to face his daughters' tongues furnished now with their tale they'd return home to tell. The story of their withered father under her spell. The fable she planned would snare, would re-adhere, her little prey who actually dared try run from her shell—Smiley's gold chalice of blood. In whom she dwells. Her chalice I loved once. Hoped to love again if from her bonded eyes the scales ever fell.

And I, who they don't believe still. I, alone alive—this pestle—knows Smiley won't stop.

Until . . .

When my aunts and cousins and them usher this mother back in—risen from her kiln—they open a bedroom door. Through which—before they barge in when they cyah take no more—they see this mother panting on all fours. In the throes of passion as her body is explored. Spread open. In front of her thrusting, naked first cousin, Donald. Tanty Marilyn's husband. The man over whom my mother cried, and over whom Tanty Marilyn, unknowingly, was bludgeoned. Then understanding cannot be denied.

This mother lies.

Tanty Marilyn will discover that my mother is her husband's lover. That this bird fight Marilyn for a man. That this mother knew her plan.

As I now know her name.

This open-armed, open-thighed Cyatrin, or Cyatrine, or Catherine, or Yolande, or Smiley, or Mummy. Each moniker summoning a crone living vilely. Whatever she gives as her preferred name—a new identity for each new life she claims. It is actually Soucouyant—vampire borne through flame.

This night. The night after the Mummy-cuss-Granny-and-take-a-bite-outta-Tanty Marilyn fight. For the first time ever in my life, I hear Mummy recite. I hear Mummy reel off words I had to discern from the lips of the child beside me in our primary school line. Watching and striving to lip-read during our assemblies. To fit in, please. These words, untaught to me, that Mummy now so easily release. Our father . . . thy kingdom come . . . thy will be done.

This night is the first time I ever see Mummy take a candle and kneel. And light this candle, when current not gone. T&TEC electricity bright. But, with wax taper in hand—tall, slim, and white—Mummy descends to the carpeted floor. Into the backroom where Mummy went to be alone, I peek. This Mummy who always want my company. While she sew, while she wash, while she cook. This Mummy who all of a sudden took a moment to withdraw. So my tumid feet tiptoe across the floor. To understand more. And here, kneeling, is another new Mummy I never see before.

Her head is bowed. Her hair is covered with a headtie. A long skirt is tucked over her knees. A single trickle she cries. Her dark face is illuminated in the black room by the candle flame. Her long nose and her bulging, Mr. Johnson-fed-up-with-Grover eyes look the same. The tattered-pages book spread on the bed, winging like a dusty moth, is the unearthed King James.

Mummy's lips move in chanting, singsong calling. Her torso rocking back and forth. Her heavy breaths and breasts rising and falling. Her small palm comes to her heart. Short fingers refusing to be pried apart. Unlike the denied daughters from whom this mother easily departs.

I stand quietly, afraid to breathe too loudly. I don't want her to discover me spying. I don't want Mummy to hear me above her own quiet crying. This time she is weeping genuinely.

At twelve, standing before a closed door and taking a peep through the hinge's one-centimetre crease, I watch Mummy kneel. She who doh believe in dem church ting. For the first time in prayer. With the psalms. Asking: Let the wicked be ashamed. And let them be silent in the grave.

Vengeance, Mummy craved. For her deliverance alone my mother prayed: Let me be saved.

And it will take me tired decades to put away the lesson Mummy teaches me this day. That when truly desperate to escape, call through flame. Call on gods by their dredged-up names. Kneel to darkness. Chant aloud your pain. Retreat. Lock the door. And conceal your shame.

7

COCONUT TREE

I am thirteen.

And my mother leaves.

My mother is a permanently departing mother, again. Just like she leave Grenada, the country of her birth, the country where her leftover daughter—the first—remains.

My mother, who came to Trinidad, first living down south. First living in the same house with her first cousin who she will take into her bed, between her legs, between her arms, from his cancer-stricken wife, in her mouth. Before she weds her own spouse. My father meeting her and bringing her—while he build his own—to live with him in his mother's house.

And on this storytelling day—the last of many before my mother flies away, before she embalms my heart in grief, suspends it in amber, preserved and petrified in a glass jar through which my heart can't be touched though seen, floating in formaldehyde, the stink of its gases seeping past the lid to weep, before she leaves to set her own self free—what Mummy say, the story Mummy relays is that Beulah, my grandmother, from jump did not like her. And the dislike, the concealment of it, is something with which Beulah never bother.

Mummy telling me, Mummy washing wares while she say, Anytime yuh father beat me yuh grandmother would just sing her hymns even louder and would have a big smile on her face. When I come out yuh father little bedroom crying. My mother, on the kitchen towel that hanging in front the stove, her hands now drying. Mummy sniffling, throat clearing, near crying. Mummy to my distressed sound replying. Mummy ramping up to reveal more early-marriage days to her not-first daughter, me, who is not prying.

Mummy sharing, Mummy not sparing how she think Granny used to take extra-long in the bathroom at night, just to spite her. Just because she didn't like her. How, first, Granny give her and my father the smallest and hottest bedroom in the house. The tiniest bedroom that right by the bathroom where you could hear everything, somebody hawking and spitting and shitting out. And then Granny used to make sure Mummy couldn't even get a decent night sleep. Because is all hours my grandmother would keep. Going to the bathroom all hours of the night and then getting up early in the morning for spite. To brush her teeth. And showering while singing some Jesus song in that long, drawn-out way. That warbling style old people getting ready to meet they maker does mourn-sing-pray. Mummy say.

My mother telling me of Beulah, of my grandmother, that she too damn lie. That Granny was only singing and whinging, with her heart condition in that crowded house, like she getting ready to die. But that is my grandmother's badness keeping her alive. Despite Granny going to the doctor frequently. And getting plenty tablet that big, and pink, and green. That Granny always looking for sympathy.

And always bawling she dying even before she and my mother meet. And that Granny eh dead yet. Mummy tells me and tells me, and I do not forget.

And when Granny does die nine years later, I will be the one who is un-devastated enough to deliver the blow. To tell the news of the unsuccessful surgery to my aunts and to my uncles, who drop to the ground in wailing sorrow.

And it will be me who Granny visits on the third day, dressed all in white, standing on her house's red front step in the bright sunlight. It will be me Granny lets see as she comes back to say goodbye. Me, who sang and prayed for the nine-day candle vigil we kept morning, noon, and night. Me who writes this twenty years later and weeps, chest tight.

I am thirteen.

And all I hear about from my father's family is Granny's care. That we must not do anything to raise Granny's pressure. The cousins inheriting their parents' fears. My aunts who pass by Granny after they come home from work every day. My aunts who does kiss Granny forehead and ask all mousy-mousy like they fraid. My aunts who scared to startle Granny with the slightest noise, asking her in they whiny, un-spiny little voice:

> Mammy, how yuh spen de day?
> How yuh holin up?
> How yuh manage today?
> Yuh awright?

And my grandmother does drop her volume and her eyes, and her head and her posture and answer in soft resign: I eh feelin evah so good tuhday buh Ah holin orn by de grace uh de lawd.

She never so good today, every day, as soon as her daughters reach. They only have to say, Guh-naffuhnoon, Mammy, for her to be sicker than she was two minutes ago when she was strong enough to scold, to pinch, to preach. Strong enough, any sickbed or resting chair or kitchen confine to breach. And teach her grandchirren a lesson. Chasing a grand around the house and under the plum tree. Chasing one a we over the roots of the mango tree, between the fallen branches of the coconut trees, around the rose garden, past the fish tanks, between the gas tanks, and under the dining room table, to take off the white school uniform before they able to play pitch with marbles in the dirt. Or shouting behind one of the grands tuh Come and do yuh homework first.

As soon as the aunts come, we have to start walking on eggshells. Because they say Granny need her rest and can't take so much noise in her head; so all fun quelled. But since the aunts does come home around six anyway, and that's time for news and the sun starting to set, then it's okay. For this to be the time when all the cousins go home to their own house. And it's Ericka, Sherrie, and I signal, when we there, to vacate.

My sisters and I would only be down the hill if Mummy let us go down to play. Other than that, when Ms. Yvette drive us all back from primary school in her maxi that does carry and drop we by Granny house every weekday, Granny would say: Iz nuh time fuh allyuh chirren tuh go up de road. Allyuh muss ha homewukk tuh go an do, nuh so.

Though all the other cousins get to stay. Though all the other cousins get to play. Though is just my sisters and I leaving. Just me getting no relieving. From Mummy and the company she needing. After spending a whole day cleaning and watching *Young & Restless* and studying what to cook on time for Daddy feeding. For Daddy to eat and burb and watch TV and sleep. And not his wife's company to keep. Nor my sisters and I, who Granny does send up the hill's steep. Because her heart can't take the trouble of three more grandchildren to make it stutter or leap.

Or if Mummy gone in town, we does get to stay down. For the hours until Mummy return. Ericka, Sherrie, and I so happy to not be spurned. So happy to play all afternoon. So happy for the chance Granny might give us food. So happy Granny might nourish us like she does her beloved brood.

Though I do not like how Granny food does taste. Granny who does water down everything, not letting any dregs waste. And I do not like having to say Thank you, Granny, ever so sweetly. And that this is my favourite yummy meal she does cook, nice and meekly. And I do not like having to fold up my language, my laugh, my bold declarations of the world ever so neatly.

And I especially do not like hearing the other cousins eat. These cousins for whom chewing with their mouth closed is a feat. Manners that their modest mothers never teach. So they smack and they slurp through every meal. That my sisters and I are still glad to attend. Working together on all our straight-A homework and belonging for an afternoon—even if is only pretend.

Because I know, I am aware, Granny don't much like when Mummy go in town; having us here. And on this last day Mummy leaves us by

Granny while she supposedly gone in town, Granny keeps glancing at the sienna clock and looking around. And Granny keep saying *hmmph* as she does when Mummy not up the hill and my sisters and I have to stay down. Except, on this last day, as it growing later and later, Granny start to say: Buh whey Cyatrin at all, all dis time. Huh, an look ah de hour. With her face not growing more worried, but looking more lemon-juice sour.

And on this last day, when the sun finishing set and the moon starting to rise, Granny say—in a wobbling voice, like it suppressing a cry—to my aunts, when from work they arrive, Buh look how Cyatrin gone in town all dis time. And she cyah mek hase an reach back yet. Dese chirren here an Ah need tuh geh mih lil ress too. Ah mean she could show me a lil consideration, man. Ah too too too tyud whey yuh see meh hey. I listen to Granny say.

And my belly begins to bubble. As Granny starts telling on my mother like that, like Mummy in trouble. Granny who complaining so loudly that, though she pulled my aunts into the good living room, her pitchy whines resound like a sonic boom. With all my cousins hearing her across the kitchen into the dining room. Hearing Granny calling my mother irresponsible, and uncaring, too. Till the cousins all start looking away from the three of us, my two sisters and I. These cousins turning their backs to us and meeting each other's eyes.

The cousins all with the same expression on their faces. The cousins all with the same whispering speeches full of judgemental traces. And when Granny comes out the living room we all know she does only use for company or to talk about serious business, one by one the cousins run up to her offering to fetch that and to get this. The cousins rushing to hug Granny around her high-curved belly, asking what she need. My sisters and I receiving no offers, no concern, no hugs. No expressions of love to us three.

The cousins happy to skip off with a smile. Happy to oblige as Granny favourite child when Granny sends them for her slippers, and for her glasses, and for her Bible. Happy to fetch Granny big metal crochet needle. Happy to bring back her colourful crocheting thread, and a pillow to rest her back on. Happy for the biggest boy to bring out a comfortable chair and the cushions with which it adorned. Happy to lift and carry the chair from the living room for Granny to sit on and sigh. The chair where she could relax her varicose-roped thighs. Happy to afford Granny this ritualised ease, to watch the news, to crochet, to read her Bible, and to get off her achy knees.

But my aunts emerge from the good living room, not to rest but to interrogate us three. To question my sisters and me. How Mummy taking so long. Just to reach in town. It never crossing their mind Mummy could be hurt or she fall down. Or that badgering a thirteen-year-old, an eleven-year-old, and an eight-year-old is wrong.

I look through the window, above the coconut tree's crown through which the fluorescent, incandescent sun is going down. Peering through and round the curved branches and between Coconut Tree's curtain leaves that softly wave to me in the breeze as indigo chases bright orange from the heavens. The sienna clock now saying is minutes to seven. And allyuh father working late as usual, so he wouldn't be home till after nine—though these aunts don't know that if Daddy go have a beer, he won't return till after eleven. So with allyuh Daddy working so hard fuh allyuh, that mean (my aunts glean) we all have to wait for him until that late hour when allyuh grandmother could well be in her bed getting some sleep. And she not as young as she used to be. And she does do a lot when the day come. And where allyuh mother could be this hour at all. I mean to say, she could be a little more understanding of Mammy situation, taking care of these grands whole day and . . .

Night falls.

On and on, with the aunts rattling over our heads. While we hang them in shame. And because it is easier for me, the oldest, to bend my cheeks, full and aflame. With my face tilting toward the floor to repeat the same: I don't know why Mummy taking so long.

And nothing more. Silenced conversation, outside cricket chirps soar.

While the aunts peer and stare over our heads with closed-lipped smiles. Smirks that twist in the corners of their mouths as they *hmmm* and *mmmhmmmm* over and over again, disbelieving, as they cross-examine a child.

I am thirteen.

And it is up to me to stage this scene. To set the example for my sisters, like my mother instructs me to do. This mother telling me, Camille: Uricka, yuh must, no matter what yuh goin tru. I must, no matter what this mother is getting up to.

But the aunts talking over us anyway. Mumbling words like *jamette* and *gallivanting* and *typical*, and shushing each other though they all continue to lambaste. Giving they mouth licence to utter what they always really want to say. Not whispering and hinting today.

Is okay. Let them keep thinking that my mother gallivanting. In one of her three town outfits and her one good shoe. The pair of shoes that was first a tan leather pumps with a two-inch heel and a small bow above the toes. The shoes that my mother then use Oxford brown shoe polish on to darken, so it hide the stains and dirty look from her wearing it everywhere she go.

The shoes that the heel and inside part of the sole—where her foot press heaviest when she walk—beginning to wear down. The pair of shoes with so much scuff marks that my mother couldn't take the shame of wearing them any more to go in town. So she decide on the shame of asking my father for a new shoe again, the shame of facing his frown.

This father, a subcontractor for a construction and engineering company. This father, the owner's second in command and earning good money. Making good good money, Mummy say. But only giving Mummy just enough cash to "manage de house" every fortnight he get pay. My father who does estimate the price of every grocery item before he give her the sum. Counting to the last red dollar the amount to buy groceries that have to last the month.

And at the end of the month when the cupboards start to empty, and Mummy might only be able to make dumplings and lentil peas for her and her daughters three, she still need to make sure that my father have his four pieces of stew chicken, fry rice, pigeon peas, callaloo, macaroni pie, coleslaw, potato salad, and orange juice aplenty. All without beseeching my father for any additional money. For anything. My father does not like to be bothered with financial problems my mother bring.

So when Mummy brave the shame of asking my father for new shoes, he went in the closet for Mummy one good pair and bring it in the living room. My father put the shoes on a sheet of *Guardian* newspaper he spread to protect the tiles my mother did tell him not to buy. The tiles Mummy say would get dirty too fast and look too dingy, but that he select anyway. The tiles that Mummy must use grocery money on purchasing polish and cleaners to mop every day.

The newspaper making big black marks over the tiles when my father spread the sheet. Then my father examine the shoes carefully. Inspecting the shoes for ten full minutes while he lay stretched out on the couch to his six-feet-two length. While the four of us—my mother, my sisters, and I—squeeze into the two single seats and onto the footstool of the living room set.

At which point, my father turns back to watching the Western that the channel he put the TV on showing, though *MacGyver* on too. And *MacGyver* is what the four of us want to view. Then my father waits till advertisement to talk about the shoes.

He smiles, wide, pleased, sublime. With the top row of his front teeth showing and the corners of his cheeks turned in and little gatherings of saliva making his lips shine. His eyes smile too, but they seem hard, like he concentrating. My father's eyes, red and glazed from the du Maurier cigarette he was just smoking without ventilating. The cigarettes making me cough and Sherrie's eyes scratch and Mummy's hair stink and Ericka wheeze. The cigarettes that accompany the Carib beer that making him belch louder than the TV.

My father turns from stretching out, spinning to sit. My father turns to his wife, to his daughters three, and he points at the shoe while talking about it. But his hard eyes are looking straight at Mummy, and his lips eject spit. Then he looks at me like he wants to see if I will say something. Because I usually answer him back. Then he looks at my sisters, too, who quietly blink and silence their coughing hack.

Nuttin wrong wid de shoe. Ah mean juss a lil touch-up it need hyeh an hyeh. He points to the scuff marks, and to the tilting heel, and to the worn-down sole. Then my father leans back on the couch with his bare legs spread apart, feet on either side of the newspaper and the shoes, in his posture of control.

His muscles, big from years of hard construction work, flex as he spreads his arms to rest on top of the couch. Ent nuttin eh wrong wid de shoe? As if daring us to deny what he is talking about.

My mother says nothing. My sisters and I decide we don't want to watch TV any more. We go to our room and gently close the door. My mother sleeps with me this night, as usual; it is what my bed, and my space, are for.

And the town shoe becomes black after that. My father takes the pair after my mother goes to sleep in my bed with me and covers it in liquid black polish. The tan, then the chestnut brown of the leather is abolished. It is now streaky and brown and black. The shoes look like the brown pothound my uncle covered in black machine oil to get rid of its mange, that none of the cousins wanted to go near, and neither did its pack. My mother has to take the pair of shoes to the shoe repair down the road to have it professionally dyed to make it decent enough to wear in town again. This different-colour shoe whose worn-down sole remains the same.

Though, if my aunts could see Mummy this evening as they interrogating me—this whey-yuh-mudda sunset day when I have a splitting headache; this twilight day, approaching night, when they wondering why she taking so long gallivanting in town—they wouldn't see the black shoe that used to be brown. They would see a new pair of shoes on her feet. And my aunts would ask my sisters and me how yuh mother manage to be so fancy. With smiles on their faces and voices sugary.

And we would hang our heads so the aunts would not see our faces when we tell them: We don't know. And they would step in close. And chorus their *hmmms* and *mmmhmms* like they done judge and have the answer anyway. No matter what we say.

But the answer these aunts don't possess, the answer their *mmmhmms* cannot guess and cannot access, is that my mother knows how to leave her children best. That, months before this gallivanting day, my mother asked her sisters in England to lend her money that she take and buy a new pair of shoes. Western Union funds that my mother used to buy a bag to put her better clothes in, too. But not a bag that conspicuously look like a suitcase. That would give away her running escape.

These head-shaking aunts don't know. That this mother additionally used the money to buy a light coat, because we in November, and she will be cold. And that—most importantly—she used the money, also, to buy a plane ticket to New York City. To go. To live with her father, Cuthbert, in his Brooklyn home. Cuthbert, Mummy father, who file for the whole family. Cuthbert, who file to sponsor Green Cards for my mother, for my father, for my sisters, and for me. Though, on this day, this mother alone flees.

And the aunts and their talking eyes don't know. What my father only find out ten o'clock this night when he finally reach home. When he park his car in the garage in Granny's yard because he can't park on the hill. When he has to pick up his children because, for once, his wife is not in the house obeying his will.

Not my grilling aunts, nor my pilling grandmother, nor my stilling father have a clue. My mother leave her first child; they don't guess what she can do? They don't guess that my mother went behind my father's back when he said No to any damn Green Card, going to the embassy in her shabby one-town shoe. They don't guess when my mother calls on the phone this night after eleven p.m. to talk. They are stunned when she answers my father's Cyatrin whey de fuck you is dis hour? with Brooklyn, New York.

And what my aunts also don't know, what my grandmother doesn't guess, and my father could not care less about, is how—now that we are forced to live with *him* alone in this house—we are terrified of what will happen with his anger roused. Nor do they perceive that I feel my mother is my world. That my life has no meaning without her near me—a cold, deserted girl. And that my spirit is breaking. That I could kill my father. And I wish I know a way to do it without going to jail. No, none of them know, and none of them are paying attention to my uncontrollable trembling, or my chest's silent wail.

I am thirteen.

And after my mother flees, my grandmother gets even less of her rest. My father leaves us to sleep at Granny's house every weekend while he takes his new one-night stands and new girlfriends out late at night and brings them to his house for audible sex. Now, he gives Granny the budgeted grocery money to cook for us every day, too. But during the week my sisters and I learn to stay home by ourselves on evenings after school. Three girls, alone till my father comes home at his usual time after nine at night. Granny says the whole week taking care of us, when she has the other grands to mind, would be too stressful on her heart, and the aunts agree she's right.

Then when Granny begins to complain about how she need some rest on the weekends too, my sisters and I learn how to stay home by ourselves for the whole night and make do. While our father sleeps over at his women's houses with his graphic VHS blues. We also learn now how to stretch the little money our father now gives us for food. The exact red-dollar amount. To take care of all our own groceries and all our toiletries for the month that my father sits on the couch—legs spread wide, with his hard eyes, his spitty smile—and counts.

8

SOURSOP TREE

I am fourteen years old.

And my mother calls weekly from Brooklyn, on prepaid five-dollar cards that count down our minutes on the phone. You have thirty seconds left. These last thirty seconds that Mummy uses to interject into her thus-silent reply to our litany and cries: I dunno, I really expect Ulric woulda treat allyuh good when I gone. Accompanied by her sighs so forlorn. Before the Well-keep-good-till-next-week, bye-bye speech she delivers just before the beeping Boss Card connection is torn.

And when we, her daughters three, pick up the receiver between designated mothering time each week, and we cry and we moan. And we say We miss you, Mummy, we can't take this alone. And we are afraid and we hungry. And we plead and we beg when, Mummy, when, and we groan. And TSTT cuts our service over exorbitant, unpaid, overseas charges, and our father curses and threatens, overturns, thrashes, and smashes. Then my sisters and I receive Mummy calls on Granny's and Tanty Acklyn's phones. Which Daddy does not condone. How it go look that he can't afford this basic utility in his home?

So he installs a phone lock. And his raised temple vein demands What de fock?! Allyuh mudda tink she min'ing, cockroach in here?

And when I learn to pick the catch placed over the keys, I take the money Mummy sends to buy us underwear and I pay TSTT. Paying as soon as the bill print and before the bill envelopes from Granny mailbox share. And give us away before I have time to intercept them there. Before my father and his bulging arms read the balance and barge into the backroom, my bedroom, where my belly churning and my throat gulping air. Where my stomach refluxing and my bowels loosening, not holding down food chewed with care. Where my knees knocking, tongue pooling with bile, and my trembling fingers clutch my sheets in fear.

I am fourteen.

I am shell-shocked, walking grief. Every month I bleed, with no relief. No paracetamol, no Gravol, no ibuprofen, no Tylenol, no Motrin, no Excedrin contains the diarrhoea, the vomiting, the drill-stabbing, ovaries-crabbing, uterus-contracting, cervix-dilating, leg veins-spasming pain. The five horizontal days till I can walk again. The ambulance rides on period first days when every neighbour hears me all day, all night scream and cry. When my pitching wails out the window fly—above Uncle Ken peering-staring Soursop Tree looking in through the louvres at me with her hundreds of stalk-stem eyes that rise out of her skin's hush-my-baby lullabies, over Baptist Hill, up the surrounding mountain rise.

With nurses asking me every single month, Yuh try tuh trow way chile? While they inject doses hospital-strength high. That finally, temporarily, makes my howling womb subside. That soothe the insidious, undetected fibroids that therein swell and reside. My womb's growths shrieking aloud the sedimented memories of which they are comprised.

Their remembrances lodged in membranes that are by words—called loving—unbeguiled. Retention, resentments the truthful body does not hide. Knowledge that syringed medicine cannot override. Even as the injection staunches the glide of the bitter, orange lining of my stomach up my throat. Allowing me to sink into fitful sleep on hard, scratchy, serial number sheets in the A & E alone.

While my two younger sisters are at home. The two children I did not birth, and must mother on my own.

I am fourteen years old.

My mother mails pictures of herself garlanded, head to toe, in urban New York, nameplate, washed-out 10-carat gold. Smiling photos tucked in her letters of hope, sent to fill in the blanks she cannot say on the phone. Meant to fill in the hearts she pledges to help cope.

My mother mails postal money orders I use to buy bread—hops, coconut bake, and plaited loaves. From Freddie's on the bank, whose friendly shop girls know me on sight and know the sugary, sticky buns I like, and does sneak a couple in my bag if I don't have any extra change after I count it out that night.

And to my right, on the other side of the main road I does cross alone, where a speeding taxi knock me into a somersault two years ago, I does buy sharp Anchor New Zealand Cheddar from Kelly's grocery to pack school lunch for my sisters and me. For myself, for Ericka, for Sherrie, whose classmates does tease that we's rats since we does only bring cheese and nothing else. Only these sandwiches from our empty-cupboard house where my father hardly dwells.

Where my father big, rough hand that smells of wood shavings and gasoline intermittently tosses a few extra dollars or a greasy Kids Pack meal, Hyeh allyuh share dat fuh allyuh tree, while he and his young woman of the week dine on buckets of KFC.

My father every payday fortnight treating his lured girls well, so they join him in this house that is a hot, stagnant hell, where my feet and my ankles with un-draining fluid swell. Ulric's house that my mother says she had to escape or she would kill herself. My father's house that my mother left us in. That she calls every Sunday to check on my health. Calling to say I love you so much, and to make sure her daughters three are well.

Stay strong, Mummy, our litany quells. Keep the faith, Uricka, Mummy privately tells. In the ticking time allotted by the Boss Card her Brooklyn bodegas does sell.

9

ZABOCA TREE

I am fifteen.

It is two years now since my mother leave.

And it is some time before my sisters and I learn about Luvern. Luvern, who is twenty-one. Only six years older than me. Luvern, who has a two-year-old son. And done marrid and divorce already. Luvern, who my father meet when he is thirty-eight. Luvern, another teen mother my father gallantly rescue from her burdened state.

In the before, Ericka, Sherrie, and I didn't know where my father used to disappear to after dinner. After he noisily fed. He would just say, Arite chirren, Ah goin an take a breezer and relax meh head.

When the need first arose for my father to leave us in order to cool down, he would amble around. For two hours or so after he clean the plate Granny cover down with a kitchen country towel, fluffy and light brown, to send up the hill to keep her big boy fed. He would dawdle, not getting ready for work tomorrow or to go to bed. In those early days he would act as if he suddenly need to stretch his legs. Ahhhh, yessss. Because his hours plunging steel poles and laying floors with decorative tile shards was so long and was so hard.

And in those days, before this preamble he discard, my father would take extra precautions to lock up safe and sound. The doors, the windows, the top gold bolt, stuff toilet paper in the bottom keyhole, and tuck in his dark house all around. To keep his three little girls protected from Covigne Road gang dangers that abound.

He would check the side door.

He wanted our pumpkin vine cousins who live below us on the hill—who hear everything, who smell everything, and everything saw—to think he home still, because what again he have to go out for? A good father, they must view him as now and ever more. A caring father under the same roof with his daughters tucked in tight. A doting father, bunking down, and everybody turned in for the night. Nothing to see here for these cousins who eye too bright.

He didn't trust these cousins.

Uncle Errol children and grandchildren and great-grandchildren in one pack-up house, reproducing by the dozens. The way they live—add-on-a-bedroom-here, add-on-a-bedroom-there, more and more extended family moving in to share, one back bedroom housing eight children and two parents on a double-decker of raw yellow sponge that smell of pee when they put it on their roof to air—annoys him bad bad bad. And in those days, before we learn of Luvern, my father didn't want any of the pickney in a tear-up jersey and a jockey shorts clad coming to asking for sugar, ice, condensed milk, matches, ketchup, or to make a quick phone call, and discover that he had left unguarded his prized, mr-big-shot pad.

He would check the back door was locked just right.

The last time one of my sisters left this door ajar, after hanging up clothes on the lines outside, the gold bracelet that my aunt in England send for me disappeared, never again to be spied. My beautiful, 24-carat-gold bracelet, delicate and bright. Gone from a brief open-door oversight.

We knew who stole it, too. We knew it was the older son of the new family that just move. The family with dirty sons. The family who, to live in the back of us, just one day come. Setting up house behind the backyard tree laden with white flowers for green plum. The family that reach from who-know-where. With no relatives in Covigne to welcome them here. And before my mother leave, she catch this older son one time. Not on the same occasion when I see him tugging rough and fast with his hand down his fly, standing on a branch of the plum tree he climb. When, after that grip, after that drip, the plums was more sour than lime.

When my mother catch him, she had see this older son creeping through the sprawling, thick, St. John's bush—emerald green, straight-spined and high. Crawling through the heart-shaped leaves and the little offshoot fig trees that divide our land from Uncle Errol's side. Uncle's land, on which our cousins' ever-extending house was being built. Uncle's piece of Baptist Hill that also thankfully separated us from the land where the new family's rented house was perched, leaning on chipped gravelly stilts.

This oldest boy who my mother see was only around the age of thirteen. He didn't go to school. He thought no one was home in our house during the day, so he could well play the fool.

Except, my mother was always home.

She ketch his yellow peering eyes and muscled bare chest peeping out from the bushes' splay. She watched until this boy with no slippers on his feet crept past the plum tree that had only buds on it and was no good to him for a raid. She watched him while he stole green zaboca from our tree—most likely to try to hustle down the road later for money to eat. Zaboca he put in his crocus bag, hidden among the roots. She watched him stealthily on the move. Through the holes in the fancy blocks in the wall over our back door, standing on the old, splintering table from the dining room. The dining table that my father build by himself because it was cheaper than buying one at Courts. My handy construction worker father who eh need no dear dear furniture stores.

She watched him—my mother—while standing on the old, woodlice-pocked table that was moved to the backroom. The furniture my father carpentered as a new groom. The pinewood, unvarnished table that was relocated when my father replaced it with the store-bought dining set. The purchased furnishings my father reminded my mother she ought to be grateful she get. Thankful she collect it as a Christmas present at all. When what de ole one needed was a good tablecloth. That, if she knew how tuh do tings properly, woulda hide any little mark de table have. A nice lacy lil linen and de table wouldn look too bad.

She watched the boy and his half-filled bag of too-young zaboca he tief from our yard while standing on the one-leg-short, limping table, trying—and barely able—to reach the ceiling that was waterlogged from the rain that, in the last week, begin again to leak. Seeping in past the piece of melting tar that my father had stick on the galvanise, over a hole. A hole that had only grown bigger from bearing the toll. Bearing my father's weight the last time he climbed up the sloping bank of dirt that underwent wet season landslide growth spurts at the back of our house. The mound of dirt Daddy climbed to pick zaboca when his pelau meal demanded something else sweet in his mouth.

The dirt my father promised every year to rouse himself and backhoe one of these good Christmases, because it reaching from the ground to our roof. The bank of dirt that he used. That he scaled up to walk atop our house, his heavy pounding sounding like hoof. As he clomp over to the right to pick rose mango from the massive tree in our yard blocking the light. Rose Mango Tree—spread out wide and tall and pretty—blocking the living room. Blocking the louvres and blocking gusts of air from coming through. This Rose Mango Tree that my mother asked my father to cut down every hurricane season. This growing tree that my father kept for the primary reason of making mango chow to snack. While waiting for my mother to finish cook his Sunday lunch without answering back.

My mother watched this grown-looking boy tiptoe up to the empty water tank stand that stood where it was placed, on the raised square of concrete my father paved himself. The concrete square my father built as a cover, as a shelf. As a platform resting over the septic tank concealed. The septic tank that leaked. Down into Uncle's yard below us once every year because my father let his workers come on weekends to fix it, to make some overtime away from the construction site, and they have no idea what de borse really want dem tuh do, and foeman need a good plumbah fuh dis kinna wuk man, *steups*, allyuh muss tell allyuh fadda dat, iz a good man who train in pipewuk he need tuh come an see bout dis. And allyuh never tell allyuh fadda is da wuh he hadda do self. Dis kinna patchwuk he doing all de time so eh go wuk tuh hol dis ting fuh long. Ah mean, Ah sure it does be backin up inside, mussbe cracking de bottam uh de toilet and leaking out cuz de ting full, Ah tell yuh. Yuh fadda hadda fin a way tuh let de man dem who know de job come een and handle dis ting fuh him, dis eh go lass no kine a time. Look ah de smell it causin. Ah sure allyuh neighbours an dem mussbe does fret, and dey ha chirren down dey playin in de yard, man. Dey doh complain? Ah sure dey does mussbe want tuh tell allyuh fadda sumtin, buh dey biggest boy is he godchile and de modda wah allyuh fadda tuh hire de chile tuh wuk wid him, buh even so, tell allyuh fadda . . .

Watching, my mother saw when the yellow-eyed, bare-back, barefoot, zaboca-stealing boy passed under the iron tank stand that wobbled as he touched it with his ashen hand. The tank stand that swayed on the uneven land because my father weld the fourth piece of iron shorter than the other three legs. These four uneven pegs he meld to the flat square surface top meant to be where the tank would sit, the tank for which my mother begged. Three tall legs and a limping fourth that tilted the ten-foot stand meant to bear the grand tank aloft. The empty tank stand with no water tank on it to hold court. No 2,500-gallon water tank my father was meant to have bought. That was supposed to be similar to the water tanks all my father brothers and sisters, living but yards away from us, had done donkey years ago sought. Water tanks brought to make their lives easier when WASA gone on strike, as they well like to do. Or for when the dry season decide to evaporate too much water on the isle and leave the pipes and all parch, too.

A water tank for which my mother plead, so she wouldn't have to scrub blue buckets to carry down the hill to my grandmother's house she dread. Blue buckets that once held asphalt or paint thinner or some other high-fume material from my father construction job sites—that deep well of leftovers hell my father plundered regardless of toxin or smell to avoid acquiring anything that people make to sell. These noisy clank-a-lank blue buckets that tell every neighbour they going down the hill to get fill. Down in Granny yard where, because the water pressure don't have to build up so high, and don't have to climb the incline, does come stronger and for longer times through the pipes. Granny yard where the scrubbed blue buckets make to stand up and wait. Till my father come home in the night, after eight. And could load these heavy blue buckets onto the pickup truck tray. This roomy bed of the new-model grey truck his boss give him tuh do de people dem wuk. But that was really my father's personal vehicle that he clean and polish and shine and keep free of any muck.

My father would drive the buckets up the hill and carry them through the narrow track. This slender lane brokenly paved along one side, with dirt and gravel on the other where intended construction material pack. This path that does plunge into complete dark after sunset and, once traversed, I does never want to walk back. This track waiting till my father become less busy so he could cast the whole a it in concrete. Cementing where the thick roots of the trees, broken glass, drain water, fragrant mud, and sour black mould does meet. Planning to plaster where manicou, lizards, snakes, and spiders does hide. But until that promised time, my father would tote the buckets down the steps that growing moss on one side. Slippery green slime flourishing because the gutter above it too clogged with mango, guava, plum tree, and St. John bush leaves that fall when the rain come down in sheets, making waterfalls and whirlpools and tidal waves in the drains that overflow their banks to create gravel deltas on the steps Daddy promise to fix as they get eroded from the rushing water and silt mix so their big cavities and small nicks wouldn't yank one of us into a trip and cause us to get a bad lash, he say, when we coming home a day.

And after passing through the track and down the steps, my father would bring the buckets through the gallery with its vinyl flooring that every Christmas we changed. Plastic vinyl flooring that my mother had to mop up and dry up every night in tight-lips rage.

Sopping up the buckets' drool as the blue brigade make their way through the front door, onward to the washing room. My mother hated when my father bringing in the buckets and is the front door he choose. *Steupsss*, wetting up de carpet, and because it doh look good, man . . .

My mother saw, watching through the fancy blocks above the back door, this neighbour boy slink across our land. Looking down from the table, my mother lifted her hand. Raised her palm as she watched the yellow-eyed, zaboca-filled-bag boy with no shoes, who she knew was going down the hill and see how he could get tru in the market, tiptoe in the backyard's bush round the trembling tank stand he touched with his hand. Then up to the backroom door. This exit through which my father would bring one or two retired blue buckets to catch rainwater from the mouth of the galvanise spout, and she had no more. What he coming to the house for? Reaching his dry, ashy hand so bold to the back door to take hold. Out of patience, with nothing left to give this stealing boy who just show up to live in the back a we and now breaching her security, my mother pick up a dipper full of rainwater she didn't purchase at the price of smiling as the good in-law daughter filling the blue buckets in Granny yard and, putting the dipper lip up to the fancy blocks over the reaching, tiefing boy, she poured hard.

It was not the back door, above which she poured hard, but a fancy front door that my mother walked through two years before when this Trinidad-living life—and her daughters—she discard.

This is the front door my father checks again. Before he goes out overnight to some place he never explain. Before we learn about Luvern.

But, before she arrives, we just watch our father lock up for the night. In our new life, where a parent deserts a fifteen-, a thirteen-, and a ten-year-old with a parting, Arrite.

Before he alights from the living room's one-step height, into the gallery and into the black, frog-croaking night, my father lingers at the front door. Not regretful or hesitant to leave his three daughters alone with five dollars and nothing more. Is just—this is a piece a furniture he well like.

This door bonafide. Store-bought. From big-shot Courts. It have carvings of flowers and leaves. It thick and don't rumble when the wind breathe. And into its heavy wood, my father install a peephole after my mother say he should. He realise—grudgingly—that my mother right. That we still need to see outside. After he change those old double doors, with their thirteen years of varnish and three-quarters glass panes. The glass doors that had to be curtained to keep people from passing and minding we business plain plain plain. The new door prompting my mother to pose the, How else yuh would know who come to yuh? question, again and again. Till my father cede the game, put in the peephole, and strike a balance between exposure and an impenetrable wood frame.

It is this peephole that is the last thing my father checks before he leaves every night, after eating the dinner my grandmother sends up with one of his child. Now that Mummy is gone, and the dropping-down-the-blue-buckets duty is another one on us that is piled.

After checking the locks on the front door, my father shows us again how to stand on a stool or on the fat yellow phone books. Though I am tall enough on tiptoe, he teaches us how to look. How to gaze through the peephole and check to see who calling if anybody come and he not there. When he heave himself off the couch after his dinner wares clear. Then, after this warning, he would lock the deadbolt and say he'll see us in the morning. And in those early days, my father would return through his front door, giving it a brief dawn-time fawning. My sisters and I would hear him come in about five o'clock, and when we wake up he's there getting ready for work with his Brut aftershave adorning.

I am fourteen in these early days. I am still in form three in high school, at Bishop Anstey. And Ericka, at twelve, just start Diego Martin Secondary. And we big enough now—it seems—for our father to stop ironing our uniform shirts and skirts, navy and green.

My school is in town. At least forty-five minutes in the traffic that abound. Ericka's is in Diego Martin self. She can walk to school, and she often walks home with her friends. But thas in the afternoon, when no one in any particular hurry. On mornings, she would welcome a drop from Daddy and an early arrival without worry.

But my father, in the morning, is always flurried. He can't be late. His workers depend on him to open up the construction sites and their assignments bam-bam-bam communicate. He need to start their day. To tell them which way, what flooring or roofing to lay, how to cut, and which steel to solder and burn, and which cement to mix with water and sand to churn.

My father, who has in every area of construction served. Working his way up after dropping out of school at fifteen to help his mother with money he could earn.

Though my grandfather was labouring hard, too. But no matter how much his gardening, their shop, his odd jobs, and the rest brought in, there is only so much that money can do. That amount was still so little between my grandmother and eleven pickney. Especially when it first divide for my grandfather to mind his other families. The one just down the road primarily. This right-there, everybody-know household of girls who take Gold Grampa whole face. These gold-skin, green-eyed girls who are Gold Grampa's inside children same age. Gold Grampa genes visibly seen by Granny when she go een supermarkets and schools where Gold Grampa offspring going too. These children, these women, these satellite families who will thin out the walls of Granny heart, furthering her disease. These women, these children breathing evidence of her husband doing as he please. These same-age pickney who will attend her funeral when she later dies, coming to support their siblings as they grieve and cry. These outside children of Gold Grampa's who then get fully embrace. Living with, dining with, minding babies with the extended family bearing Gold Grampa congenital traits. This Gold Grampa, who in Sunday church services, does sit down at the altar, holding the shepherd staff, preaching the beatitudes with his loud voice raise.

My Gold Grampa who money cyah stay. Not when he have families needing the same supplies for school, and the same healthy food, and the same outgrowing clothes. With the marital and common-law wives in his life demanding the same curtains, utensils, and utilities for their homes. And so my father, who say he was never good at schoolwork anyway, decide to drop out. Food presiding over clout. His sisters, he say, brighter. They should be given the chance to study books and make something of themselves, while he make Granny burden lighter.

So my father worked as a gas station attendant for three years. And he did other small-wuk here and there. Till he started cleaning up on a construction site. Then a little carpentry, then a little joining. First to reach every morning, last to leave every night. Learning the breakdown of everything. Following everyone; no job beneath him. No irresponsible teenage whims.

He did it all, and upward, till he became a foreman and a subcontractor boss. He could teach and critique his workers in any job because he had been doing everything years now, like an apprentice course. Teaching himself with his hands, there was nothing he couldn't make, no design he couldn't erect, no concept he couldn't materialise from his vast know-how. My father's brilliance earned by the sweat of his brow.

He built mansions fuh dem big shots and dem, and high-rise company buildings, and housing complexes, and so much else that he would take my sisters and me around on Sundays to see. He would take us in and break down the blueprints so we could perceive how he took this setta lines on a page and made it into a million-dollar home for which he was just about to hand over the keys. We marvelled, then, at everything we saw, the sunken pools, the ascending balconies. His craftsmanship was so gorgeous it took our breaths away. We were so proud and our father loved hearing the oohs and aahs of the family he work so hard for, he say.

And we admired our Daddy. Stunned by everything his strong hands could create.

It was only when my sisters and I, as we grew older, saw more, and started asking why. Why he didn't do this with our house? And we started reminding him of the questions my mother would state when he used to take her round about—before she started being busy sewing every Sunday—only then my father stopped having any new places to show us that he make.

Still he invests in every new beauty—that we no longer see. Taking each construction just as seriously, and goes off to be the first on the job site, to examine, to measure, to touch. So if Ericka and I want a drop when we see him in the morning, after he come home, we have to rush.

I need it more. Much.

Getting a taxi to town in the morning is the hardest thing to do. And I am always exactly on time—my-time, late-other-people time—competing with town workers and other school attendees, too. Plus, taxi fare does cut into the money my father give me that I can save and spend on a cheese pie. The cheapest lunch item from the tuck shop I could buy. And I could make the money stretch for something else for when I come home. So that day I don't have to go get food by Granny—a meal with a side of eyes not warm, but harassed and cold.

And even if doing so—being on time for when my father ready to go—means skipping hotting water in the kettle on the stove. Means no hot water to add to the blue bucket's cold. Means bathing in chilly water early early in the dew-dark morning. Then so be it. Because it bends my neck and heats my eyes, being obligingly given food like a pothound stray, with my grandmother's scorning.

Three blue buckets stacked inside each other and a school bag each, and Ericka and I would tear down the hill as the hour hit. With Sherrie between us, three of us hoping my father still there and not silently cursing and catching a fit. My blue and red Bishops tie loose around my neck. Ericka's green skirt pleats billowing around her legs. Sherrie plaid overall buttoned at her chest. Three girls my father makes run and play fetch. Get to Daddy before the grey van drive off in a huff. Pant, cough, wheeze, belly bubble, eyes scan, breaths puff. Reaching the yard with the van still present—engine gunning, doors done flung open—though, is not enough.

Remember those blue buckets feting in the down-the-hill excursion with all our school stuff? Them same blue buckets for all our household water needs have to go and get drop off to their daycare by Granny washing machine. And een that space of time my sisters and I settling in the empty blue buckets to fill when we reach back from school in the afternoon, our father could leave. Though he done see us reach.

We kiss Sherrie bye because she is still nine. And she goes with Ms. Yvette, the maxi driver who takes all the little cousins to Diamond Vale Government Primary School on time. Driving them fifteen minutes from home but safely across the main road. All the aunts fearing their children crossing, finding dem drivers does steer too mad and speed limit is something them doh know. Indeed, the aunts' concern not unfounded as my still-aching, bowled-down, flipped-over, hit-and-run leg could show.

And then my father stops coming home on mornings, and starts returning earlier from work instead. He visits the house and make sure everything in order, his forefinger wagging as he Bam-bam-bam ticks off the checklist in his head. And when he done assure himself, in those fifteen minutes, that we safe and we sound, he give each of his three daughters our money for the next day and say, See allyuh later, his back never turning around.

He don't even eat the food Granny send up the hill with us, each side dish on another plate covered under folded towels in Country Kitchen design. All piled high just under the chin of whosoever turn it is to go down by Granny since we all hate doing it now, never easily resigned. To going by Granny and getting the food both. Equating this responsibility that we loathe to walking the plank. I sure some of the torture with which pirates dealt must have been the shame they felt at first being exposed in front their shipmates, under whom they sank. And for all that hefted load, Daddy would say he go just pick up something down the road.

My sisters and I don't know that down the road means by her. Luvern. Is Renee, the distant cousin my father pays a lil change to clean the yard every so often, who tells us that my father van park up at the foot of the mountain. Jess go up tuh de top top a Cemetery Road an tun right. That road, two streets from ours, Renee tell us, the van does be dey every night.

Marcia, the cousin older than me by a year, who needs braces and reads the dictionary on weekends, once tell Renee to hurry up and done de antibiotics he was taking cuz at this rate jess now he go have too much blood in he alcohol stream, the way he abstaining. And granted, Renee does drink. Like a fish. But Renee also know everybody business, and is facts whenever he dish. Plus, Luvern is his distant cousin, too. So what he say mussbe true.

He know before my sisters and I that my father planning to move Luvern into our house, too. Know that my father has been begging Luvern all this time to come and stay by him because he don't feel ever so comfortable leaving de chirren dem by deyself in de night. Which—discomfort or not—he does still manage tuh do. But Luvern find with three big gyuls she might be crowded, and she prefer her two-room shack in de mountain any day to any grown-ass children she might have to live with squeeze up tight. She don't know if we go accept her in our life. My father assures her we will. Naturally. And when she finally feels convinced of that, and the benefits of indoor plumbing, she decides to move in on Baptist Hill. But, she say, incrementally.

Luvern who as dark as burnt sugar, and does wear light hazel contact lenses. Her hair straightened and, when it out of the weave, she does wear it then with some pulled up in the middle to create a mountain-like effect, with two streams pouring down either side of her face, and the curling-ironed-flipped ends of the streams touching her cheekbones she grace with fuchsia blush pens. Luvern gels the sides of her hair up tight so there are no flyaways, and no mistake it is her real hair when the exposed scalp is displayed so clearly through the hairline strands and beyond, with no track marks or panels glued down. The back portion she flips under, courtesy the curling iron and Vaseline again. But she always make sure the ends aren't tucked too tightly because she wants to illustrate that her own hair long enough to touch her shoulders. Barely, but undeniably to any beholder.

Luvern wears bright-coloured, spandex tops with cap sleeves that don't hide the stretch marks on her shoulders, and with sequined words across the front. She might be SEXY on Monday and DIVA on Tuesday or HOTTIE on Wednesday, but Thursday's BITCH is my favourite one. I might have told her something about self-fulfilling prophecy if at any point I deigned to speak to her and her son. The spandex tops are always too thin, made out of the cheapest, one-wash fabric, and too short. They might have been a normal, just-below-the-waist length on someone for whom they are designed. But Luvern's DD's and triple rolls of belly fat bring the tees up past her navel and the stretch marks there that people also see, which she don't mind. The people she limes with say the stripes show she is a woman. I think her hips sufficiently negate any remaining doubt there is about her being a woman, but this is just another point on which we disagree, this Luvern and me.

Luvern thinks that corduroy, slim-fit, gun-mouth, crossing-river-length, bright-coloured jeans on her size 22/23 frame are a good fashion choice. It is all she wears in Trinidad humidity that make everything hot and moist. Light-blue corduroys, dark-blue corduroys, Pepto-Bismol-pink corduroys, curry-yellow corduroys, hunter-green and lime-green corduroys, and a white and black zebra-like pair for special occasions. Formal attire dinners requiring a dress and with Luvern there is no persuasion. Luvern also thinks that alternating between gold slippers and silver sandals with three-inch glass heels and sequined patterns and with openings that reveal her dry, cracked heels, complemented by black nail polish to hide the discoloured and thickened toenails, are a good fashion choice—especially because they make her look even taller than her six feet, perfectly sexy and sweet. My sisters and I are not inclined to agree.

Nor do we quite agree that Mr. T is the trendsetter one particularly wants to emulate. Gold rings on every finger, thumb included, and on two toes, and she will have music wherever she goes. Long acrylic nails that she clacks together; popping gum that she chews mouth-open, forever baring gold teeth; and a high-pitched voice with a chalk-on-blackboard laugh accomplish that feat.

Luvern makes my father happy.

This is what he says to my sisters and me when he introduces us to his "friend." My father skinning and grinning, his half-denture smile thinking it winning us over to his end in this game of pretend. Introducing us to Luvern who he tells his children will, from now on, spend one day of the weekend. That, and the fact that he wants us all to be happy.

Why we would need to be happy if she only staying one night out of the week, we wonder. We just ignore her and go off to our rooms when she come into this motherless home ripped asunder. A simple Goodnight lets her know that our mother raised us right, and that we not looking for a replacement for her either. Luvern is just going to be just another in the line of domestic helpers that aren't actually here to cook and clean. But to serve our father and his needs.

We ponder how long this one will last, a two-month "employment" stay? And whether she will make anything as disgusting as that citrus orange chicken that Sharlene-was-it-? baked and we'd promptly thrown away. Granted this one is doing overnights, but since my father thinks we've grown up in the little time since our mother left, maybe he feels he doesn't need to hide the actual relationship between him and the help.

But then we get the picture as weeks pass and overnight stays become weekend delays and weekends don't end with the weekdays. And when her black garbage bags of clothes start appearing, we realise this one isn't going to go. We are fearing . . . she is in fact coming. Into our house. To stay.

To shack up with my father.

And the woman brought her shack with her.

In every way.

She cooks eggs and leaves the broken shells in the kitchen sink. The freshness that my mother taught me and my sisters to always remove from the egg is left in Luvern's omelettes, and the kitchen stinks. For days.

The blood and fat, skin and undesired parts of the chickens Luvern cuts up for frying, stewing, baking, or for steaming when she is on a week-long diet—during which time she complains about migraines and weakness so-as-to-make-me-want-to-drop-where-you-see-me-here to such an extent you think she on death drink, so advertising her two-hour deprivation of food, that my father pleads with her tuh eat something nuh, reassuring her she looks fine just as she is with a butt pat and wink—are left in the sink.

The blood and fat, skin and undesired parts of the chicken are left on the draining board. On the kitchen table, the kitchen counter, the kitchen floor. On the outside of the overflowing garbage bags, and on the kitchen louvres' glass slats through which Luvern throws the scraps—not relieved that the stray dogs eat her crap and so clean up most of the mess that brings fat green flies buzzing around our house. Not stressing that she encourages all the strays' friends to come into the yard unbound for a treat they rarely get anywhere else about. Raw chicken free throws. So few people think to fling animal parts out their windows.

Luvern pees in a posey. She keeps the posey under the bed. She comes out every morning from my father's bedroom carrying her posey full of pee with her heavy, shaking tread. She walks the length, too hard to traverse at night—through the living room, through the kitchen, through the washroom, and to the bathroom—to empty her nightly pee that stays under the bed for hours and the ammonia sours, waiting to be poured from her arms, shoulder-height. Never close to the bowl, splish, splash, flush, announcing her delight that her man has plumbing inside his house built right. Pronouncing her joy that she no longer required to use a latrine in the dark bush under moonlight.

Make her feel at home, my father say.

I think she does. Look at the way. Stripping sheets off the bed, Luvern spreads them on the hard, vinyl-floored concrete of the gallery. She wraps a threadbare thin sheet about her, too. Showing off every calorie. Luvern wears nothing underneath. Luvern wants to catch the breeze. Uncle Ken passing to go to his house, a little higher up the hill, sees. His wife, Tanty Acklyn, sees. Their child, Avanelle, sees. Luvern naked with a sarong bed sheet. Every neighbour watches Luvern lie, revealed, in the front of the house. For hours of loud phone calls and open-leg naps from which she does not rouse.

Everyone can see Luvern bathe nearly naked at the side of the house. At first, Luvern wears a half-slip about her breasts and soaps through her slip, and pours water from the rusting barrel in the yard over the polyester with the pan she use to dip. Then she dispenses with the ceremony, and now wears just her bra and panty. In the yard, in front the barrel, at the side of the house. From which point, Uncle Errol, my grandmother's eldest brother, and all the pumpkin vine family of his offspring, crammed into that ever-expanding residence below ours that extends to hold eight-week- and eighty-year-olds, can see my father common spouse. Luvern. Bathing. Her see-through underwear doused.

People passing in the road going about their business can glance up between the chenette tree leaves, and under the plum tree branches, and clear through the shaved mango tree in Grampa Biscuit's yard, and see her. Can see up the hill, into our yard, and can either be disgusted or get a thrill as Luvern bathes straight from the barrel that my sisters and I stay up late on Friday and Saturday nights to fill. My sisters and I remaining awake long into the night when WASA finally sends water to Diego Martin with enough power to reach through the pipes, and up our hill.

My sisters and I fill the barrel, angling the hose under its cover in a way that the flow won't be cut off, or the hose slip out, or the water lose its pressure. In a way that we can watch TV inside the house and not have to stay outside for the hours it takes the barrel to finally fill, while sitting on the cold, hard, rough concrete steps the chicken scraps makes fresher. The jagged concrete steps my father added as an afterthought, unsmoothed, when he joined the two last rooms on to this house he built. The steps he didn't really use a trowel on, and on which our butts can feel the unpolished silt.

The last two rooms with one of them being the washroom my mother got my father to construct after six years of washing his clothes, her clothes, her three young daughters' clothes by hand, on the jooking board, in the concrete sink. My father building the washroom to enclose the washing machine he bought three years after his mother and his sisters had theirs and freed their fingers from their handwashing crink. My father buying my mother her washing machine for Christmas so she didn't have to go down the hill to use his mother's any more, or his sisters' own, entering—with dirty laundry—their yards and their homes.

My father buying my mother her washing machine and building the washroom to keep it from getting wet with rain and dew and to keep it clean. Only when his mother tell him If yuh eh find iz high time Cyatrin have she own lil machine. And stop use mine. Granny telling my father that his wife could stay an use her own instead uh walking dong de hill tuh come when Ah trying tuh get meh lil washing done. Granny being the person to make household suggestions to her married son.

And looking out over the side door in this washroom, peering outside, my sisters and I are glad when the water pressure is sufficiently high. That means neither Ericka, nor Sherrie, nor I have to fill the blue buckets directly under the short pipe. Under the drip drip dripping tap. This tap that drips because it want a washer that Ah go bring home wid me one uh dese good days as Ah comin as iz jess tuh screw it in, my father says with a doh-criticise-me snap.

And when we don't have to use the short-fuse dripping tap, my sisters and I don't have to pull the bucket away and off the cement block that my father lay over the roughly hewn drain to form a platform on which the buckets can stand. The cement block over the six-inch open drain, where raw chicken parts stagnate and slime over with moss along its length that winds and snakes. The drain my father promises the health inspector to clean again and again when dengue fever starts to reappear in Trinidad and they want to fine him for mosquito larvae breeding in his place.

They are heavy.

The blue buckets are heavy. To lift the buckets off the block, and across the three feet between the pipe and the barrel, and up over the five feet of the barrel's height, and pour the water, not too hard to unsettle the rust at its base, is arduous—it is a task for which our young girl bodies are not ready. And it is my sisters' and my job we have been assigned. Our plight. We have to take care of the water situation, my father says, my father recites. We have to stay home on weekends to do it, too. Securing all the cooking, bathing, cleaning water needs for a household is work my sisters and I have to do.

My father is never home on Friday or Saturday nights. These are the nights when Luvern treats herself for maintaining her diet all week, for keeping up the good fight. My father takes her out to get KFC or pizza, roti, or chicken wings, or some chicken foot or pig foot souse from on the promenade, and always ice cream as dessert. My father takes Luvern to Independence Square for fast food like he would treat a woman who works. A desperate "chickenhead" young girl. A woman on the road bargaining for something to fill the stomach hunger corrodes by pledging to serve. A girl who is spotted by a man in a car that makes the claim that she is a gasbrain on the streets. And plies and pays his way into her skirts by providing her something to eat. One-off fast food on the go. Not loving meals cooked together in an intimate home. Quid pro quo. It is the way of this father from that family of men, what they know. And if my sisters and I likely to be awake because it kinda early, my father might bring my sisters and me two Kids Packs from KFC. To share. We girls don't warrant his money spared. That's budgeted for no-good-home girls he has to lure to get in his front seat after his dollars pretend to care. My motherless sisters and I already in my father's house, we not going nowhere.

And though my father not here and we have to manage the water collection as he declare, at least my sisters and I don't have to carry the blue buckets down by Granny if we fill them at the side of our house on weekends. We are happy about that, and having the living room to ourselves, and time with just us to spend. So the sound of water rushing through the taps after nine p.m. on a Friday night is always met with excitement by my sisters and me, who wouldn't put on our home clothes yet. Waiting to see if we will still be forced to go down the hill for all the water we have to get. Making sure to call Granny first, disturbing her rest, to let her know that we coming down to full the buckets that hour. Calling first so somebody can look out to hear us because the hill always so dark at that time under the trees' bower, and nobody know what could be in the bush along its side to make us cower.

And if Uncle Donald, Tanty Marilyn's husband—who resent having to live in the same yard as his forever-ailing mother-in-law—has a particularly bad dog at the time. A dog that Uncle Donald training by keeping it tied up on a short leash, angry at being confined. Tied to the pole for the electric meter right outside Granny's bedroom. A bad dog that Uncle Donald feeding dragon blood to. That red powder he sprinkles over the chicken he makes his wife cook for his dogs. Chicken that Uncle Donald himself doesn't eat except on Sundays and at Christmas because he is a six-day, eleven-month vegetarian and meat is for dirty hogs. If Uncle Donald have at the time one of these violent dogs then my sisters and I have to stand outside the gate and loudly call. Like strangers, like intruders, like we not family at all.

We have to explain what we even doing down here this hour. And watch the disgust, or the amusement, or annoyance crawl across our aunt's face, or our uncle's face, or our cousins'—every now and then our playmates'—face that goes sour or even more dour.

Never pity or understanding. Never questioning or a glance toward the car section reprimanding. A look askance over to the garage where my father's van not parked at eleven o'clock on nights. In the gloom of black clouds shielding moonlight. When his daughters brave snakes, bandits, shame, and fatigue to get water that flows automatically up to their tanks. Their 2,500 gallons of water banked in cisterns that they, our aunts, prudently bought and that flows easily when their taps are cranked. When they turn on the taps in their houses, evenings or mornings, our aunts waking up refreshed after not waiting up, angling a hose in a barrel till two a.m. Our father's sisters so displeased that we inconveniencing them.

Luvern bathes with all this water in the barrel that we fill. Luvern takes a cake pan—that my mother used to pour her home-made sponge cake mixes into to bake on Sunday evenings, on birthdays, for company, and at Christmas—to bathe, in view of everybody on the hill.

But first, she turns the cake pan into a container for ice.

Luvern puts the tin pan in the freezer fulla water to get hard. And when there are too many bumps and holes in the tin, formed by the ice pick after the ice stick, then she takes it and makes it a dipper in the yard.

Luvern does not take out some water from the barrel for her needs. She does not fill a bucket with some water for her use only, to clean. Luvern dips her ice-picked, cake-tin dipper in all the water, in the whole barrel that full to the top. Between pouring water on herself, Luvern drops the dipper on the hard, cold concrete steps on which my sisters and I used to sit to fill the barrel—making sure the hose stayed straight, talking about how much we want to leave, wondering when Mummy going to send for us, pondering how it is we will finally get away. And how long we have to wait.

Luvern puts the bar of soap in the dipper, making it slippery and sudsy. Luvern dips this soapy dipper into the whole barrel that the hose work so hard to fill, staying at attention, not being clumsy. This cake-pan dipper that she placed on the steps—that we never sit on any more since she come to stay and start throwing chicken parts out the kitchen window, that rot and make maggots, and that attract stray dogs that lie in packs that continue to grow—gets dipped into the barrel of water my sisters and I in sleep refused, and with the wiggly hose fused, and from the dark hill excused filled for our use.

And when Luvern is done bathing, she wraps her towel around her and shrugs off her panty from underneath the towel's stretched length. Then, Luvern washes her panty by hand with the bar of bath soap that always holds some of her pubic hair in ultimate tensile strength. Luvern washes her panty with bath soap, in the cake-tin dipper at the side of the house. Where every man Jack could see what she going on about.

Luvern dunks the dipper—with the soap, and the dog fur, and the remnants of her son's urine, because boys must learn to be man and pee outside and what yuh is, a gyal, go and pee by de step—back into the barrel of water that we are all to use. Luvern does what she wants because she pays her nightly dues.

But my sisters and I prefer when Luvern bathes outdoors. Then there is less chance of her leaving her clots of menstrual blood on the white tiles of the bathroom floor. When she bathes outside, there is less chance of my sisters and I getting caught smelling like the bleach we use to clean every inch of the tiles and walls before we shower to stay home or to go to school or with friends go out. Doing the little we can to counteract the influx of germs and infestation Luvern brought when she moved into our house. Creating a home with this man she calls by his last name, Adams, like his workers who extend de borseman his clout.

Luvern brings her own stove to my father's house, from her wooden shack on the mountain, about six months after she moves in. The mouse droppings on our stove every morning bother Luvern. We are ungrateful children not to clean the stove after her food—that she cooks with water out of the very barrel that to bathe she does use—bubbles up. Rumbling out of the pots and falling on the stove top. Luvern's barrel water food creating dark, sticky, messy muddles that feed the mice who moved in with her as her brood. And we are thankless children because we will not touch her food.

She curses her grievances aloud. Luvern stands by the windows of the living room and puts her ringed fingers on her exaggerated hips, spread wider by her opened legs, backing a stance and she shouts. Luvern cries. Loudly. And long.

Our neighbours come out of their houses to stand in their yards to hear her lamentation song.

The Christian ones only pull their windows open wide. Sticking their heads through, looking to see if, again, my father beating one of his women's hide. But my father never hits Luvern. Maybe because she is as big as him; not because he learn. Maybe my father doesn't beat Luvern for the same reason he has started dressing like a young boy. For fear that Luvern will leave him and his feed-her-junk-food ploy.

So Luvern first wails, then sobs, and follows that up with a long unleashing of her fed-up-ness with his nasty children who Won't clean up after theyselves and look how long the bucket full, and nobody will empty it. The bucket that my father put under the kitchen sink and squeeze een to make fit. To catch the water leaking from a burst in the kitchen drainpipe that he repairs every two months or so with some tape. Because a plumber would only charge, and want to bust big price to do wuk he could do himself when he find time this weekend and put it back in shape. Look how long it is this bucket full and these chirren wouldn't empty it. And look how the water smelling. Like grey landfill shit. And watch how the garbage under the sink overflowing outta the bag that my father thought was sufficient, no bin necessary to actually put the bag in. Because it easier like that for him. Faster to take out the garbage, now that he has to do it, since my mother—who was the one that tied up the garbage and carried the heavy bags down the hill every other night for the rubbish truck to pass and take, since it can't drive up the hill and brake—has left.

And these fucking chirren of yours only bringing rat and cockaroach in the kiss-me-ass place. And I not accustomed to this kinda stupidness. Luvern wildly gesticulates. Look when I sweep out the bedroom and leave the stuff in the living room, these bitches won't even say lemme pick up the stuff with the hand shovel. And look how long they greedy selfish ass does leave the food I cook in the fridge to go bad, and with they bad mind go and cook they own. Luvern hollers and moans. I tired say is not me drive they mother away yuh know. It wasn't me and I tired being blame for this. They mother gone, they mother gone. Luvern loudly informs. That have nothing to do with me. They don't even fucking say morning dog in this place when they see me. And it not fair, I don't have to put up with this shit in here. I tired say I have my own place. Iz you who beg me to come down here with you, and iz this I have to go through. I don't need this shit from nobody. Iz time for me to pack my fucking bags and go. I iz nobody chile. I doh have to stay anywhere I not wanted, Luvern moans. And I not wanted here.

After she share, my father begs her to stay.

And when, on that occasion, she curses about my sisters and me not eating her food; and her not being able to cook on the stove we have here that could never clean properly, and that two burners never working good on; and if my father think she is our mother; and she don't know how our mother used to make out on a stove that couldn't work good, then my father goes up her mountain and brings Luvern's stove to our house. After she yell and curse and grouse.

My sisters and I are forbidden to touch Luvern's stove. My father puts a separate gas tank on it for his woman, her son, and him alone. And when the gas tank on our stove runs out of gas and we can no longer do for ourselves as he told his daughters to do, we still aren't allowed to touch Luvern's stove to cook our food.

And when my sisters and I wait until our father and Luvern leave to quickly exchange the gas tanks on the stoves—so that we could cook something and then switch the tanks back, because Uncle Ken who lives right smack above us is not home so we have nobody to buy and bring a heavy gas tank up the hill for us to use—and Luvern returns later and finds that her tank feels lighter, she curses yet again, loud and profuse.

Curses my father's ungrateful, stealing, conniving, motherless bitches-for-children, who jealous she, and can't leave she things alone. And always putting they blasted hand on she things, and this time she really tired of this shit and she going, for sure, for sure, for sure. Going home.

And she does.

Luvern goes back to her shack on the mountain for three tense days while my father drinks rum, smokes cigarettes, smokes weed, swears, and cries. Then on the third day he asks my sisters and me—after lining us up in the living room for a serious talk—Why?

The first he speaks to us after three days he spent ignoring us completely—no good morning, no food to eat, no drops to school, no money to travel to school, or for lunch, no good evenings, no goodnights—is to enquire Why? He asks us, Why?

Why we don't want him to be happy? Why we torturing him? Why we deliberately trying to take away the best thing that ever happen to him? Why we can't just stand to see him live his life? And believe me, he tells us, we not going to keep him from living his life, and from being happy. And Luvern makes him happy. And he want her here with him in his house. She belongs here. This is her house now. And if we don't like it. We can leave. We can find where *we* belong. We can find somewhere else. Don't know where, don't care where. But this is Luvern's place now, with him. And if we don't like it, we could go.

Go. Go where?

I am sixteen years old. I am seventeen years old. Living in fear.

Go where? The United States embassy just rejected my mother's suit after the step-by-step of two years. From hush-hush in small Trinidad, in the capital of Port of Spain, where we are afraid our father would see us going for our medical testing step. To our police record, fingerprinting in the police station just down the road from our house step. Two years of the steps it took us to finally get in for our interview.

Our interview, for which my sisters and I snuck away from school. Without telling our teachers, who might alert our father. Teachers who will ironically believe they doing the best for their charges, but would be harming us rather. Telling our father of the wrongdoing of his daughters being out there, on their own, without parental supervision in town alone.

Our US embassy interview, for which my sisters and I put down candles in the church our aunts invited us to. While they smiled, happy that we were finding their lord. Not knowing what we were praying for. Our interview, for which we put down candles in prayer that everything would go alright when we finally got a date to go in. Our interview to apply for our Green Cards so we could escape *him*.

Our interview, where the American officials finally denied my mother's bid to file for my sisters and me. Denied my mother even being able to apply for our Green Cards so we could join her in New York City. The American embassy declaring that, with what she makes, my mother is below the poverty line to sponsor her children three.

Our interview that my sisters and I had to come home from at our usual times, as if returning from school. As if returning in our usual moods. As if all in the world is all right. My sisters and I had to come back to my father's house, no exit in sight. My sisters and I had to go back to Luvern's home. My sisters and I had been rejected, at noon, from entering our mother's own.

Go?

Where?

My father lines us up at the foot of the hill, at five o'clock, on what will be the last of Luvern's three-day strike. Everybody passing in the road and all our family in the surrounding houses see us, my two sisters and me standing outside. Standing there waiting.

About half an hour goes by before my father pulls up in the van alongside. His hands grip the steering wheel. His knuckles stand up under his stretched skin through which his throbbing veins are revealed. He leans forward over the dashboard, staring hard through the windshield. He does not look at us three. He tells us to get in, silently. Our limbs are trembling violently.

He drives slowly, easily. We thought he would drive fast. He keeps checking the time, and letting other cars on the road pass. At twenty past six, he pulls over from this drive of his depravement. He partly rides up onto the pavement. He gets out the van. He still has not spoken since he told us to get in—with a red-faced man. We three sit in the back seat looking at each other. His car door does not slam. My father crosses the road and walks away. My sisters and I look into each other's face, and nothing we say.

He crosses another little labyrinthine street and continues walking away. We sit, twisting our hands, and mentally pray. He enters a small bakery that looks like it has seen better days.

Fifteen minutes later, my father re-enters the van. Everything going to be okay, he says. His eyes pierce the windshield and wildly scan. Not to worry. He manically smiles. Everything going to be alright in a little while. Luvern will hear our apology now and she will take him back. Just do dis fuh me, chirren. She willing to take me back if allyuh would just come in and show her dat allyuh really want her to come back. Tell her dat we all need her. And that home wid us is where she belong. Her shift at work just done, iz she alone in dere, allyuh could go in now. She will see allyuh now.

My father jumps out the van and into the middle of the two-way road. He stands on the median line and puts out his hand like a police officer directing traffic before a cricket test match make town overload. He stops the approaching cars and then frantically signals, waving us to come, to cross the street. My sisters and I quickstep in front honking horns, screeching brakes, and shouting drivers sucking they teeth.

He walks in front of us, like a demented goose under possession. He leads, looking back, to make sure we are in procession. Looking back with that bid-no-contest expression of unfailing faith and unflagging hope that must attend those seeking the Holy Grail. We bow our heads so that we cannot see who watches us out on Diego Martin Main. On this road, following silently behind this man with the clenched fists and eyes crazed. We cannot see what lies in front of us either this way.

My father opens the door to the shabby bakery and steps aside to usher us in. It's dark and smoky, and the air is thin. The glass panes are smudged and flies buzz around the few pastries sitting on oily grease paper. The walls are bare, and the floor is sticky, and the crusted ceiling not much safer. The counter is covered with a dissected newspaper, strewn black-print guts all around. Behind the counter stands Luvern, working at the job my father begged her to quit because she does come home so tired and down. And because he doesn't get to see her as he want. And why she fighting up sheself when she does get anything she need from him. And if she quit, she could get pregnant faster and easier and rest any swelling limbs.

Luvern wears a cheap, cap-sleeved, black spandex top with a keyhole cut for her peeping cleavage, but there are no printed words. It is her concession to professionalism that she observes. And instead of her usual corduroy, she wears plain black jeans with an orange wash—still slim-fit, still gun-mouth, still camel-toe tight. Instead of her gold sandals, Luvern wears black, ballerina-laced, cork-heel sandals that lean to the left, worn down on the sides. Borne down upon by her Slim Tea–undiminishing 280 pounds. Her skinny plucked eyebrows are in the upside-down U shape of a clown. Her lips, lined in black eyeliner and rouged with fuchsia-pink lipstick, tremble when she sees us walk in. The corners of the fuchsia lips tightly grin.

She is on the brink of tears. Why, when we treat her so badly and run her from our house, we now in her workplace? Why we can't give her some peace, Luvern sniffles and say. She know what we really think about her at de end uh a de day. Her building tears threaten to dissolve the clumps of mascara thickening her lashes. But my father stops her before any actually fall, before the greasy countertop catches. The children here because they have something they need to say to you, my father enunciates. Waving his daughters forward like we on Aunty Hazel variety show competing for a Disney trip in the States.

Luvern drops her eyelids and tries to make the upturned corners of her mouth go down. She drums her gold rings on the glass and says that she done working and is time for her to go home, to her house where people like her around. And that she too busy to hear anything my father's children don't really mean from their hearts, deep inside. My father promises her that we mean what we're about to say. He made sure of that. Luvern smiles.

In the years following, my sisters and I live in Luvern's home. My sisters and I live in my father's house. We live in the house wherein she, and in which he allows us to stay, once we know our place.

My sisters and I know our place.

10

BAMBOO TREES

I am nineteen.

And my mother wants to come to Trinidad six years after she leave, to visit her daughters three.

I am nineteen.

And my mother books a holiday to Trinidad, renting a small vacation stay on the beach. A calm, restful place forty-five minutes away from my father's house. And asks him to let us come, my sisters and me. To come stay with her while she recreationing for two weeks.

And since she never return to Trinidad in these whole six years, my father feel it not likely she going to try to steal. Kidnapping his children away. But just in case, he checks every nook and cranny of our luggage for any ticket that say New York–bound. Because if—god help allyuh—any kinda ting like dat is to be found, allyuh could stay by allyuh granny while I hunt yuh mudda down.

But the real reason Ulric relents and gives his consent for my sisters and me to see our mother is because is Christmas time and he doh want to bother having us around. Our spending Christmas away frees up his house for Luvern's guests over the holidays to come, sleep over, drink rum, and lime in numbers that abound.

But my mother's vacation, our vacation, is not a time of rest. It is a time wherein my sisters, my mother, and I work on our quest. We work between offices, between appointments, between requests, between replies. We work faxing, phoning, forwarding money, letters we write, sorting the information supply, providing signatures, and anything else that the United States embassy thinks to demand of my mother, my sisters, and I.

It is not enough. Our work. It is never enough. And we labouring on our mother's lover's dime. Another document, more photos, another background check. More money. Always more money. Just not enough time.

The US embassy erected around the Savannah as judge, jury, and gated governing body getting to decide that what Smiley say she could provide is something to accept or deride. The US embassy assessing the supplicant open palms of a woman toiling to make things right, returning from Brooklyn where she safely reside. The US embassy evaluating the dependability of a mother 14-carat stamped, tramped in her first name she now chooses to go by. A mother decked out in *Yolande* dull, dead gold. From head to toe they behold.

The mother that greeted me at Piarco. Her small hands bearing the shackle bands of her *Yolande* brand across her wrist. In flat, unshiny, tarnished gold and large cursive script you cannot miss. Her tidy ankles bearing her name in chains displayed around the joints of both feet. And when after years I finally get to hold and touch and smell her perfume sweet, and I hug and squeeze and kiss her cheek again and again, the *Yolande* at her neck and ears are cold and dig into my skin with pain.

The 14-carat plated gold is the gift of her lover, Lenworth, her children three are told. The generous head waiter at the Brooklyn branch of Junior's where my mother works also. The married browning Jamaican man that paid for this trip as his wife coming up from Jamaica over the holidays and so, this is a good time he tells Yolande to cross the Atlantic, with a ticket he funding to see how her children grow.

And what do you know, the appraising embassy is not pleased. My mother's two weeks come. My mother's two weeks go.

Our hopes, risen, fall.

My mother returns to New York. Alone. My sisters and I ~~crawl~~ return to my father's house. My sisters and I return to Luvern's home.

We hide, again, our manila envelope—the one with our documents and applications—in our wardrobe. Behind the mirror. In the centimetre of space between the glass and the wooden backing, we jam the envelope. Using a break, a missing mirror chunk, in the left bottom side of the pane that leaves about six inches of the board behind exposed, to conceal our hope.

My sisters and I never slam that wardrobe door, never jiggle it too hard. We treat it with the greatest of ease. Lest one day the envelope should slide down and my father should see. Something is hiding here. Lest my father ever see *what* is hidden there.

And our passports my sisters and I hide in between old schoolbooks and papers. Our father, we think—our father, who never attends parents' day meetings or asks anything about our schooling about which he is never aware—will never look there. He would never care. We think.

This night, he does. This night, he goes psycho. This night, my father literally froths at the mouth and his bulging, bloodshot eyes roll in his head. This night, five veins stand up in my father's temple, under his face flushed red. My father, normally the colour of nougat, looks like a beet spitting and cursing—about to burst in front our faces. Where the fuck is your passports, he crazes.

We don't know what makes him ask for our passports all these days in. A day like any other in quiet January. A couple of weeks after we return from vacation by the sea. From holidaying with our mother in the beach rental not far. We do know what makes us say that we don't know where our passports are. Whatever the embassy asks, however long it takes my sisters and I to finally get our Green Cards and go, we could kiss all hope goodbye and accept our lifetime imprisonment if we hand over our passports. This much we know.

In the hours my father spends questioning us, lined up in front of him as he sits on the couch fiddling with his belt, punching the wall, and cursing us out, my sisters watch my face and read. My sisters follow my lead. My sisters simply relay what I say. I don't know, I say.

He sends us back to our bedrooms. He not taking this shit. He not getting played for a fool. Not by a setta pisintail chirren. Not by your fuckin mudda neither. All this time since your mudda leave, she ever send money to buy a spoon in this house? She wukking for Yankee dollars and she gehing on like is cockroach she mindin in here. An now allyuh chirren want tuh play allyuh doh know is me fuckin takin care uh allyuh all dis time. Dat everyting I do is for allyuh I doin it. And now allyuh want tuh turn on me. On me. Jess fuckin go and get de blasted passports wey evah it is allyuh mudda tell allyuh to fuckin hide it, and bring it shittin come now or is trouble inside uh here tonight, tonight, tonight.

It is trouble inside my stomach. I am queasy. I am sick. I feel faint. My heart is banging too quick. My belly bubbling. My breath racing. My hands trembling. My whole body jerking, shivering. My father isn't joking. He gone mad. Luvern is off to the side smirking. My younger sisters and I are in this by ourselves, in a house with a cutlass and knives and fists and anger clad.

So much for family living right around us. They've been ignoring everything all these years anyway. They're ignoring my father's cursing now. It is up to us to survive this rage. It is up to me. My sisters are looking to me to take us through this red mist. I need to get us through this.

In my sisters' bedroom, I tell them to make noise, as if they looking and searching. I creep under Ericka's bed. The bed in front the door that my father build into the middle of the wall—the doorway in the middle of the perimeter like all the doorways in this house that my father build and my mother complain about.

The doorway in the smack-dab middle uh de way, whose placement my mother had so hate. Griping that it make the rooms much smaller when everything have to fit on either side of the damn doorway that my father, in construction, shoulda have better sense than to put in the exact centre. The doorway that Ericka put her bed alongside, using the other door to the right instead as the main way to enter and leave their bedroom. Giving her and Sherrie more space, instead of this door dividing the room in two.

I use Vaseline to ease back the bolt in this unused middle door, and put some along the hinges, too. Then I open it slightly. And I pass through. Into my own bedroom. This way I do not have to walk out into the kitchen and through the washroom to get to my room which, before I turn fifteen, used to be the backroom, like I usually do. This way I will not be seen.

Now in my room, I tiptoe on shaking knees up to the back door, where my mother stood years before, watching the bare-back, barefoot boy sneak up to our house to steal. I touch nothing. I make no sound in the dark. The pitch-blackness I must maintain. No sound that will alert my father and his fists and his veins to me being in my room now. I ease the back door open with Vaseline again. I wait.

My sisters are still making noise. My father still cursing in his loud barking voice. Still banging everything around. Knocking glass down, throwing figurines to the living room ground. Luvern is still silent. My fingers are shaking. I need them to be pliant. I sneak outside. Into the dark night. I stand in front the empty tank stand, the one-leg-short stand balancing on the concrete casing my father built over the septic tank that leaks every year. My teeth chatter in fear.

I stand in front the tank-less tank stand and I fight the urge to run. To just run, now that I am outside. Not in there. Run. Run. Run, and go where?

I look at the giant, green Bamboo Trees. The towering stalks fed by the rain spout and red earth dirt spurring massive growth spurts of the sighing, soughing, singing, ringing Bamboo Trees. Help me, please. I am standing on shaking knees. I pray to think quickly. I pray to get out of here—alive. My sisters and I.

The moonlight moves. Moon conducts her light. Moon beams a stream of white.

In the bright moonlight that moves, the moonlight that comes through all the bush my father hasn't cut in over seven months. That he won't pay Renee a little small change to come and cut, because now he needs more money for the weekend KFC jaunts. But more so because Renee does talk his business too much. In the moon's shine, the only piercing light that comes through the bush making our overgrown yard look like an abandoned lot that care never touch.

In this moonlight that comes through the fig and zaboca and soursop trees that hold little wild and stray animals and frogs and snakes that have slithered as they please into my backroom-bedroom, through the gap between the floor and the door. In this moonlight that moves, in the moonlight that penetrates that thick, hulking bush, this beam of moonlight falls on the discarded door.

And I see.

This thrown-out door is not the old, three-quarter-glass front door that my mother had to beg my father to buy a replacement for. This rubbish-piled door is another door my father built, and then updated with a store-bought upgrade Luvern only had to request once—nothing more. A Courts door for their bedroom. A door she could lock in all the fumes they produce and the blues they consume, and all her cheap unenviable clothes, too. A door my father locks every time they leave the house. To keep his children out. A door I once picked, that was guarding the groceries my father and Luvern brought into the house and did not place on the empty kitchen shelves. Groceries they bring into the house every Friday for themselves.

In this old bedroom door, on which the moonlight shines, I see now a hole in its plywood surface that's a small fist size.

I look around quickly in the moon's headbeam shine. I pull the three passports—my sisters' and mine—out my bra and shift around the running sweet potato vines. Clearing away from the door's top the bush and other junk piled up high. More old trash and scraps that my father says he will take down the hill one day for the garbage truck to haul to Beetham side.

Balling up my fist, I slightly fold the passports and grease my palm. I push my hand, slick with Vaseline, into the hollow of the home-made door, keeping my claustrophobia calm. I push my whole hand with our three passports past the rough-edged ply. And through the small hole, exactly fist size.

Passports hidden, I readjust the dirt, the bush, the junk, and sneak in the way I come out. Slink back, easing open the locks, easing closed the hinges, easing under the bed in the middle of the doorway. Creeping back to the searching that Ericka and Sherrie still portray, into my sisters' room. Leaving the passports in trash under the moon.

Five minutes later. My father enters. My father breaks down the shelves where we first held our passports among our books. My father rips the sheets off Ericka's bed where I then cut a hole in the mattress to hide the passports in its foam, thinking there he wouldn't look. My father turns the whole house upside down, dashing, crashing everything as he roams. My father breaks wares and furniture as his daughters' belongings he violently probes.

When he is done, my father drives his van up the hill and loads us into the back while Luvern sits in the passenger seat. My father takes us to the rental house on Carenage beach. The restful place where we stayed for those two weeks. Down there to get de muddafuckin passports if daiz where allyuh fuckin hide dem. His foaming mouth spits fury and phlegm.

Pat, the Trinidad-white woman who rented my mother the house, pleads with us to stay and let her call the police. She is afraid my father will drive us all over the seaside cliffs. Pat has never seen this. A man so mad. We have never seen this man this bad. This terrifyingly, psychotically, evilly out of control. We fear for our lives. I am afraid tonight we will die. But my sisters and I tell Pat no. It will make things worse. We tell her we will be okay.

We will be okay, we say, but our teeth are chattering, we are holding each other's hands. We are praying in our minds every time our father wrenches the van. Round another sharp Carenage mountain bend. Don't let it won't go over, I chant in my head without end. My father veers inches close to every edge. Teeters the van's tyres over every ledge.

Still, he drives us back to his house, back to their house, back home, in one piece. Without peace of mind. This is not over. He says.

For six weeks my father hounds us. For six weeks my father threatens us. For six weeks my father curses my sisters and me. Every day we have his spit in our face for six weeks. And he pleads. He wants those passports.

We don't know where they are. We report.

My father is still cursing, he still curses my sisters and me the day we leave. The day, like any other, we leave his house in our school uniform shirts and skirts and socks and washrags to sop sweat from the heat. With going-out clothes to change into filling our bookbags.

My sisters and me, knowing that we will never see that house again. Nor him. Six weeks after, over Carenage narrow cliffs, his speeding tyres bucked and spin.

The embassy has finally been satisfied. Our Green Cards have finally been issued. Our tickets could finally book. Our tickets to leave; only six and a half years it took.

And our little blue booklets, my sisters' passports and mine—though the clerk at the counter for BWIA airline looks askance at the dog-ears, looks aghast at the dirt rimming there, looks appalled at the grease oiling their covers, looks incensed and hovers over the fold along their lengths, looks disgusted and tense—our passports, my sisters' and mine, stay in our possession. In my hands, without a mother's protection.

11

SILK COTTON TREE

I am twenty years old.

It is June 19, 2000. And my sisters and I are fleeing our father and his house, Luvern's home.

We are leaving Trinidad with the clothes on our back.

Ericka, eighteen, wearing the blue skirt and white shirt of the Jamaat. The uniform for her A-level study at a Muslim girls' school. Study she will not conclude. Sherrie, fifteen, is dressed in her uniform too. In the black-and-white plaid overalls of Diego Martin Junior Secondary. Her school bag packed with only a pair of jeans to change into for the plane, her birth certificate, immunisation card, and ID.

And me, bringing our dirty passports, retrieved from their hiding place in the backyard. Our freedom passports together with our long-awaited, red-stamped papers for our Green Cards. The escape credentials I had to stuff deep down in my long Rasta bag.

I, who am taking classes on Frederick Street for the SATs, supposedly. And am dressed this day as a Spiritual Baptist, completely. With cotton headtie, shapeless blue dress, and silver cross necklace. The picture of grace. Looking older than twenty with an unadorned face.

A look I wish is a disguise. And not a desperate subscription to my aunts' church-people lies. About sacrificing vanity. A way to ply their god with offerings of piety, so it would hear my secret prayers to finally set us free.

But, luckily, my gown and headtie is also an aesthetic that serves to avert eyes. Do not pry. A necessary entreaty in the middle of a weekday. As three teenage girls make our unshepherded way to Piarco Airport on an isle where everybody know everybody. And making report is something they too much like. A report we cannot afford as we run for our lives.

Three teenage girls making our don't-see-us way. To board a plane. To not return to our father's house this afternoon like a normal school day.

Hopefully.

This is your captain speaking, we apologise for the delay. Ericka's head swivels round. Suppose he find out? Sherrie's frenzied eyes search the aisle. I hold a King James Bible open on the tray to Psalm 69. Let me be delivered from them that hate me. Ericka's nose blooms red. She start crying. Again. Hide not thy face from thy servant; I am in trouble. Sherrie nearly out of her seat, bend over double. No one else reacting to us not taking off yet. To our plane not even taxiing from the gate. Trini time, plus everybody know BWIA. Them always late. But not today. Please. Hear me speedily. I offer frantic pleas to an invisible entity.

I look through the oval window, searching the tarmac. Any six-foot-two muscleman in construction boots running to call us back? To hold up take-off? Would officers get involved? View us as minors in the eyes of the law? Unable to run away to a whole new country just because?

Just because our father make us have to trade in Coca-Cola glass bottles at Spikes' shop. Trade bottles like cokeheads do for deposits to buy powder milk, cheese, Crix, and hops. Sweet drink bottles we tote down the road after we use Squeezy, water, and care on them to wash. Heavy glass bottles for butter bread. Three girls feeding ourselves. Since our father prefer to spend his construction-manager salary on his fat girlfriend and her son instead.

Just because our father say Two shirt enough fuh allyuh fuh school man, jess wash one de next day. Allyuh hand eh break. Learn how to make do. So he could fund the KFC, pizza, rotis and Chinee food, the Johnnie Walker, the Vat 19, and the weed, since he now doing that, too. The father who taught me to associate all drugs with fear, now needing harder highs than regular beers. Needing to be cool for the girlfriend and her sisters, and her cousins and fellow gutter peers.

No, we may not have the right to run away to New York on a flight that delay just because Ulric let the trash he sleeping with and her sleazy Bagatelle Road posse take over every weekend, then weekdays, then school nights. Them openly accessing our bedroom, without pause. Rifling through our drawers. Them using Ulric's allyuh-chirren-go-somewhere-else-if-allyuh-doh-like-it house at all hours to lime at top volume. To screw, to drink, to get stoned, and black out on carpets we have to sweep. Them passing out on Ulric expensive armchairs and couch we have to clean. That's if we want to keep the vermin away, mice and cockroach that don't bother people who accustom to latrine and no electricity and filth and decay.

Even Ulric's driving recklessly around sea cliffs. May not grant his running-away children a legal premise. Even though Ulric very nearly plunge us to our deaths in his raging attempts to get his hands on our passports I kept lying about not knowing where they gone. Passports for which I had to keep coming up with different places they could have been borne.

No, not even a father's open threats or violence or near-homicide merits coming to inspect. Not in a country where neighbours and police officers does stay inside and doh bother and hide. A country where neighbours and police officers does shoo-shoo and mind-yuh-business and smile behind their curtains. Lurking. All responsibility shirking. Saying me'en getting involved in dat schupidness. Leaving children to they father, however wutless.

No. Trinidad's femicide-allowing authorities don't vouch for children. Don't vouch for women. Don't vouch for girls.

I make my sisters turn around in their seats and slouch to keep their heads beneath detection. I hand out Royal Castle napkins. Dry yuh eyes. Look calm. Take deep breaths in. And don't draw attention to yuhself. Act like everybody else. For ten minutes, fifteen, twenty, half an hour. Stop biting yuh nails. Yuh doh have to go to the bahtroom yet. Keep it together. I, my sisters' tether. While I must submerge and calm my own upset. And fight my fingers not to fret.

But, on that idling plane, Ericka's breathing never regulate. Her hazel irises stay swallow up by her black pupils that can't undilate. Sherrie don't unfreeze. Her hand never stop clenching mine. She don't stop holding onto me.

This morning, earlier this morning, before the plane. Before we run away. This morning we plan to spend our last day in Ulric house, I kiss Ericka's cheek and hug her extra-long in the kitchen before she leave. To stop her trembling, for minutes I just hold and squeeze. You have to play it off. Be normal. Just walk out the door. Don't look worried. Act casual. I'll see you later, I assure. Our plan hinges on everyone performing like we practised before.

Promise? Ericka asks. She grasps both my hands. Looks me dead in the eye. I promise. It'll be alright. I'll get us out of here. Just don't let him see you acting weird. Don't cry. He'll hear it in yuh voice. Say yuh going when yuh reach the front door. Doh make him have tuh call yuh back. My heart beating wildly, but I can't show my sister that.

And you'll come and get me? Suppose he see yuh in town?

I going to go the other way around. I gonna take a Maraval taxi. Just be ready to go. Leh dem know that yuh sick from the time yuh reach, and I'll sign you out when I come. I could sign my sister out officially now. I could act as a guardian, being over eighteen years old. Having turned twenty just four days ago.

You'll be safe? He wouldn see you? Suppose he ketch us an we miss de flight? Ericka's face flush flush in fright.

Shhhh. We going tuh make it. I going an get ready now as soon as allyuh leave. I going to give myself plenty time. Fuh this I would be extra early. We leaving today. Now go on.

I'll see yuh later?

I hug her again. There can be no more repeated words to explain. She has to be brave. I walk her through the beaded strips into the living room. To the mahogany front door, still shiny and new. The store-bought door with the peephole half-covered in varnish. I look through the oily lens to make sure he not in the gallery. That our plan not going to be tarnished. That our father not somehow waiting in the yard. Not stand up by the fence. That he not under the cashew tree and won't see Ericka's red liquid eyes, hear her blowing her nose hard as I get her to go, and wonder what it mean, and cuss loudly, and make Ericka babble nonsense. There must be no impediment as I push Ericka to leave. Finally.

Ericka always crumbles spinally in the face of Ulric's rage. If she does this day, again I will have to step into her place. To bear the brunt and be the shield if he outside to interrogate. I will have to stare him down, in the face, if our father's bulging biceps lifting, threatening a blow. For Ericka not to be winnowed, our father must not be outside to question me why yuh sister looking so.

So I look first to make sure Ericka could uninterruptedly go. That he not outside to tell her Fix yuh face, allyuh does want tuh get on like I treating allyuh so bad in dis place. Like I'z de worse ting out hyeh. I'z allyuh fadda and I care about allyuh. I care about all my chirren. I does try my endeavour best tuh put allyuh first but like allyuh doesn want tuh see dat. Is like allyuh does do tings jess tuh see me upset. Allyuh like tuh geh me vex. I could be de kine Daddy yuh know, but allyuh . . .

Luckily, he en leave his bedroom yet. Luvern still giggling. Luvern en turn into the slamming-everything beast yet that she does hold back when Daddy home and receptive to her finagling. This as good as it gonna get. It'll be the last day we have to bear a grown woman's fawning and pitchy tittering. This siren serenade of Luvern's that keeps my used-to-be-disciplined father procrastinating.

My father who, before Luvern become a full-time project to woo, used to drop us to school in the morning. He used to drop Ericka, Sherrie, and I right in front our schools' iron gates. He used to go to his job sites after. Check on his foremen. Used to take charge of his workplace. He used to check and make sure his workers dig the foundations deep enough. That they cast the concrete clean enough. That they drop the steel posts in the ground, in the right place, at the correct angle. That was before he move Luvern in and outsource his every responsibility to someone else to handle.

My father used to go around to all de big-shot buildings he managing simultaneously as Trinidad construction boom keep climbing. He used to take pride in getting up early. Going to his second job to clean Diamond Vale Primary. Then coming back up the hill to get ready. Eager to go and tump up some uh dem fellas if dey en doing de wuk properly.

But then he start making Gold Grampa go and sweep our old primary school. And he start calling from the house phone in the living room to make sure them boys en on the job sites playing the fool. He start staying in bed with Luvern, glued to her side. And my sisters and I start taking taxi rides.

This morning, the morning of the day we plan to escape, I walk Ericka past their closed bedroom door. Morgan Heritage on the radio, playing loud and long. One of Luvern's favourite remix rocker's song. I'll be down the river waiting for the good lord to pass my way, oh yeahhh. I'll be down by the river, singing songs of joy on this lovely day, ohhh yeahhh. As Luvern warble along, spewing confusing word salad. Only she could make a lamenting praise into a sappy love ballad.

With the music, at least they mightn't hear us. It still have the louvres of their bedroom window, though. Ulric could still open the louvres onto the front yard to watch us go. He could still open these glass panes on the front yard side wide to let us know he not done. Not by a long shot. That when we return to his house after school, he gonna resume his interrogation. He could still open his sneering, peering, glaring, glass windows. To let us know: He allowing us to go to school. But we still have to come home. And when we do, he want those fuckin passports.

I walk my sister through the store-bought door of mahogany, walk her out the gallery, out the front gate, out the yard, under the poui tree. I keep my hand on Ericka's back. I can't walk her through the track. Not all the way to the hill. That would look weird. This is a normal day. I in my nightie still. But my hand is steering, gearing Ericka spine to make sure she don't turn around to look at me. That she don't turn and let a peeping Ulric see she vibrating anxiously.

That she don't turn around and undo all the months of undercover Green Card work. That done fall on me.

Just like all the labour this morning, now that we finally escaping, and the work of actually ferrying us to New York City falling on me. Getting us there safely is my duty. From Covigne. To Diego Martin Junior Secondary. In a taxi. First to pick up fifteen-year-old Sherrie. Turn back around. A short- and then a long-drop taxi into town. Up to Maraval. Second, pick up Ericka. Her loving teachers calling, See you tomorrow, have a good day and feel better. We smiling, replying, we shall. Frowns seeping back into our sober faces. Leaving Maraval. In another taxi.

Here my heart racing. We back in town. Weaving around the Queen's Park Savannah now. Thrust into the open expanse under a sun shining bright. It's mid-morning. Ulric should still be fastened to a job site. Not on the road. Not able to see all three of us together out of school, not detecting something not right. It's not lunch break. But Ulric might be wandering anyway. Quick strides down to City Gate. But not too fast. Trinis does stroll, lime, linger. Our good, sweet time we does take.

Board a bus. Make it to Piarco Airport up in the east. Tired and running on nothing to eat. While the hot sun beat. Walk up to departure. Deal with the employees who hafta cut style and prove who in charge. Act deferential, pay the extra fees. No luggage, but we still getting taxed what they please. Look out the side of my eye for Ulric large shoulders and arms. Vigilant out my periphery for Ulric reaching to keep us from crossing the threshold, departing from his perpetual harm.

Through the door. Make it to the gates. Retrieve our paper tickets from my deep Rasta bag. No letting agent stares intimidate. No letting agent questioning eyes humiliate. Hiding in the lounge. No drinks, no fries. No expended cash after all the taxis, no sandwiches to buy. Ducking the watching, glass-walled gallery on this side. Where Trinis doh need no flight to just come and lime and view jumbo jets fly. And anybody could know Daddy and use a payphone. And alert our father. To come drag us home.

Me, a twenty-year-old. A ferry woman navigating an underground railroad. Staving off River Styx by sacrificing clothes.

We flee Trinidad with the clothes on our back.

We did not pack. We could not alert our father with that. We cannot provoke his fists, his speeding van, his tantrums around sharp cliffs, his umbrage that his "possessions" ran. We cannot provoke that man into attack. We cannot provide the means for our father to bring us back.

We won't survive that.

Allyuh could get out my house an go. On my right, my eighteen-year-old sister still trembling from head to toe as if she cold. Shaking, quaking visibly. Allyuh doh like it here, fine somewhere else tuh stay. On my left, Sherrie, staring straight ahead, unblinking, unresponsive, like a mannequin on display. Sherrie, eyelids heavy, breathing unsteady, tongue-sucking at the ready to calm the thready pulse that the shut plane door does not cull. This is what being stripped of shelter and a home—by threats of a father telling you to go, whereupon you escape with no clothes—looks like. Shell-shocked children on a BWIA flight.

Seven years of living with Daddy after Mummy leave. Seven months of Ah want de fuckin passports. Seven hours of getting in and out taxis under will-he-see threat. My straight back does not lean back in the cushioned plane chair yet.

Me, a new twenty-year-old silently pleading with an open Bible, with my younger sisters on either side of me sat. Me who looks up from the book, through the oval window, when the plane still won't move, over Sherrie's head where everything trembling, down to her plaits. Out through the Plexiglas into the long, lancing rays of the bright afternoon sun. Spearing, yellow light that into the waiting plane comes. Please, let this done.

I hold my sisters' palms, breathing deeply, looking through the sunlit windowpane. On this near-airborne plane that finally taxis the runway without giant, violent Ulric bursting through the doors, wild and insane. Without Ulric and his throbbing temple vein storming to explain that we, his three prisoner daughters, can't leave. That we can't fly free of Trinidad soil and song and him if he don't agree. Though he threaten us directly. Telling us if we don't like his girlfriend and them building a life together, we could go. Seven years. And now we doing so.

Ericka quivers on the whole flight. Even as she doze. Sherrie, Sherrie is quiet, though, completely froze. Sherrie is fifteen years old. She was fourteen mere days ago. Sherrie is going to live with a mother who left her when she was eight. A woman who left me, her not-first child, to mother her daughters for seven years while she told me to keep the faith.

I was only thirteen years old on that November day.

Thirteen when my mother told me to take care of my sisters. To take her place. To become their mother as she secretly arranged to get out my father's house. Out the country. Out the Caribbean. And to leave her three daughters behind. I, a mere child.

I was thirteen when I had to learn to comb Sherrie's wispy hair. I couldn't plait canerow. I was thirteen when I had to learn how to cook rice and veggies and pigtail, after we failed at accepting Charlene's food and making ourselves swallow. Charlene and her terrified, experimental concoctions. Charlene, the first of my father's mother-substitutions.

Willow-thin Charlene who put whole, hard pigeon peas in split pea soup. No blender, no swizzle stick, no soaking overnight, no clue.

Whisper-quiet Charlene who baked her chicken legs and thighs with orange-slice goop. With the rinds still on. Crying Charlene who told my father she couldn't take children sobbing that's not the way their mother make macaroni pie. Twenty-year-old Charlene who didn't last long, despite needing the wages from the boss who'd promoted her to his girlfriend when she approached him for a job at his town site.

For seven years we endured all the Charlenes who came and went as cooks, cleaners, and girlfriend-employees. We survived tall, fat, cussing Luvern of the gold teeth. Luvern and her garbage bags, who came and stayed and didn't leave. It took seven years for our mother to bring her deserted children to her in New York City.

Our Bee Wee flight lands in JFK at nine p.m. By the time we make it out of immigration, it is way after ten. They have questions, these uniformed, armed, white officers and them. Where are you going to stay? Why are your passports filthy and bent? These are official documents. Does a parent know you travelled? Are your clothes arriving on a different day? Green Cards mean you can reside in the US permanently. But we don't have to let you through that gate.

Sherrie creeps close to me. She stares silently. Ericka speaks in a high pitch, with high-flying hands, and at high speed. I pray, don't unravel. My whole body trembles. My throat is dry. I am suspicious in my shapeless dress and blue Baptist headtie.

We are suspicious to the US immigration officers because we have no luggage by our side. No bags with any clothes inside. We are suspicious because we leave Trinidad with the clothes on our backs, and this is how we arrived.

I answer every question. I joke. I am polite. I lie. I smile. I keep the panic inside. They watch us, eyes narrowed, no-lips folded tight. They watch us, guns and badges repeating: Why?

Don't send us back there. For the crime of not bringing any clothes to wear. Not to that man. Not to die.

It is June 19, 2000. And I am twenty years old when I realise.

Our mother meets us after the airport glass doors slide. We're in New York City. Officially. Arrived. In our new, prayed-for lives.

I am conducting my two younger sisters from Trinidad to Mummy. Delivering myself and an eighteen- and fifteen-year-old. Returning us like packages, waylaid on our own. Left to roam. In a pocketed region of the globe. From Trinidad, whence our mother fled her husband's home. Seven years ago. When she left three little girls in the hands of the man she thought would kill her if she stayed. Seven years ago when she booked her own secret flight to JFK.

It is June 19, and ninety-six hours since my twentieth birthday. Two years and four days since I became mature in the eyes of the law. A couple years and four days into being an "adult" who could attempt kidnapping of my sisters, who are minors and not permitted to run past Trinidad's shore. Two years—but I, the adult, if tried and charged, would be sentenced to more.

I am twenty, and old enough to risk the charge to ship us overseas on a BWIA flight. I am twenty and, by my mother secretly filing for our Green Cards, I am granted this right. My mother who say You could do this, you so bright. My mother who has ceded to her not-first child this survival fight. To come and meet our Mummy this New York summer night. To start a new life.

When the glass doors slide, we step beyond the gun-patrolled immigration divide. There is a six-foot-three man at our mother's side. He doesn't stay behind as she strides to where we stand together, looking around at the massive airport. He does not give us room as our mother walks. Up to her children. As she does not run.

Our short mother steps in front each daughter, closes the space. Pulls each of her girls down. Doles out a thirty-second hug and a kiss on the face. She does not cry. Our mother does not weep. You're here, she laughs. She looks us up and down from our bowing heads to our shuffling feet. She smiles. Allyuh take so long tuh come out. She does not ask why. What the delay was about.

The broad man sighs. He stares at us. He has protruding eyes. And a nine-month belly. Come and meet allyuh new uncle, our mother says to us three. Her children who've just arrived in a new life, in a new country. This is your Uncle Roy. Is a long time now he waiting to meet allyuh. Roy, these are my big girls.

After seven years, we do not have our mother to ourselves for the first five minutes in our new world.

Hi, Ericka pipes brightly past her red nose. Hello, Sherrie mumbles to her toes. Good evening, I say flatly, watching Roy studying us closely.

All uh dem taller dan you, Smiley, he chuffs through bulbous lips. This hefty man puffs when he talks. He wheezes in and rocks his bulk on unevenly centred hips. He lengthens his spine two inches on the wind up. He inflates his Dizzy Gillespie cheeks. Then he exhales his speech. So long allyuh mother talking about allyuh reaching. Allyuh know dat? She waiting fuh allyuh long time, yuh know. Allyuh finally come tuh see she.

Finally?

I look up at this man. I look down at Mummy. Down at her four-foot-ten height that seems shorter than when she was in Trinidad. Shorter than when we walked together down Covigne Road, her holding my hand. Her hugging my, even then, higher-placed waist on my taller frame that bears her pear shape. Shorter than when she would take me with her to Kelly's Supermarket on the main road to trail her through the narrow aisles. Me holding the list of groceries to buy. Me being trained at thirteen to become a mother, an abandoned child.

Mummy looks shorter than when she would say Let's take the long way Saturday mornings along the back road to reach Ounce to buy provision. And she taught me how to choose dasheen. How to dig the skin and feel for it be sticky. How to pick callaloo so it wouldn't be too scratchy. How to break cassava and make sure it good, with no black veins rotting the root.

Mummy forgetting, though, to teach me is soft, black, quaily plantain that good to fry. And all her lessons are moot. When an old vendor woman look me in the eye, confused then resigned, when I try to stand up for myself and insist on the firm plantains still half-ripe. Only to cook them and realise why this old vendor woman watch me so. From under sun-shadowed eyes. In that moment I showed I am a motherless child.

Looking down at Mummy in the middle of JFK, after our extended immigration interrogation delay, Mummy seems shorter now than during those Sunday afternoons. When she would sit behind her Singer sewing machine. And talk with me about the past week as she stitched over the chalk lines she'd drawn with the hip rule. She is rounder. And I have grown, too.

After Roy's observation that we finally deigned to come, Ericka's smile calcifies. Her eyes scurry to the beat of her pulse jumping in her neck. Sherrie draws closer to my side and makes a fist to grip my shapeless, navy dress. I press my lips together. I watch our mother. None of us three answer.

Dey does talk? Funny kinda children yuh have here, Smiley. Our mother turns, and she giggles.

I look past the little accompanying shimmy and wiggle. And I see she's fixed her front tooth. The bottom of the incisor no longer has a chip. She's had it mended, just like she once stitched the rip to the front of her buttercup nightie. The pale-lemon cotton gown that split alongside her tooth and lip when my father cuffed her down. To the ground. To the washroom floor, and she'd nearly hit her head on the corner of the washing machine. And she'd slept with me that night, like most nights of the week. I'd woken to Mummy crying on the right side of my twin bed. Before she left. Before she decided that running away alone would be best.

Now we are here. And our mother twirls. You like my dress? As the sky-blue chiffon whirls around her plump thighs. The pink flowers hold my eyes. And I just nod. It's new, she shares. I was saving it to look nice today. My mother doesn't comment on what we wear. No questions, nothing to say.

The rush of people from late-night-arriving flights is dying down. And our gate at JFK quiets in the wake of the departing crowds. Beyond the glass walls is a dome of blackness with pinpricks of light. I am not eager to venture into what looks like unfathomable nothingness stretching to the horizon of sight. Roy twists his girth to peer behind him and intone, Alright, what we standing here doing? It getting late. Whey allyuh bags? Time to go.

Ericka and Sherrie stay mum. I answer what seems like a question unthinkably dumb. We hold only bookbags on our wilting bodies. We did not emerge from our immigration pulling suitcases on a trolley. This is it, I duh.

Roy guffaws. Smiley, dem children didn't bring no clothes wid dem. He looks at her, raises his eyebrows, opens his googly eyes wider, and drops his mouth into an O. He sneers and whisper-shouts only to her, as if her children are not standing close. So, what you gonna do wid dem now?

Our mother doesn't tell Roy how to not speak of her daughters. Our mother's eyes do not spill any water. Our mother does not reinforce the obviousness of there being no luggage, no trolley, no porter. Our mother whisper-shouts her reply to our new uncle in this private conversation of theirs.

This exchange being conducted before our tired stares. Us who've just arrived to regain our mother after seven years. I didn't know dey woulda do something so careless, she declares. They big enough to know tuh bring they clothes. I thought they know. I shouldn have tuh tell dem dat. Our mother says of her children who've escaped from her husband with the clothes on their backs.

Our mother turns to look over her shoulder. Her voice is high. A whip. She curls her thin lips. She turns up her long nose that she always proud say is naturally straight. Her nose that never needed a clothespin at night, a measure she tried to convince me to take. To make it point. Since allyuh get allyuh father flat nose, she'd rejoin. And down the slope of this long nose, my mother asks, Allyuh really en bring anything else wid allyuh? Nuttin, no clothes?

Doesn't she know?

I didn't pack. I could not risk that. And carry suitcases down the hill where our whole paternal family lives still? And have them lean out the windowsill? And ask what we doing with them travel bags we fill? And have them reach inside to pick up their touch-tone and rotary phone and give their brother a trill? And have Ulric speed up Covigne Road, his molten face and spitting mouth issuing pledges to kill. And his sisters and his brothers, our aunts and uncles, going back in their houses after they've spectated their fill.

No. We leave Trinidad without any clothes.

Ericka's voice beseeches, No, Mummy.

I glance at Roy, then look at our mother meaningfully. No. How could we?

At that, our mother turns fully. She drops her shoulders defeatedly and lets her chest expand with an inhalation. She opens her arms, cups her hands, smiles, and moves forward to issue a ten-second hug to her children. To Ericka, then me, and then to Sherrie, who she draws tight and melds into her side. They are the same height. No, it's okay. That's okay. Smile. I'm just happy you'll here. Nod. That's what's important.

Sniffle. That's the most important thing to me in the world. Throat clear. That I have my girls with me again. Blink. I've been praying so long for this day. Synchronised pinched eyes, sigh, and nod. Let's go home. This my mother enacts after her indignation is shod.

Roy takes the lead. Roy limps on sloping New Balance heels. He drops one leg two inches lower, two seconds later than the other. His convex waist rotates on an elliptical axis as he cuts through the parking lot, dodging slow-moving traffic.

Our mother steps quick. Directly behind Roy. Struggling to match his stride, taking second place in this convoy. Mummy's Mary Janes brush the concrete that sends tremors up her thick calves and thighs. I bring up the rear with my scanning eyes. Our mother does not turn around as she hurls, Hurry up, girls. Roy have to go to work. He can't be late. He was nice enough to pick allyuh up from the airport. And then to him, It shouldn't have traffic this hour, right Roy? What way you think we should take?

I listen to the mother, who left us with a man who she say she shoulda never marry, still speaking in this voice that supplicates.

Roy and my mother stop upon reaching a black SUV. It's tall, imposing, bigger than vehicles in my country. Roy slaps the trunk as he circumnavigates his bulk around to the left of his ride. I am confused for a minute about who is going to drive, about why he's going on the wrong side. As Roy settles behind the wheel, our mother climbs up into the passenger seat.

Into the high back seat, Ericka slides, lifting up from the running-board platform first. Sherrie shimmies into the middle. When I drag myself in last and close the door, the night's darkness and the interior's merge. The darknesses surge into the waiting blackness from the airport's glass walls I saw.

I reach over and squeeze Ericka's palm. Her hand is still vibrating. From this morning's breakout from our father and his house, Ericka's hands have not stopped shaking. I stroke Sherrie's head. Its weight resting on my arm. Sherrie is tired, her eyes drooping, ready for bed. All her energy expended from a day of needing to look calm. A day of not drawing attention to ourselves, of not letting our our faces give away our flight. I smile slightly at both of them and meet their eyes. We're here. As I promised my sisters this morning when their eyes welled in fear. We're going to be alright, my touch intimates. I've kept my promise to make sure we safely escaped.

Our mother turns around. At the lack of sound. Angles her body from the front passenger seat. She sees Sherrie leaning on me. Mummy shakes Sherrie's leg, Eh eh, doh sleep. Sit up. Wait till we reach. You have a nice, big, comfy bed waiting for you home. You'll sleep with me, and yuh sisters have they own.

Then Mummy removes her ringed fingers from Sherrie's leg. She puts her hand on the side of Roy's seat instead. And she smiles. She chuckles and replies as if her daughters have spoken with words instead of our eyes. Allyuh so quiet. I thought allyuh was going and have a lot more to say. Tell me about de trip. How was allyuh day?

It is a question I pose to friends when they return from a vacation adventure they're bursting to relay.

Roy starts up the engine but doesn't shift into gear. He keeps his car parked here. And he, too, turns around. He reaches up, flicks a switch. The car's ceiling light turns on. Muted rays of the single bulb shine down. Roy's Cookie Monster eyes travel across our faces. He smirks after he graces us with this inquisitive stare. Roy turns his head to our mother and declares, Yuh know I was planning on yuh children having plenty luggage. And I clean out de back uh de truck fuh dat. But like they didn't need dis big car. Smiley, if you did know, you and them coulda take a taxi instead.

Roy's SUV interrogation light shines like the bulb in the immigration room where my sisters and I had been led. The stark white room we'd been sequestered in with our stomachs rumbling in hunger and dread. The cold, gun-patrolled room in which we were told to have a seat. Detained when we suspiciously didn't arrive with luggage to New York City, our mother to greet.

Our mother draws back on a chortle, twists her lips, scrunches her brow, and playfully shoves Roy's shoulder. Uh chah, she laughs, and turns back to the front. Roy snickers and turns his mass with a grunt. Ericka looks down. Sherrie's vacant eyes stare nowhere. And I shift to look out the postcard window, the dreamed-of arrival photo, waiting for our prayed-for New York home to appear.

This is when Memory rears. Memory grips this postcard picture. And she tears.

Memory has returned. To share. Memory is here. To instruct. Look now through the screened veil of the truck. And see—as displayed on a cinema screen—what I, Memory, need, what I mean you to know.

There was a time before, when you also hoped. When you boarded a plane, bound to go. To wherever your mother called. There was a time before when she summoned and you, loving daughter, did not stall. You answered her invitation, her request. To come . . . to wherever your mother was next. Abandoned girl, you follow, seeking your mother wherever she may be in this world.

But I . . .

Memory does not wait, she hurls. Go, Memory scolds:

I am fourteen years old.

In Grenada. Up in St. Patrick county. Visiting from my home of Trinidad for a week. Visiting for the first time my mother who, for a year, I have not seen.

I am fourteen, visiting my mother's birth country. Where she has planned a festive reunion. A week's holiday together for all her left-behind children.

I am fourteen, permitted this trip. After my father pounded the centre table he then flipped. After my father slammed down the phone on my mother's long-distance call. After my father yanked the cord out the wall. After my father threatened his daughters with his fists. And warned we not going nowhere at all.

I am permitted this trip after my over-six-foot-tall, construction-foreman, girlfriend-spending-all-his-salary father relent. Permitted to see my mother after my father curse his children and yuh-fucking-modda vent.

Permitted, finally, to see my mother again after my foaming-mouth father examines my two younger sisters and my tickets for the plane.

Examines the stapled papers for terrorising hours and days. Upside, downside, in every single way to make sure they contain no secret keys. No discreet visas allowing us to exit the Caribbean bowl. Making sure we stay under his empty-cupboard roof's control.

My father making sure we cannot board an international LIAT or BWIA flight. Making sure we cannot go to Brooklyn where Smiley, my mother, now resides.

My father making sure that we cannot go to New York City, unbeheld. To that cold country my mother lives in after she alone fled.

Now, I am here in Grenada. Here in the isle where my mother left her first child. Here in the country where my mother abandoned her first baby. The village where this first child still lives. The parish where she, with an aunt, resides. Here, meeting an unknown sister for the first time.

Here we are, all five. Each pregnancy with which my mother was fertilised. Including the baby aborted just in time. Another daughter conceived in this isle. All five. Together in the place that sprouted such a mother we have to survive.

And I—while the first priorly unknown daughter is being maligned, while my new older sister is being deemed evil, bitter, and full of spite—drift over to the hill to take in one of Grenada's most famous sights.

From this distance, I cannot hear the last daughter's whine. The last daughter regressing to babyhood with the mother for whom she pines.

With my back turned to the rest of the excursion, I cannot see the third daughter's anxious, flitting smiles. Wanting to be Mummy's favourite, while Smiley ignores her first unloved, silenced child.

While Smiley cuddles the last. And gossips with the third, who eagerly agrees with everything her mother asks. Lest they, too, be forced into the iron mask. Of unfavoured daughter.

While the unborn foetus—with no name, no claim, no face, no trace—remains bound to her mother's past and to this place: Conception Island, as it translates from its original name. Bordered by a sea rendered, to this daughter, unpassable water.

And I—dressed in all denim my mother shipped from Brooklyn to her barrel children, binding care in a cask—step away from the jovial group. The family troupe who boarded Cousin Ashley's bus early this morning for his escorting of all of us. Up, round, and through Grenada's must-see destinations. Sites of familiarity, nostalgia, newness, and recognition for my mother and all her visiting cousins. The dozen she come to see.

The real reason for my mother's trip from Brooklyn turning out to be—her not wanting to miss out on the gathering of her England, Canada, US scattered family. Bringing her children together an addendum after a cousin enquired, And what bout yuh pickney, Smiley. As this cousin laughingly tells me, sitting on the bannister of our holiday verandah filled with family. Generations renting vacation houses on a hill whose name issues this collective's creed, Happy.

And the noise and the rum punch jokes and the cigarette smoke of my mother's cousins getting to me. So I step away. To examine the hill my textbooks say is called Carib's Leap. The hill my soul remembers in agitation, in dreams, in anger, and sorrow deep. The hill over which my remembering spirit shudders, and weeps.

Donning the mermaid-cut, ankle-length denim skirt Smiley sent in the last barrel she mailed from Brooklyn to Trinidad's capital, Port of Spain, I ascend Carib's Leap Hill. Careful not to take a spill among the stones. Those lain for commemoration in lieu of Kalinago bones.

I am fourteen years old. In Sauteurs, Grenada, where my sisters and I have for the first time flown. Here is our treat. With Mummy we get to spend a week. Samantha, Ericka, myself, and Sherrie. And the aborted daughter with no name she carries. All the left-behind daughters of Mummy, spread over two countries. Before Mummy flies back to New York City. We will feast on yellow, saffron-fragrant, woodfire oil down and pigtail at centurial Lake Grand Etang.

Before once more: I am leaving on a jet plane. Don't know if I'll be back again. That song my mother sang.

I am here to walk where it all began.

Finally in Grenada for myself to see. I stand on the hill that witnessed jumpers leap into the open-armed sea. The hill that saw jumpers fly over its steep 340 years before I appear at its ledge. In this town of Sauteurs. Named by the plundering French who made them flee. Named *jumpers* for these Indigenous people who came before me.

I stand on this inherited shelf, peering into the wealth of blue who received undefeated troops and families. My Kalinago ancestry. On Carib's Leap. The hill that keeps hold of their screams, their flails, their dives, their lives. Their dignity.

I am fourteen, here to stand on the cliffside whence ~~Carib~~ Kalinago arms flailed. Here, in the town of Sauteurs to see where my mother was born and raised. And all her mothers who before her came. And the first mother—back centuries, back generations—who before me comes. Travelling the bloodline that for aeons run. To greet me—descended descended daughter—standing in the same millennium sun. Her watching eyes pressed right up. In my space. In my taken-aback face. In my who-is-this-looking-directly-into-and-at-me line of sight. In my field of vision where she is so close I can see the whites surrounding her jet-black pupils intent, silent, focussed.

And the locus of my control slips. And in the swift horizontal tilt, I realise is not only I who longed to see. Not only my desire that drew me. To Carib's Leap. From whose rocky, beach-washed feet she rise. And extends her hand to right my gravitational confusion. Extending a warmth in profusion. Bending her come-with-me head to invite, to walk alongside, to guide. To provide me with sight.

It is she. My mother's mother's mother's mother's mother. Millennium mother of generations. This slender, bronze woman who comes. Before me as I stand in this place. It is she. My mother's mother's mother's mother's mother, with hip-length black hair, flowing waterfall straight. She who will prove to be the base. The beginning. The initial mother.

It is she in my vision, in this visitation that comes purposefully. Comes knowingly, comes familiarly. Comes, called by my questing and rousing curiosity. She pulling me back in time. This mother's mother's mother's mother's mother. Showing me first her eyes, then her whole face. The inceptive mother in whom I will trace the origin of the exponent that is my own.

Smiley, the multiplied, the intensified, nth-power-raised. Smiley, descendant of this first mother bringing me back to this place. This first mother taking me with her to watch Sauteurs before it was so named. With her to see Carib's Leap, before it was so claimed.

It is she, my mother's mother mother mother mother, on whom my time-transported eyes now look.

She who, before the sky alights with French fiery projectiles, cooks. Baking in the yard's semicircle mud oven is her lover's caught lipi and cacador. Tonight, over the feast of fish from this morning's haul, she will tell her husband of her lover. And the fact that he returns her heart, her husband's brother. That she wants him instead, and that he loves her back.

It is what she intends. Before the attack.

Darkness diffuses through the bowels of the tapia hut, made of mud. The hut red as roucou as evening light floods. The sun's withdrawing rays stretching forth its fingers to hold its quarry. To make them stay. Abide with me, gold and pink linger to say. Dirt walls and curved halls turned into a screen for the dawdling sun's display.

She drops the cotton and rattan shawls over the squared-out holes that let in light and air and some reprieve from being a vole in her husband's home. And basks in what she knows. That tonight she will claim the right brother. At last. Then this ajoupa will be the cask in which she seals the obligation she no longer feels.

Smoke ascends to the dome of the marital home where she readies the finishing feast. Along the sides: manioc, cachiman, spinach greens. Heaped on top: spices and herbs adorning the fresh meal prepared the way her beloved likes to eat.

She likes how he eats, with verve. With firm flesh held aloft in his crooked fingers. Its spurting juice shining his lips. Running in drips down his chin. Caught in the trimmed beard there. Whole jaw participating in consuming his catch.

She is his rightful match. This mother's mother's mother's mother's mother giggles aloud. He's hers, she just know. Something just tell her so. Her toned thighs longingly rub while her hands unfold the fig leaves in which she steamed dawn's snatch from the sea. She sighs. Her restless thighs' friction does not relieve the heat, but inflames the suspended dusk waiting to hear her pant his name. It draws her husband's sister's eyes to her before whom she refuses shame.

She hears the sister's snort of disgust. But tells herself she does not feel compelled to use bitter words to reply, nor make any sound in kind. Adoration elevates her state of mind. Who cares, she tosses her straight veil of hair behind her back. And reminds herself not to let her peace be brought under attack. Today is the special day her truth gets declared. Still, Smiley's mother's mother's mother's mother's indignation flares. How dare she be judged. Much less by a sour woman who obviously does not understand love.

She decides to hum.

This foremother pitches her voice higher to drown out the loud sound of that sister's silent frown. To keep at bay the sister's suspicious eyes skittering across the mud-packed floor. The appraising eyes drumming plotting fingers from its chair lair, shadowed along the wall. The squinting eyes stabbing her spinal cord.

Her husband's sister, her lover's sister must prefer her bored in this ajoupa all day. It is true, she could go out to the joined compound among the other women and cut cassava roots. Help prepare seeds for the garden's planting. Participate. Share in the fishing village's tasks. Without being asked. But those high and mighty women's lips—pinched and cast down, and laughing in whispers when her back is turned around—always stay her feet.

Tonight, though, her mind pirouettes, I will be free. For tonight, we will feast. Celebrate hefty canoua loads from the pounding, gushing, deafening deep. Triumph in prizes claimed from aquamarine salty waters that bite, that kiss, that steal. Those velvet waters that slip and slide around paddles and limbs which straddle warm waves with ease.

Rejoice in the yield claimed from those bounteous hills of teal. Those mercurial tidal flows that burn the eyes and clog the nose if one strives to deprive them beyond the gills of one's boat. Take daily only what you need. And go. Her people know. Any more comes with a scourge that urges rafts too far from shore, or down toward the sandy floor. Water watches. Sea remembers. Ocean demands manners at the threshold of her door.

Yes, a fish haul. But how to solve the need to get the men to loiter a while and stall, she ponders. She wonders, walking through the dirt yard to the tall clay oven made hard by the fire that shaped its mound. This mini volcano issuing fragrant lemon and pepper steam bursting out. Crackling flames escaping through the square mouth, south of its peak. The mouth belching heat. Requiring a paddle for food's extraction, requiring her heavy-lidded, dark-iris acous to close to half mast in reaction, to protect her orbs from the blast of steam; her eyes near sealed against the burn from the oven's cooking meat.

What story to tell to quell suspicion from filling their buzzing ichie. What tale to coax these minds of theirs into receptivity. How, she wonders—this base mother filling the calabash bowls with their hot meal—to spring my surprise most effectively? And get them to commemorate her corrected nuptial, unwittingly.

Easy. The thought comes to her, and she smiles in victory. This precursor mother of Smiley's. We will celebrate success. I will, she decides, gaily twirling in her mind as her hands take care to prepare the cassava beer she places at the calabash bowls' sides, speak to my warrior men of my pride. How proud am I of their driving back the white skins to their side of Camerhogne.

Intone pride at my men's six years of battling the vermin plaguing our isle. Battling with arrowheads of sharpened bone and pointed stone, tipped with the poison of our manchineel tree. Arrows they shoot into the backs, the calves of those spurred to flee who would have us heel and resign our lives to their designs. My men's warring resilience through six years of those marauders pushing past the agreed-upon line. Wanting all and every from us and from the Galibi. From the Arawaks and from the Taínos. Our neighbours on surrounding isles our chief visits to learn from in hopes to know how our troopers could collectively get these pillagers to go.

She decides, this progenitor mother of Smiley's, to invoke the worry that chokes the anxious eyes of her village's women, whose sons, fathers, husbands are the frontline against the invasive white skins who would have them writhe under their swords.

These ghost-eye usurpers crawling from aboard their crafts. Creeping up beaches' paths, trying to claim ancestral land as La Grenade. As if our people's nurturing forests, volcanoes, and rivers do not names already have. And inhabitants. And a rhythm and a pulse. A history. Where those filthy white skins only see dirt dug and stripped leaves to fill the bellies of their ships. Greedy maws open near the lip of our land. At the sharp dip in the sand off the coast over which they skulk with steel and gunpowder. Attacking us who would not play host.

To extermination.

No. In determination, Chief Kairouane and his warriors, this Kalinago village, and these Kalinago forebears withstand each attack unleashed. Stand on firm ground and fight destruction of the animals, the flora, the harmony of nature's order that these foreigners wreak upon the land. Succeeding little by little in driving back the death-marchers; them and their insatiable demands. In this there would be much to revel.

Yet,

even while this mother's mother's mother's mother's mother plans this—her people's glory to be her own extolling cover story—black leather boots and muskets, swords and pikes hike from the sea level's west. Over the east's mountain spires. Coming, crushing, setting her land on fire.

Her nose, her ears, her pre-scorched throat do not know this yet. Tonight, Smiley's prototype has a husband to surrender and a beloved to collect.

Singing happily, smile dancing on her narrow mouth, she struts past the cachibou fronds decorating the yard and fencing the house, on another trip to the oven and back. Arms akimbo, she bears more food to the table that the village men carved from the cast-off branches of the mapou. That beautiful wood table she will relinquish when she moves. That long stretch of wood where the family gathers, which dominates the ajoupa, in the centre of the room.

His sister is draped in the gloom of the outside oven's smoke. Smoke drifting through the hut to cloak fading daylight's sharpness. Inside, shadows fall as if there is already night's darkness. Inside, smothering disapproval falls about this mother mother mother mother mother like a shroud hurled. A pall cast over her in the sister's loud silence, bequeathing no words.

She is unbothered, though, Smiley's forerunner mother. Judgement does not cull the flutters in her taut tummy. Hands to her slender waist, she inhales, giddy. At this, the mirroring dusk holds its breath. And she knows the night is hers to orchestrate, to command. In concert, the very atmosphere awaits the arrival of her man.

This waiting is how she accounts for the oncoming tranquillity. The front moving in from the indigo sea. The vacuum of air that precedes the storm's flurry. The evening gone silent. No crickets croon. No throaty calls and no lilting bamboo-flute song of the tree-nesting fou-fou and si-si rou suddenly reticent.

Her neighbours in their own ajoupas dimly muted. Their wicks aglow, gauzy orbs flickering through the cloths sealing their windows. But still. As if it suited every man, woman, and child to lower the volume on their lives. Their pre-sleep ritual denied. The shared compound's unprecedented dumbness clued into the magic of tonight. Supplying her with ceremonial quiet.

She cannot hear, this mock-up mother of Smiley's, anyone over the riot of joy pounding a surf through her ears. This is the night her destined love will be declared.

Antecedent's sinewy knees lock when her husband and her beloved enter. The beads and shells about their lean hips dip and swell. Their chains chime like bells, with the sway of their defined legs bringing in her leading husband's scent of the bush where he must have lain in wait for the large green iguanas over his shoulders draped. Ni lamaha tina, is the second thing her husband takes time to say to her. And his words are confirmed by the growls emanating from his centre.

Laying now, in a rush, the cacao on the table as her last touch, this mother's mother's mother's mother's mother retreats from the feast at which the women will not join the men to eat. She makes her feet clumsy. Their stumble cause her to brush past her beloved's sweat-slick arm. Seconds of calm wherein she allows herself an inhale. A moment to be charmed by aroma of ash that indicates her beloved didn't wait. He came straight from the slash and burn of the field the women will, in due season, seed. Which proclaims, he must have the same eager need.

The bows the menfolk are shedding stay strung. But their day's-done arrows are un-nocked. Their spears and clubs being set to rest in the walls' bend will rise again at the crow of tree-roosting cocks. Exhaling, she rocks back on her heels. All are at ease.

Against man or beast, she trusts the defence of their lives to the knives her men now put aside to walk their bare feet over to her laid table to eat. To dine on the sumptuously prepared feast. To dine on the health of the land, on the gifts of the sea. On the message she, stepping backwards from the table to the shadows to watch the working warrior men eat, is communicating.

Her husband's sister glares, baiting her, Smiley's predecessor, to look where her wiry outraged figure stands strong and tall along the other wall. But this mother's mother's mother's mother's mother is waiting. Waiting for her husband's brows, now lifting. Querying how is it his brother's favourite meal of cassava wrapped in fig leaves, and his haul of lipi from the sea that you've worked all day to prepare and serve. And not my hunted agouti meat I, your husband, prefer.

Oh, yes. Now it's her turn. Satisfaction, salivation positively churns. To slake her husband's questioning by laying claim to that which she is entitled. To fun. And to the fanciful. To the person who gives her days purpose, so vital. At long last. All these months of discretion relegated to the past. By running off. By joining her beloved in a new life. With her now as his forever wife.

She steps forward, Smiley's forerunner, from the wall's bracing side into her husband's line of sight. Her life begins now. She smiles. She opens her mouth. And a whistle pierces twilight.

The sun reverses course to puncture descending night. Orange, yellow, red bursts into the compound's dusk. Brightness thrusts through the curtains' veil meant to keep out mosquitoes' whine and frogs' sonorous bass that would upstage the speech which has raged in her chest every time her husband's balata skin pressed into hers.

Feet outside pound the dirt. Frantic. Distraught shouts. A second whistle whirls. Another crash. Another flare. Wild screams now. Crackling blares. A whoosh of air, consumed, as sounds of fattening flames penetrate the room. Alarms raise in the gloom.

Her husband and her beloved immediately rise. They push the food aside. They stride from the table to leave her feast. To dress again in weapons to meet the threat that has found them yet. Despite their treks through the woods to the encamped shores every day. Despite their labour, their strategising, their battling to keep those white evils at bay. Their scratches, their cuts, their bruises, their losses. Now at the door of their village. No matter how they tirelessly fight to stave off pillage.

These men. Hearts in their girded hands, guarding what those aliens would take from them. The land where they grow ornamental acayou, fragrant papaya, medicinal karata, and their young to whom is promised inheritance of their own island ever after. Their home. Where they call out to the sun and dance for the rain. Where they weave cloth, feather crowns, sculpt, sing, paint. Where they thrive in the way of their ancestors whose bones they glorify. Among whom they will come to lie.

These men—keepers of their culture, the earth, their archipelago friends—hustle through the exit to attend the savagery hunting them.

But no. How can they go? She protests. How can they both leave to run into the inferno, into the rising heat. She has not said her piece. She vaults onto the back of her beloved and drops her forehead between his shoulder blades. Stay. With me.

Disbelief widens the eyes of the man from whom she won't be pried, not in this life, as he turns to unclench her fingers. That clamp. Her own pleading eyes grow damp. She stamps his face onto her mind as she feels someone tugging her from behind.

That voice, dripping with derision, at the base of her skull. That disgusted sister of theirs who tugs. And pulls her grip free from the shoulders she clutched to keep her lover with her. To feast. Noooo. Pitched high, tremulous, an ascending wail. They have gone through the door into the night made day.

And she has not yet had her say.

Projectiles rain. A deluge now. The sister—so strong, so assured, always so bossy—commands she behave like she knows how. Lift her head from its tear-streaming bow. And act. She has responsibilities, remember.

Her weeping, her wringing hands, her immobility, this mother's mother's mother's mother's mother's descent into grief has no space to be centre. Selfish she is called. Without tact. Without grace. Pushed to the window. Look! See what's assaulting your ears. Look at our people. Watch our place. Villagers running. Wide mouths screaming. Fear. Animals skittering from widening flames licking thatched roofs that will not house them again here.

Come now, their sister scolds. Their armed men venturing forth to fight. Some women, too. The children of the village amassing needed provisions, treasured possessions. The communal collections for withdrawal into the forest and evasion to higher ground they must undertake tonight. Come, help pack. Help fight. Help gather the young, the old, the infirm, the pregnant out of sight. Out the path of arcing fire strikes.

But she does not listen. This Smiley's pattern. She does not join the women. Her beloved is out there. She wants only to be with him. Where he is. Not up a distant mountain. Not hiding in a dense forest. She closes her ears to that sister of theirs. Does not hear. Does not care. Does not see her responsibility. Does not taste the smoke wending its way up the trees. Does not smell the inferno's roar. Not any more.

It is 1654.

And the French have brought their filth to Sauteurs' shore. "Discovering" Grenada, driving all the Indigenous away. So they story say. That's a lie. We didn't all die.

Seeds survive to rebirth through time.

Spin the compass needle. Pivot on the grid's line. Stand with me in Sauteurs, at Carib's Leap cliffside. At fourteen, this hill I climb knows me. Has pulled me 340 years through dreams, through visions, through the coming of she to show me. Through genetic memory. Called from primary school textbooks showing a last stand that resonates in my remembering belly. To come be where my mother mother mother mother mother shed this life. And her responsibility.

She calling: Crystalline waters at the foot of these rocks, embrace me. She gathers speed, summons courage. Grows wings at the cliff's top. Daughter, hide under the eaves, secreted in the walls of the silk cotton tree. Her last words to her child before she does not stop.

My beloved is gone. And without him, I cannot be.

Head over feet somersault. Crescendoing blasts of exploding glass resound through the air as she vaults.

Behind her, fires caught in charring fences. Trees extinguish brightly under barks' burnt defences. Forest's released soul leaps across the sky that weeps.

Waves over her grave. She is free.

Oh! Did we not mention she had a child by this time already? This mother's mother's mother's mother of Smiley. A young one this mother leaves alone to survive and find a way amongst her people escaping French slaughter? The little one this mother leaves to thrive, barely weaned, without her. The dependent one this mother left to strive in the reduced quarters in which the Kalinago—owners of

Camerhogne, now marginalised—are forced to get by since colonisers bought the rights. Purchased the deed to their flourishing country with bottles of fancy brandy.

So they say.

But I am there that day. That night. The night on which a civilisation fled for their embattled lives. The night on which a proud people would not die. The night on which their strength would not break, nor bend. The night their pride would not be quenched before the guns of the French.

The night on which this mother mother mother mother mother chose to follow her heart. And left the child she does not spotlight, in any part of her delivered dream, to me. The feast is the important reveal to she who cooked, baked, and steamed the cassava, the kingfish, the carite, to declare her vows publicly. The ones she makes under the sea.

It is the hill who shows me the daughter cowering in the folds of its silk cotton tree. It is Hill who speaks, Camille turn your eyes, peek under the leaves. You see? The tucked-in daughter wrapping skinny arms around her knees.

12

SEA ALMOND TREE

I am twenty.

I am in my head. I am at a crossroads; the light is red.

And on this arrival night, in New York City, sitting behind my mother in Roy's car, I do my best to hide. I do my best to stay the tide. To keep the sorrow spilling out my eyes from being shared. With them.

I do my best not to sniff. I do not want even a whiff of that foetid, something-rotting, New York smell coming through the windows travelling further up my nose.

I do not want the city lights to refract off the water in my eyes. I don't want my two sisters, also in the back, to know. What they may not yet see. These sisters of mine who I retrieved from a house of hell. My sisters, who I delivered safely to their mother, who made me theirs when I was twelve.

I sit behind this mother, who I've been keeping the faith to see these seven years. And blink back tears.

Keep the faith, this mother said to me. The phrase I'll hold on to for seven years. Till Mummy finally sends for us. Seven years until my sisters and I get our secret Green Cards processed. Though Mummy's Brooklyn father applied for ours at the same time that he applied for hers. But Mummy didn't think that all us leaving was for the best. Seven years before I'll put that phrase to rest.

I sit behind my mother who I've been keeping the faith to see these seven years. And blink back tears.

This mother who for seven years I wrote a letter to every week. When her husband wouldn't give us enough money for clothes, for books, to go out, for food to eat. When her husband keep all his construction foreman salary to pay for his girlfriend of the month. From out the allyuh doh need no money, doh be greedy, how much more allyuh chirren want pittance our father dropped into our hungry hands, I made sure I bought writing pads, envelopes, ballpoint pens, and stamps.

When our father wouldn't let us speak to Mummy on the phone, I wrote. Like Mummy made me promise to do after she go. Five, six, seven pages, front and back, full of script. Full of how bad it is here, full of how much we lacked, full of how much my Mummy I missed. Letters full of longing for love and to hug her in person. Full of how lonely I was, of how much I was hurting.

Pictures of what we looked like now. Pictures of me in the leopard skirt and the blouse she sent in her last barrel. A stuffie baby Simba I bought in town, hugged and sprayed with my perfume, wrapped, and sent her in a parcel. This stuffed lion I sent for her birthday with a card that I kissed after I wrote, See you soon. Simba will keep you warm in winter and you can put his head on your belly and he'll hear the funny noises instead of me, Mummy. I love you, too.

Seven years of stopping at the post office after school. Seven years in that dusty, grey Diego Martin main road building under the ceiling fans' cool. Seven years of being recognised by the postal workers who watched me address my letters and intercept any my mother sent. Intercepting hers before they were delivered to the mailbox in case Ulric decide to take them for minding his own children rent. Our father stealing the postal money orders in the envelopes that Mummy sent us to cope. The little bit of money she mailed to help buy our uniforms and food in an empty-cupboard home.

Seven years that I didn't have my mother come to parents' day at school. To see me perform on the hall stage, or march for sports day. Or to set any rules. Any boundaries about who could just walk in and through our house. Parental rules of care about the days and nights I partied and petted just to get out.

Seven years.

And now I am here. We are. Her children who survived her violent husband to make it back to her. Her children she now allowing a new uncle to jeer at. Her children on behalf of whom she will not infer—why we have no clothes.

I wonder at this mother.

This mother who sits in repose in Roy's front seat. This mother who has forgotten how she not-packed to leave. How, for weeks before her flight, she'd subtly shifted around her stacks of folded clothes. How, from the wooden closet my father built, she stealthily extracted any garments better suited for New York's November cold. The attire she would take. How, in the rough-hewn closet he never varnished that they shared, my mother had to arrange and rearrange. My mother had to manipulate her side. So my father wouldn't notice anything missing from her slender piles.

I wonder how this mother doesn't remember that she confided in me, her not-first daughter. How she whispered about storing the few outfits she would sneak out with inside the barrel her own mother sent from Canada. Hiding these cold-weather clothes under special-occasion satin sheets we never used. Under gifted assemble-it-yourself stuffies she never sewed. Hiding her new-life clothes under other items for the household. Knowing, since my father never bothered himself wid dem kinda ting, they were concealed and she'd be good to go.

I wonder at this mother who chooses to forget she had no suitcase for her trip. That it was a blue, white, and red crocus market bag that wouldn't draw any notice that she held in her fleeing grip. Ulric wife could just be going in town to get some shopping done. No neighbours, none of his surrounding family members should pay any attention to our mother venturing out, not on the run. This mother with one big handbag and a zippered shopping sack in her hands. This mother escaping the man she left her three young girls alone to withstand.

I wonder that this woman doesn't recall how she run from Trinidad. How she worked so hard on her singular Green Card. While filling my twelve-year-old ears with endless talks at the side door about how Yuh father so bad.

I wonder at this mother who chooses not to recollect how she shrouded her whole journey in secrecy. How she burdened her children, but especially me. Hours and hours-long conversations plotting how she would leave. Because she couldn't take any more, while I had to offer this mother comfort without ever asking What about me. What about Ericka and Sherrie.

Now Yolande—Cyatrine for Catherine in Trinidad, Smiley to her Grenadian family—sits, no she preens, in Roy's front seat. This mother who when finally having her children to hold decides to ridicule. This mother who decides to play up to another man and make her daughters look like fools.

Like we schupid for not taking all our clothes. When this woman should know that we wouldn't have even made it down Covigne Road. Burdened with clothes. Not without every single man jack alerting our father. A-A, Ah see yuh big daughter and dem wid some heavy grip. Yuh en tell meh allyuh was travelling. Whey allyuh going fuh allyuh trip?

Is this what this mother would rather? Our father being alerted and keeping us prisoner in his house? Maybe it wouldn't matter. After all, this mother already got out.

And, besides, the clothes are gone. The sheets, the pillows, the towels, some sandals and all. To sea. Literally.

Those piece-a, piece-a bags of clothes weren't easy for me to carry. Incrementally. Down to Carenage. Down to the beach. Down to the lip of the ocean. But it had to be done.

Down through the crowds who gathered, the swimmers who scattered. And got out. The women who collected their children with Come here now! shouts. Obeah, they whispered. Black magic, they mumbled. As they bundled their snacks and backpacks and got out the way, lest jumbie descend and attack. Obeah woman, they surmised. Noting my head tied in Spiritual Baptist style.

Madness, those beachgoers muttered. Noting that every day, as I stood in the sea almond tree shade while I dumped a whole wardrobe into the waves, I prayed. Let us be able to go, please. Let us get away. Let the embassy grant our Green Cards. Let this be over today, tomorrow, this week. I can't hold on any more. Our father's house is filled with trash people and their gore and weed and nothing to eat.

To get something, you have to give up something. To balance the scales, you have to remove some weight. To stay afloat and sail safely to another shore, detritus must be jettisoned. To fly, to be unmoored means sacrificing that which you've outgrown, that which should be left behind. Peel the skin, strip the binds, and prove, in a big gesture, your clean break from all that's held you before. I don't remember the genesis of this philosophy I live by, but I know it works. I knew it at that shore.

At nineteen, under the Sea Almond Tree, standing by the sea, dumping beloved diaries, childhood picture albums, teddy bears, jewellery, I showed we were ready to leave. Blue candles and incense in the first corner of Melchizedek Church at the feet of a statue of Mary, syncretised over Yemoja, great sea mother of the so-called seven African powers, were not working for me.

Visit after weekly visit for two years to the US embassy on my own, while Ericka and Sherrie were at school and our father was at work. Visit after visit every week when my mother cried and said she couldn't send any more processing money and for harassing her I was made to feel like a jerk. When she threw tantrums and bawl, what more they want from me, blood? And my aching head would fall and my hot throat would flood.

Visit after visit alone when my mother stopped taking our phone calls because this application business was stressing her out. Visit after weekly visit to the embassy by myself to line up in the hot sun in dark clothes and pray my father don't drive through the roundabout.

Visit after weekly visit, except when my terror and finally-diagnosed milk allergy landed me in a hospital bed. Week after week with no resolve. When no after no, more after more requirements, was all the embassy said.

I went to the water. I threw it all.

I entered a contract with the sea who, when I return to Trinidad eighteen years later, will rise to reclaim me.

Seven days after the final purging, seven days after the clothes-throwing was done, the more friendly one of the consulate officers compiled our police reports, our chest X-rays, our mother's proof of above-the-poverty-line employ, and all the papers that showed the ways my sisters and I would be good immigrants to the United States. She stamped a red "Approve" across our files. At her booth, I openly cried. She touched my hand through the slot and smiled.

I was finally going home to Mummy. To my mother. To my new life.

13

POMERAC TREE

I am twenty.

It is the black of night. I am in the day I leave Trinidad, the day in New York City I arrive. I am in my mind. I am at an intersection. Under road signs.

And there, in the jeep, my mother in the front seat, where I am seated behind, Memory is unspooling her scroll. Before my eyes. Memory her parchment unrolls. That tells no lies.

In the jeep, Memory, my history unfolds. Memory calls her roll. First up in her assembly line, Memory checks attendance for Smiley. That mother of mine. This mother who, when she left me, is only cornflakes and milk on which I fed for long, empty months I pined.

I—on whom Memory shines her spotlight—standing under fragrant, fuchsia-flower Pomerac Tree in Granny yard. Pomerac Tree with whom my dripping, shirt-seeping tears aren't barred. Pomerac Tree who doesn't scold me to done all the deep weeping I cried. Anguished I that my mother was no longer by my side.

In her white lab coat, Memory litmus paper tests this mother's bloodline. Memory recalls the origin I travelled to see through time. Memory bangs her gavel and pronounces a legacy of mothers who does leave. Women who does conceive and does abandon all they child.

Memory denounces: there is Smiley. That mother of mine. Camille, Memory chides, she deserted each and every daughter of hers. All five.

See—says Memory—in Smiley, that first mother's mother's mother's mother's mother's way of choosing. In concentrate. See in Smiley the continuation of the choices that first mother make. From that first revealed mother, the beginning of the traits Smiley chooses to replicate. Chooses, Memory restates. A mistake, Memory orates, a mother does not enact upon consideration. A mistake, Memory narrates, is not made through deliberation. Nor by volition. With knowing intention. A mistake, Memory firmly communicates, is not etched into repetition.

At the judge's bench, Memory not done with her attestation.

Then there is Theresa, Smiley's mother. She who discarded her own mix of sons and daughters in her time. Theresa who—before the spirits of the bottle throttle her will to leave Grenada and roam like she used to, restless, haunted, without a home—dragged her different-father children from pillar to post. And left her children to come back and go. From Windrush England, to Canada, chasing a man and a job. Back to Grenada. In embarrassing poverty. To another needed partner. Hunting love. Refusing ever to be alone. Theresa who has the same birthday as Smiley's own.

And before Theresa, there is her mother: Elvira. The Carib woman. She a descendant of the original Amerindian people in our isles. This Carib woman who, too, went away from Theresa when her daughter was but a child.

And looking all the way back. I see, says telescope-peering Memory. The mother mother mother mother mother, the antecedent, who jumped from Carib's Leap. Into the sea's deep. This origin shedding flesh the night of the colonisers' attack. Diving to her death, not to fight. Not to courageously withstand French ruthless might. But taking flight, taking her life, because without her beloved she could not face the night. Here, Memory pulls out her marker to highlight. Dons her black-framed glasses and peers over the frames with bright eyeballs white. My dear, Memory sonorously talks, she left her daughter to hide in Silk Cotton Tree roots' towering walls. Memory baulks. She left her daughter—in her deserting path—to follow and fall.

Should she—Memory draws a crossroads fork on her blackboard in chalk—so choose to walk . . .

14

BOIS CANOT TREE

I am twenty. Just touch down in New York City.

I am in my new life. Which, for seven years we wait to arrive. Whatever, it's okay, it'll be alright. This is just the first night. We with Mummy. When Roy gone, it'll come back easy. Let's just reach home. Where we'll all sit down and stretch out and finally be alone. It's okay. It'll be okay. We'll hug Mummy and talk and tell her everything when we get off the road. We here, after we pray. This is just the first day. With our mother, who for so long we wait.

Our mother who now says, Girls, we gonna make a stop on the way. We'll get some Mickey Dee's and sit together and eat when we get home. That'll be nice, right?

What? That was me. Why?

Ent you'll hungry, she says. Like fast food is a given in that condition. Continuing her conversation with, I know I am. Is a long day for me. I tired. You'll get something to eat on the plane, right? I make sure allyuh tickets come with a meal.

Ericka replies, We did, Mummy.

Just a snack, answers Sherrie.

Well, we'll stop off and get some burgers, some fries, a few sodas, even some ice cream milkshakes. That'll full allyuh up tuh sleep tonight. Anything allyuh want. My mother glances into the back seat and her generosity is compounded in the smile she flaunts. And you too, Roy. Thanks for taking such good care of me and my girls. My treat. My mother takes time with the latter to be sweet and say.

Roy snuffles a laugh, Smiley, yuh know I could put away.

Roy's princess passenger turns her head his way, pouts like a two-year-old. Then smirks and titters, I know. The streetlights glitter on her grin. Trust me, I know, she says again. Yuh fuhget I live wid you a few years ago.

Such a cosy sealing of intimacy between them in this SUV's front row.

Our mother looks out the windscreen, So whenever we see de next one. This McDonald's that the two in the front seats are proffering as so much fun.

Roy doesn't leave her waiting. It have a drive through on de right when we cross de next light. Yuh want tuh pull up dere? Dey quarter pounders does be nice. Yuh ever try their own, Smiley? She nods, this Mummy, confirming having been at the particular branch Roy speaks of so excitedly. Aren't all this franchise's fake plastic from the same factory?

Or, he says, We could do de bigger one about fifteen minutes down de road. Of course his fat ass would know. Probably have a memorised map to show where each and every McDonald's locate. A map of Ronald clowns across the whole a New York State. In which I will not now nor ever partake. And when—twenty years after this trip to McDonald's—Roy's head hits the tiled floor of a Mickey Dee's, it will be too late. Too late to save the body that quit. Too late to intercede with the amputated toes on both feet, with the raging diabetes and kidney disease that ravished it. Roy's head will bounce and split. He will die in a branch of McDonald's where he hop-drop-flop up to the counter for a meal, something nice to eat exactly twenty years after he and my mother park under the golden arches to buy their treat. To nourish three girls who just pulled off the feat of running for their lives. To New York City, to a mother who wants to give us junk food the day we arrive.

I'll just wait till we get to your apartment, is my declaration to this McDonald's invitation. Ericka ventures the same, Mummy, we'll be fine until we reach home. We will wait. My mother's children who have flown for seven hours. After being up at dawn for showers. And dressing in school uniforms. And acting like this day not out of the norm. While saying goodbye to our home country. Secretly. To be greeted by a mother who offers us Mickey Dee's. Us children she has not seen. Us children with whom she has not been. Us children on whom she is not keen.

Well, this mother states. Girls, iz dat or nothing. I didn't cook today.

Ericka glances away. Sherrie returns her head to lay on my shoulder. And I ponder. When the fuck did McDonald's become food? And your children now coming up from Trinidad and that's what you do. It don't occur to you to cook no food?

McDonald's tried to set up shop in Trinidad. Our country where is either home cooking or purchasing our own real cuisine that don't resemble the sad, indistinguishable shapes McDonald's does issue and bold enough to say is good food on which to chow down. The franchise ventured one branch, in the middle of town. In bustling Independence Square. It lasted one year. McDonald's had was to fold up and return to the US.

We like nourishment that don't make us guess. Trinis, who home-cook most of our meals, didn't like the taste of McDonald's sour ketchup when ours is sweet. We didn't like their flat patties of ambiguous meat. We didn't like their fries when ours are cut from real vegetables, wedge style. We didn't like their junk, and so we didn't buy.

This mother hadn't been in Trinidad when McDonald's had pushed its way into our isle. She hadn't been present for a lot. And apparently the information she did receive she conveniently forgot. Like the fact that I spent one whole year of my teenage life in and out of being warded at Port of Spain General Hospital. Spent years at clinics and private doctor visits across every parish and throughout the capital. Spent a whole year succumbing to illness and fear of a mysterious condition no specialist could diagnose. Not until one homoeopathic practitioner was able to determine that cow's milk is at the centre of my medical woes.

And now this wutless woman want to propose that we have buns, and shakes, and cheese, all laden with poisonous-to-her-child dairy. Because, hey, you know what would be a splendid feast? Manufactured junk of which we should be wary. Yes, some shitty dollar menu trash should go a long way, don't you say, to soothing the stupefaction of your youngest child. Soothing the still trembling of your middle daughter who was petrified just this morning. Before the sun even rise.

Your children terrified of getting caught by the man in whose beat-his-wife-black-and-bloody hands you left your own damn daughters. So yes, feed us now cows delivered to slaughter just like the children you abandoned to an abuser when you fled alone across Caribbean waters.

This mother now munificently offering us McDonald's hamburger goodness with a smile. After we have just arrived. After we just escaped with our lives. This is her treat. She has not cooked for our deliverance to her. We will have no hot meal. I will not eat.

I turn from looking out the window in this jeep. I turn from the sour smell of rubbish and pollen from strange trees. I turn from New York's darkness to stare at the back of this mother's head now facing me. I turn to take in the sight of this elevated uncle's face, awash in a flood of red light behind the wheel. And the pupils of my eyes turn inside. Turn the key.

The pupils of my eyes draw back the curtains across the cinema screen. To let me see.

Memory comes here insistently to me. In the gloom, Memory comes near to make me now undeniably see. Through the dark, starlit tunnel of the windshield, Memory streams. Painting projected images with focussed beams. Memory, dear to me. Here to share with me. Seating me before a cinema screen.

Remember, Camille. What you have seen . . .

And I am twelve again, hearing Mummy scream. A grown woman shrieking like a banshee in the middle of the afternoon. A grown woman uncaring her children are being brought into melee we cannot process. A mother unconcerned that she making us stressed. Making her children embarrassed and stand out from the rest. A mother apathetic to her cause and effects. That we would never want to show our face again after she make a mess of an easy lime. A woman making her children stand outside. Ousted from the familial space. After our mother just behave like she insane in Granny place.

I am twelve, carrying crying Mummy up the hill, who cannot hold up, it seems. Lifting her heavy body, passing watching Mr. Bois Canot Tree. Mr. Bois Canot who studies me and rubs his *shhhkkshhh* scratchy, open-fist leaves to hush my heart that hiccups and grieves. As I nearly stumble under the floundering burden that nobody comes to relieve. Me hefting Mummy after she fight and bite in Granny house, and now on me leans.

I am twelve again, sitting on those cushioned seats in the living room after we trek and reach, watching Mummy suddenly reanimate and become upbeat. Watching as she positively beams, launching into this story that she repeats. Telling her story of bacchanal-bawling-family-cussing Tanty Louisa to Ericka and Sherrie, who smile unsure and sweet. And me asking, Is she mad. Me asking: Why? Asking how she could behave so. Asking. And Mummy sighs.

I doh know what tuh tell yuh. I can't take this much more. The embassy, I just . . . and I had to send and ask yuh Aunty Ann for money again to pay fuh de . . . and I worried about allyuh.

At this, Mummy adopts an attitude that reflects I-am-sombre. She deflates her breastbone and drops her shoulders. What gonna happen to allyuh when I leave? Who going tuh take care of allyuh? She says this directly to me, quietly. Entreating me to relate on a special, grown-up level of intimacy. She can't say too much in front of Sherrie. Her youngest baby. Who doesn't yet know her Mummy is forging a plan to leave.

Mummy drops to her knees in front of me, whispering. Promise me you'll keep yuh sisters safe for me. And that you'll write me all the time. I going to buy a stack of writing pads, envelopes, and stamps and put them up fuh when I get through. Yuh know I going to have to leave right after de embassy finally give me de Green Card, right?

Mummy holds my hands tight, still talking low, And you'll remember everything I teach yuh? No, I not worried. You don't forget anything.

Indeed. I, Camille, forget nothing.

Mummy's engagement and wedding rings dig into my palm. She repeats, No, I not worried. I know you'll take good care of my babies. I nod. My throat burns and bobs. I don't want Mummy's Green Card to come through yet. I don't want to be left. But Mummy speaks like she'll get through in the coming weeks. Like her Green Card should have been issued already. And she getting antsy at the suspense.

My sisters watch from their chairs. Out of focus of this lens. They look on as Mummy hugs me, sniffling. Her eyes are full. Her voice trembling. Mummy now crying. Mummy now earnest in quantifying. I know is juss for a little while. We'll be apart only for a little while. But we'll talk on de phone all de time. I'll buy phone cards. And we'll send letters and pictures, right? Allyuh will be alright. Mummy says to me. Looking at her Bambi eyes, I blink rapidly. And nod once more as Mummy's entreaty implores.

She sprinkles salt in my heart's sore. And allyuh have allyuh whole family around here. They mightn't like me too much right now. But daz still allyuh grandmother and aunts. Juss, juss hold on fuh me.

Hold on to the family Mummy make sure and cuss out. Before she leave.

And, lastly, into my ear, separately, my mother whispers her mantra: Keep the faith. The refrain my mother does state. The phrase to my weary, seeking-love heart this mother donates. The secret declaration my mother uses to placate, to consolidate my soul. The one she breaks. To pieces. As she goes.

Seven years. From a child to an adult. From thirteen years old to twenty. Head of the household my mother left to me, her not-first daughter. The first daughter of my mother is her first child she deserted long ago in Grenada.

Seven years. Through humiliations and cellulitis infections and hospitalisations and my digging for money in town-people's dirt under increasing desperation. And my being tardy at school and developing a don't-care reputation. And my partying and being solicited by big, hard-back men seeking a child with no home supervision.

Seven years. Of cut phone lines and Mummy saying, I working hard in Brooklyn, writing does take too much time. And us children pleading When, Mummy, when? Daddy only buy us two school uniform shirts again. And he not giving us money for groceries when he taking all his salary to party and spend. And Daddy bringing in his girlfriends and their drinking, smoking, drugging family and them. And we have no home. And Daddy telling us if we don't like it we could go.

Seven years. Through which my mother reiterates, Keep the faith.

That useless, deceitful phrase of my mother's that my writing down thirty years later dissolves me into a geyser flooding my carpet with tears. I was a child, my mascara-running reflection shares.

And, as a child, this phrase, uttered in the living room with Mummy kneeling before me, is one to which I adhere. This phrase Mummy knows I need to hear. The phrase with which I tuck myself into bed at night, convincing myself Mummy cares. As Mummy prepares to leave.

As my ripping soul grieves. As Mummy sings, I'm leaving on a jet plane. Don't know when I'll be back again. So kiss me and smile for me. Tell me that you'll wait for me. Hold me like you'll never let me go.

This phrase my mother turns into a joke.

Keep the faith. Is the manipulative phrase with which Mummy punctuates the end of her private talks with me. For my sake. Togetherness to imitate. As she dumps and offloads. And buries her negativity in my throat.

As Mummy overshares and orates. As she talks about how much she hates Daddy. Who her mind tell her not to marry. And talks about Daddy's women and how he so cheap. And the woman who daily calling, and the outside daughters Daddy does mind and keep. And talks about Daddy nasty hygiene. And talks about the violence in this man she choose to marry. And talks about Daddy's every fault that requires her alone to flee. And talks with me about where our birth certificates and important documents are tucked away. And talks about how to mother her ten- and seven-year-old daughters when she boards her non-return flight on BWIA.

And talks, this mother, not about the concerns of her not-first daughter. About how my lymph vessels are already bursting under the strain. And how the tears my body cries have already begun to interiorly drain. Past their walls. Leaking fluid past the lymphatic channels of a vascular system that cannot hold them all. And I am developing bilateral primary lymphoedema. With no source medical professionals can determine as the originator. Them not knowing the diagnosis that is the weariness of Atlas showing in a growing twelve-year-old girl. Who cannot shoulder the world.

Outside, in the confines of this black SUV on this long Queens to Brooklyn ride, this mother's hands flutter like moths at Roy's side. This mother choosing to simper to a man in laughs and giggles and high-frequency squeaks. My ears want to fold in on themselves, horrified. A country away from Luvern, a whole plane ride, and my assaulted eardrums again have to abide another woman smarming from a man's front seat. Another woman choosing not to speak.

My consciousness wants to cringe back into the jeep. To be present with my set-adrift sisters in the back seat. They need me.

But unfurling has begun in my mind. Like the curls of a peeling orange rind.

My mother's voice reaches from outside. Still chatting with Roy. Not to my sisters, nor I. And the rivers on my face evaporate and dry. My tears seep back beneath their permeable riverbed. Mere damp now, reflecting the streetlight's red.

Seven years, I begged. Seven years I counted down time, in phone cards we had no money to buy, and TSTT phone bills run up too high, and Daddy cussing and threatening my sisters and I, and phone locks, and disconnection, and cut phone lines. Seven years of my suspended life that my mother took to next year, next-month-fuh-sure, next week, just now, any-day-now finally file.

I look out the windshield past my mother in the front seat. Over her teased-up, straightened hair. The woman who left me for seven years. Before she cared. Before she dared believe our pleas, we need to come now. Because, my mother vows, I tought he would treat allyuh good. Ulric always sayin how much he love his chirren.

How?

How did, how could, this mother believe? This mother who would tell me that the man she chose to marry will one day put her in her grave. That Ulric will kill her through the cuffs, and the kicks, and rapes. If she didn't escape. How then did this mother believe? How did this mother perceive? How did this mother conceive that her husband could or would love and care for his daughters three?

She didn't.

She knew!

What she was leaving us to. She knew what she was leaving us to do. She knew what she was leaving us to go through. What she made us endure, too. She knew. And she left. By and for herself. She choose.

I thought he would treat allyuh good, keep the faith, we'll be together again soon, I love you—is just words that she told me. A child. At thirteen. Then for seven years. Repeatedly. From safe overseas. While her children experienced what she put us through. Purposely.

After my mother secretly told a thirteen-year-old girl she'd be alone in this world. To lovingly make me prepared. So she said. After my mother left her three daughters in Trinidad with the man who she feared would take her life. After my mother left me at thirteen to mother an eleven-year-old and an eight-year-old, near-catatonic child.

In the back seat of the jeep, truth creeps. Down the column of my spine. From my turned-inside eyes. I am apprised.

All this time, my mother lie.

She chose to leave. She chose to dispense with responsibility. She chose this as her way of being free. She chose to desert us, to be unfettered, like the un-mother she will always be. My mother chose to abandon her daughters three. Eight years old, eleven, and thirteen. My mother chose for us the grave that she flee. In the house where she could not safely be. My mother chose, knowing. My mother chose going.

Just like she chose to desert her first child in Grenada. Pretending all the while that I am her first daughter. This is the modus operandi of this mother. This is my insight, unsmothered by keeping the faith. By yearning to see a mother who did not run to the airport arrival gate.

And I do not bother to read the street names. On this drive to Brooklyn from JFK. I do not look out the window at my new home and store mental freeze-frames. I do not talk kindly to this mother to whom we came. My eyes do not warm when, in her apartment, she stares into my face.

I am not the same.

I am not my sisters. Who call this mother Mummy and repeat how much they missed her. Who kiss her.

I resist her.

I am twenty years old. And there are times ahead of me wherein for shelter, for documentation, for food this mother controls access to—just like the husband who she chose does do—I will be forced to tell this woman I love you. But, in the new uncle's jeep, on this day that we finally reach, it's the last time this obligatory speech will ever be true.

We arrive in June. For three months, my hard eyes watch this mother before—during one of the fun outings she takes my two love-you-Mumsy sisters on, working purposely to break our bond, wanting always to be the only one, my sisters allowing their bullying mother to between us come—I dig up this mother's envelopes that store her waitress-tips cash in her chest of drawers.

A summer season.

I come to see. This woman never love me.

Click. The brass lock springs free.

I live with this woman for one, two, three. Three months before my soul says no more, Camille. No more. Run away. Three months before my soul hails a taxi. And heads for JFK.

ACKNOWLEDGEMENTS

INCITING INCIDENTS

Thank you to my soul who—at life's precipice—spoke and reminded me of this incarnation's goal, then made me obey when I tried to run away.

To the music that powerfully, powerfully, powerfully summoned my soul and the memories and perspicacity it holds, thank you:

"The Journey" by Chris "Tambu" Herbert; "Buss Head" by Bunji Garlin and Machel Montano; "Feel The Love" by Freetown Collective; "The Struggle" by Bunji Garlin; "Tanti Woi" by Blaxx; "Drift Away" by Dobie Gray; "Hallelujah" by Leonard Cohen.

Thank you to Florida's guardian trees and listening seas, who opened me up to writing honestly.

THE BOOK DOULAS

To the Restless Books team: how, just how can I ever thank you for facilitating the fulfilment of my dream, of my heart's needs?!

Thank you abundantly to the readers and judges of the Restless Books Prize for New Immigrant Writing! Grace Talusan, you are so lovely. Thank you for reaching out to me. Thank you for all your support and championing behind the scenes. To Ilan Stavans, thank you for hearing the words of my heart in person and on the page! My abiding thanks for the best Brooklyn breakfast meeting and your receptivity. To Jiaming Tang, for all your enthusiasm and positivity, thank you truly. To Jennifer Alise Drew, my word, how do I thank you? From the very beginning, your joyful support has been wondrous. My deepest appreciation. To Lydia McOscar, I am so grateful for all your hard work, support, energy, communication, and guidance. And to Jennifer and Lydia, thank you especially for all the dimensions your developmental editing opened and for seeing the strength in the choices I made—priceless.

To noam keim: dearheart, a million times thank you for "yelling at [me] a little bit." You brave, loving, genuine, open soul. It's a treasure and privilege to have your friendship, you must know.

THE COMMUNITY

To Jaquira Diaz, when I sought memoir craft lessons your Miami Book Fair workshop beckoned. Twice thereafter, in other venues, I enrolled to learn from you. Thanks for your knowledge, your writing, your support, and all that you do.

To my Miami memoirists, Flávia Monteiro, Monica Medina, Patricia Azze, our words grew up together as we workshopped. We have seen each other through so many iterations, and all of them bountiful, perceptive, and joyous. Deep thank you.

To Lance Cleland, A. L. Major, and India—thank you for assembling the best memoir workshop ever. From the very beginning, I could see why you put us all together. Thank you for the magical Tin House Summer Workshop 2022! I received talented, kind, beautiful community and craft that lasts, all stemming from the thoughtful, caring work that you do.

Thank you to Ingrid Rojas Contreras, for the knowledge you shared in our Tin House workshop, and your continued support.

To my merry band of bad parents-orphan memoirists, thank you so much for our continued workshopping after Tin House. Bureen Ruffin, Connie Pertuz-Meza, Ebony Haight, Elda Maria Roman, Gionni Ponce, Justin Chandler, Kani Aniegboka, Leslie Nguyen-Okwu, Sarah Chaves, Shuxuan Zhou. Thank you for your friendship, your feedback, your love, your vulnerability, your laughter, and your light. You are all wondrously, wonderfully, the warmest embrace and feel like home.

Abundant gratitude to Nicole Shawan Junior and Vanessa Mártir for all that Roots. Wounds. Words. gave me. Never has a workshop been named so aptly. You doing the writing community a service for which we have no words. Keep on. You are appreciated.

To Marcelo Hernandez Castillo, you are so generous and genuinely kind. Thank you for all the feedback, the fellowship, and for facilitating the greatest workshop of poet-memoirists. And thank you for really getting it when you read my work.

To my poet-memoirists, my peoples, my lovelies, my heart is full—thank you, Dr. Cecilia Caballero, Celeste Chan, Desiree Brown, Elina Zhang, Mayookh Barua, Misha Ponnuraju, noam keim, Phillip Dwight Morgan, S. G. Huerta, Victoria Lagunas. I laugh till my sides hurt wid allyuh; I weep and worry wid allyuh; I workshop words that allyuh cherish and challenge, diagramme *ahem* and big up. The friendships and support I didn't see coming and for which I will always be grateful. Love allyuh bad.

To Lisa Quinones, Shannon Marcec, there was <u>no</u> way I was making it through the lockdown in de bush without allyuh and our workshops. Your brilliance, your real vulnerability and deep compassion, your belly-cramping humour, your realness, and your beauty. My love and gratitude always. Thank you, Runako Taylor, for putting us together.

To my GrubStreet Gals—Erika Koss, Jess Witkins, Katie Baptist, Valerie Dimino—thank you for holding space, for cheering, goal-setting, accountability, patience, and the pleasure of your goodness.

Thank you! to *Passages North*, *Citron Review*, *Hippocampus Magazine*, *XRAY Literary Magazine*, *Variant Literature*, *The Forge Literary Magazine*, *Kweli Journal*, and your readers.

THE EDUCATORS

Thank you to: Tom Sleigh, whose poetry workshop taught me to play with syntax, embrace metre, and in which a new poetic voice emerged. Susan Daitch, who said "show me the outside." Harold Veeser, who so so so wonderfully pushed me and said you have to finish this! You're a true treasure. To Elizabeth Stuckey-French—the best doctoral committee advisor I could have asked for: thank you for all your curiosity, support, challenge, vulnerability, guidance, and care. You are fantastic. David Groff, Veronica Gregg, Barbara Webb, Michelle Valladares, Ravi Howard, Candace Ward, Jerrilyn McGregory, Joyce Toney, Elaine Equi, thanks!

ACKNOWLEDGEMENTS

To each and every single one of my brilliant teachers at Diamond Vale Government Primary School, the deepest thanks for educating me so well. Your foundational lessons in writing calypso, in music, in story, in history, and the ways in which plants grow, this memoir now joyously tells.

To all my remarkable teachers at Bishop Anstey High School, I learnt so very many lasting lessons from you. To KerrieAnn Jack and Tiffany Drake, my first "I know you" readers, your amazing energetic support and heartfelt words literally changed the game. Deepest thanks.

To my sociology, history, and psychology teachers at Elders' Classes, thank you for the lasting insights. They are with me as I write.

ALSO

This is also a memoir of chronic illness. Thank you forever to Dr. Johnny Siu Chong, to Dr. Veta M. Mobley-Johnson, and to Terese N. Herring—Tally therapist—for taking care of my body, allowing it to today bear witness.

To Freida's Specialty Produce for taking care of my body while I wrote this book during my PhD in Tallahassee.

To Earl Lovelace, the master historian and griot whose words always prompt my pen the few occasions when I am blocked. I have learnt from your content, your prose, your purpose, and I am grateful your words are in the world. Our Trinidad and Tobago teacher, thank you.

To Jamaica Kincaid, your books have saved me time and time and time again. From childhood till now. Thank you for committedly telling the truth about evil, cruel mothers.

To Emma Ramadan and Sherri Wolf, thanks for listening and supporting in kindness.

To friends, to lovers, to partners, to my peoples who will never be in my books, thanks for the goodness in real life. ☺

SELF

To me—thank you for staying alive. Thank you for listening to yourself, for trusting yourself, for honouring your talents, needs, wants, and perceptions. Thank you for remembering who you are and being true to who you have always been. Thank you for acknowledging and embracing disillusion. Thank you for, when you needed to, standing alone. You are your home.

READERS

My early readers, my now-reach readers, my social media readers, my coming-to-come readers: thank you, abundantly, for letting my words speak to you.

HOW TO BE UNMOTHERED: A TRINIDADIAN MEMOIR

Cheers to telling the ugly truth. Beautifully, baby. The book has agency, you have taught me. You know what you wanted to say. Thank you for making me do it your way.